The Transhistorical Museum

Pedro Cabrita Reis, *One after another, a few silent steps*, 2011, installation view. Courtesy M-Museum Leuven. Photo: Dirk Pauwels, 2012.

Aurélien Froment, *Double Tales*, 2017, installation view. Courtesy M-Museum Leuven. Photo: Dirk Pauwels, 2017.

'Hommage Arnoud Holleman', installation view, Frans Hals Museum, 2015. Courtesy Frans Hals Museum | De Hallen Haarlem. Photo: Gert Jan van Rooij.

'Kasper Bosmans: The Words and Days (mud gezaaid, free range)', installation view, De Hallen Haarlem, 2017. Courtesy Frans Hals Museum | De Hallen Haarlem. Photo: Gert Jan van Rooij.

'Erkka Nissinen: God or terror or retro dog', installation view, De Hallen Haarlem, 2015. Courtesy Frans Hals Museum | De Hallen Haarlem. Photo: Gert Jan van Rooij.

'Erkka Nissinen: God or terror or retro dog', installation view, De Hallen Haarlem, 2015. Courtesy Frans Hals Museum | De Hallen Haarlem. Photo: Gert Jan van Rooij.

'Conversation Piece V: Glenn Brown and the Old Masters', installation view, Frans Hals Museum, 2013; right: Glenn Brown, *The Happiness in One's Pocket*, 2012, oil on panel, 225 × 180 cm; left: Hendrick Goltzius, *Hercules and Cacus*, 1613, oil on canvas, 207 × 142.5 cm. Courtesy Frans Hals Museum | De Hallen Haarlem. Photo: Gert Jan van Rooij.

'Conversation Piece IV: Maaike Schoorel and the Old Masters', installation view, Frans Hals Museum, 2012. Courtesy Frans Hals Museum | De Hallen Haarlem. Photo: Gert Jan van Rooij.

Editors
Eva Wittocx
Ann Demeester
Peter Carpreau
Melanie Bühler
Xander Karskens

Contributors
Mieke Bal
Melanie Bühler
Peter Carpreau
Bice Curiger
Penelope Curtis
Ann Demeester
Olga Fernández López
Hendrik Folkerts
Hanneke Grootenboer
María Íñigo Clavo
Xander Karskens
Christa-Maria Lerm Hayes
Jean-Hubert Martin
Alexander Nagel
Ruth Noack
Nicola Setari
Jasper Sharp
Abigail Winograd
Eva Wittocx

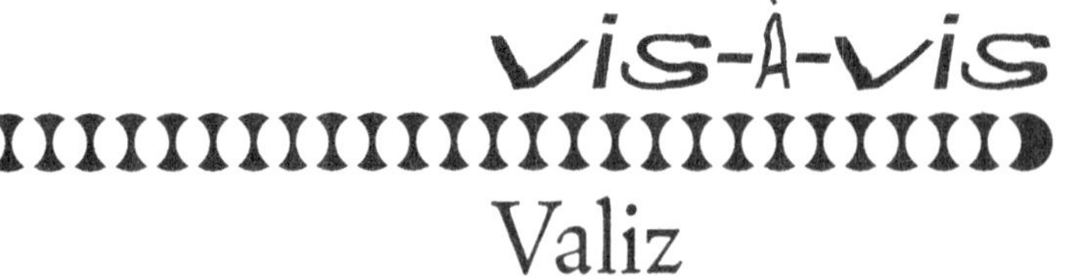

The Transhistorical Museum

Mapping the Field

Valiz, Amsterdam
M-Museum Leuven
Frans Hals Museum, Haarlem

Contents

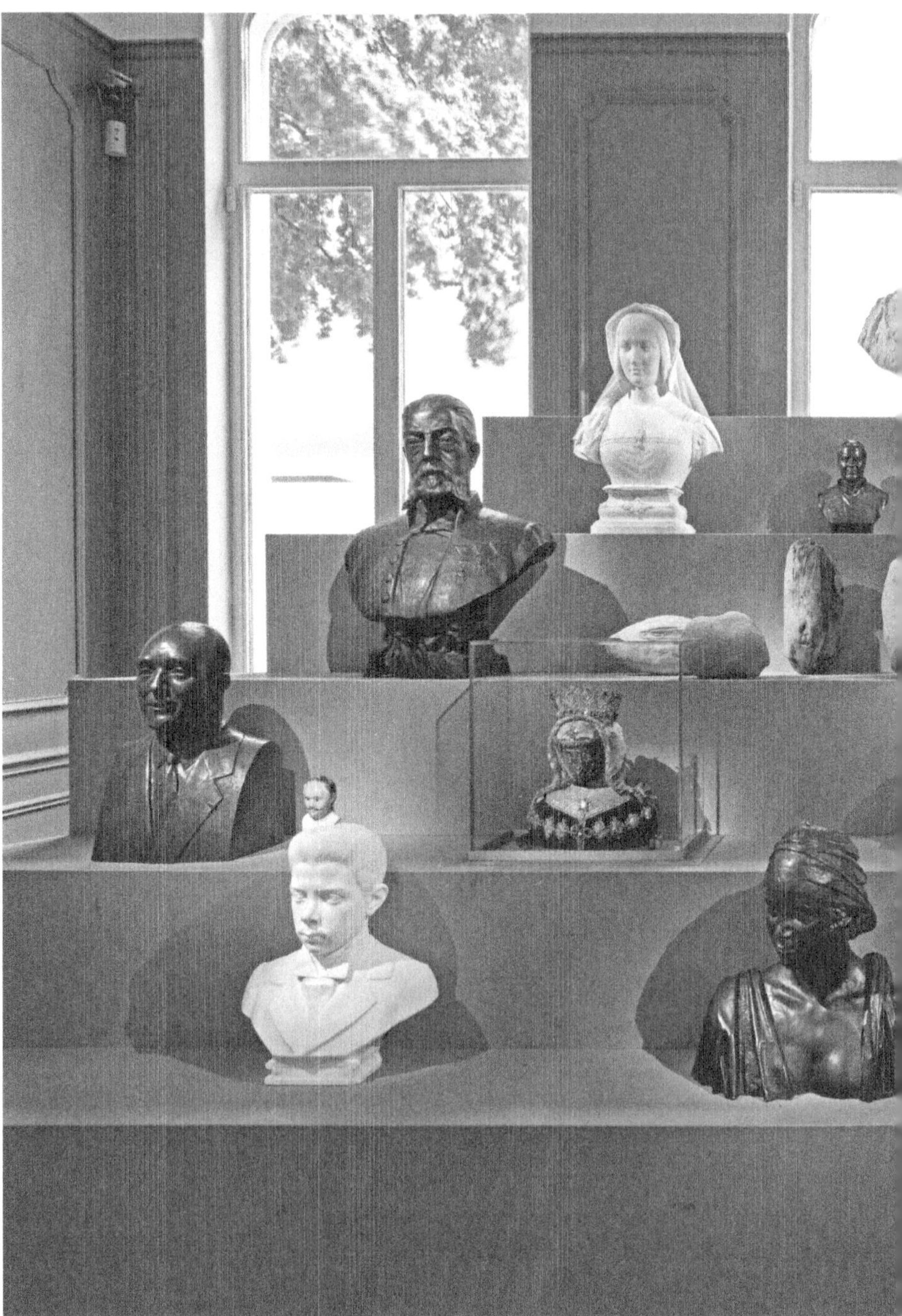

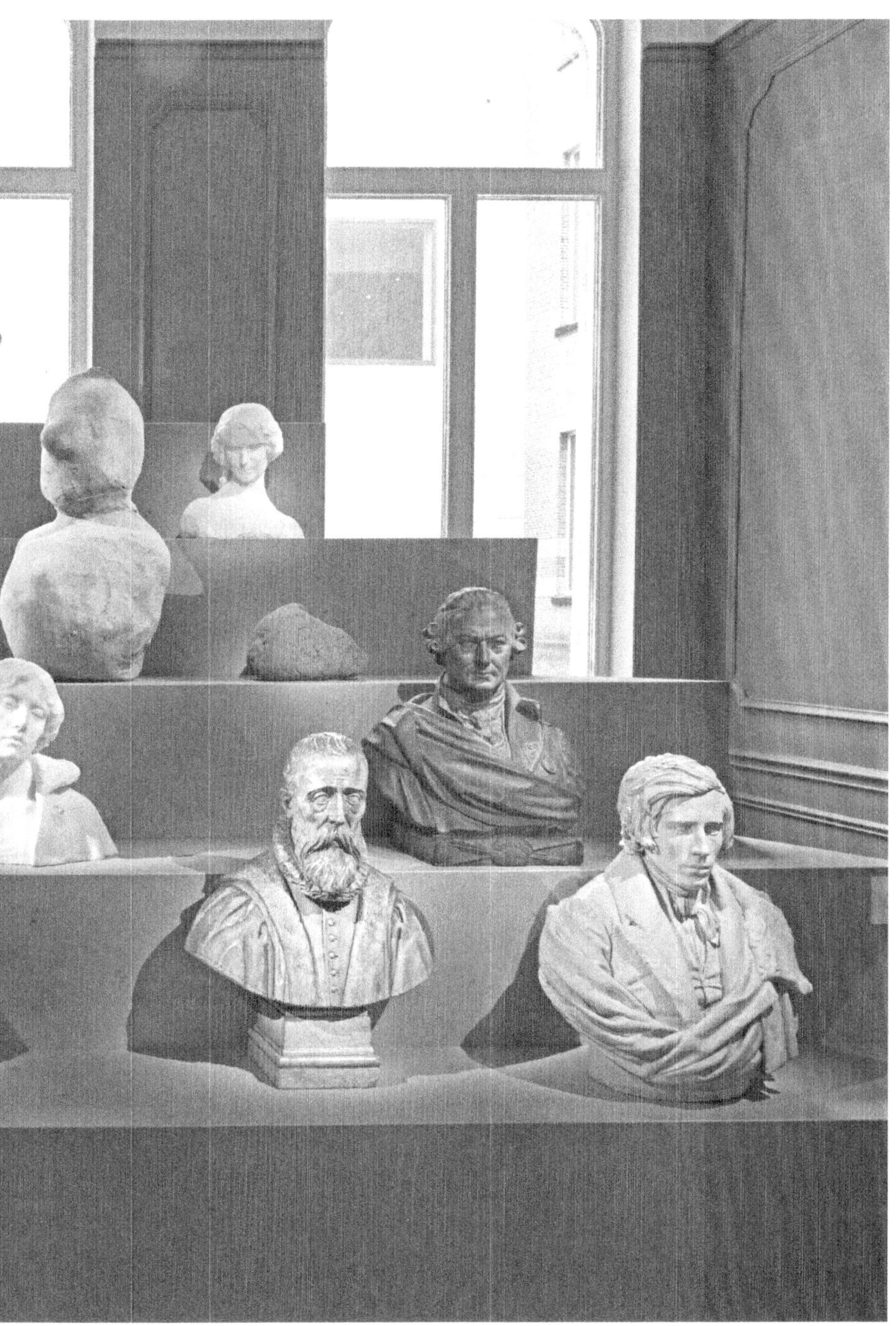

Collection presentation, installation view, M-Museum Leuven, 2017. Courtesy M-Museum Leuven.

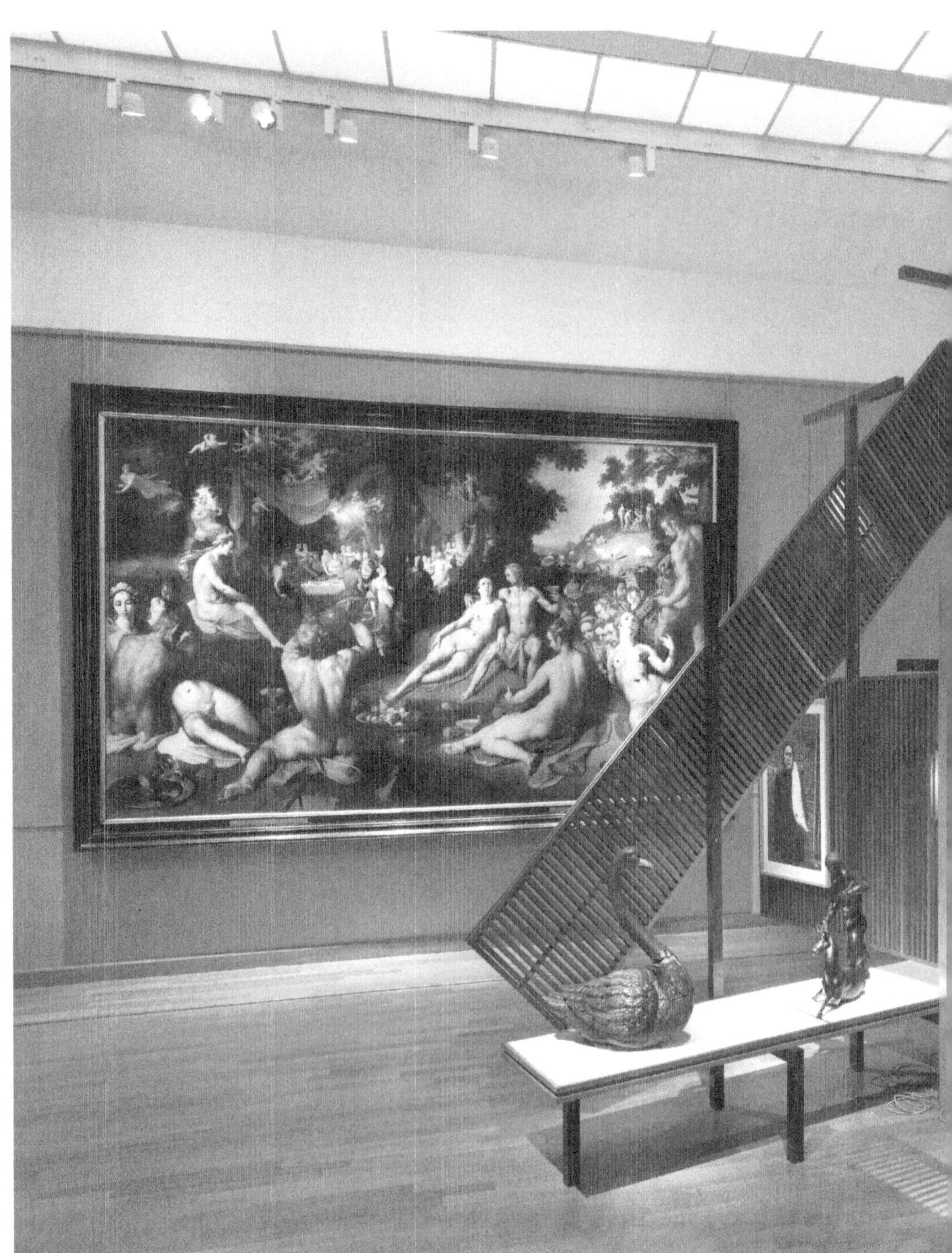

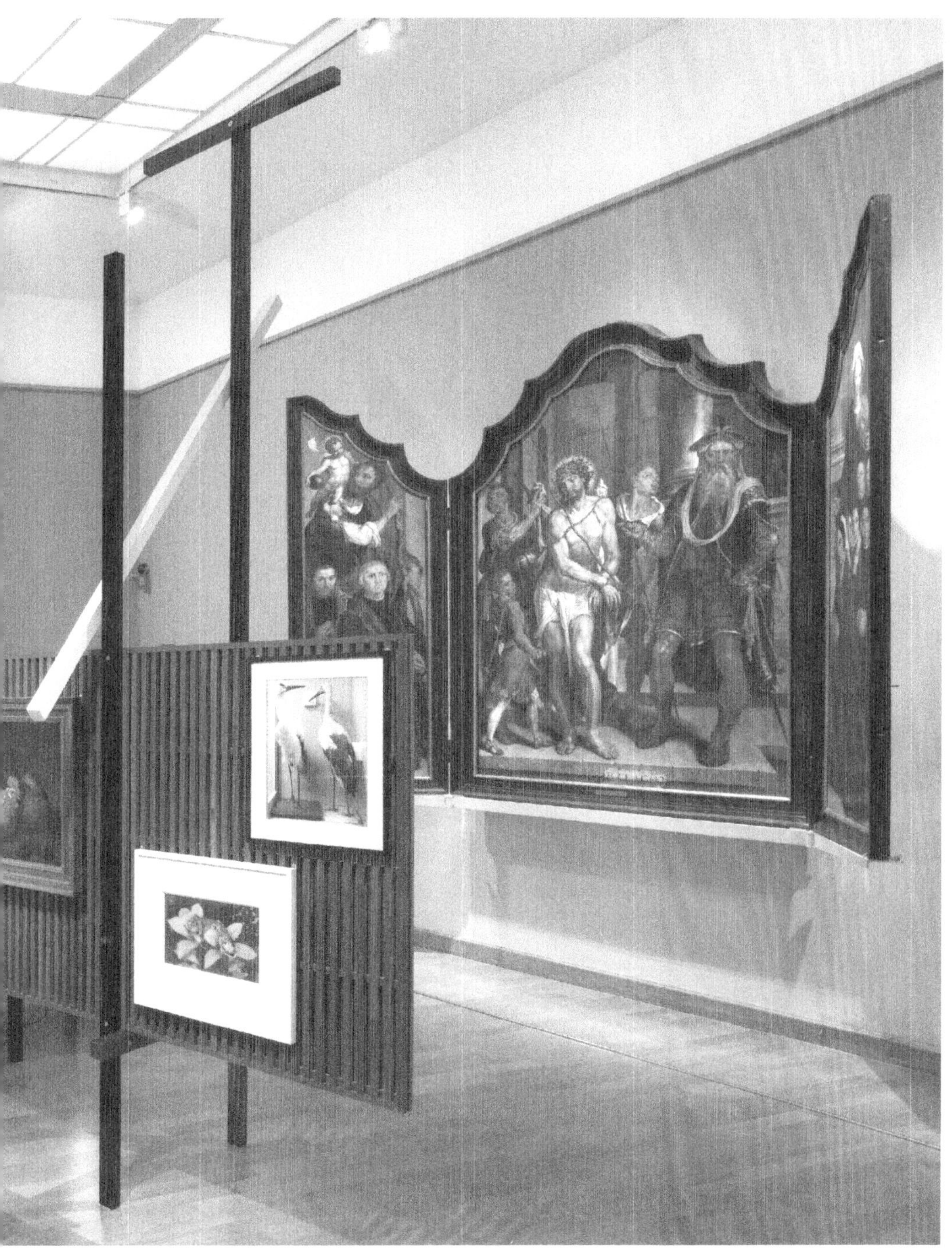

'New & Old—Z is for Zoo: Gavin Wade', installation view, Frans Hals Museum, 2016. Courtesy Frans Hals Museum | De Hallen Haarlem. Photo: Gert Jan van Rooij, 2016.

1 From Ben Okri, *Mental Fight* (London, 1999).

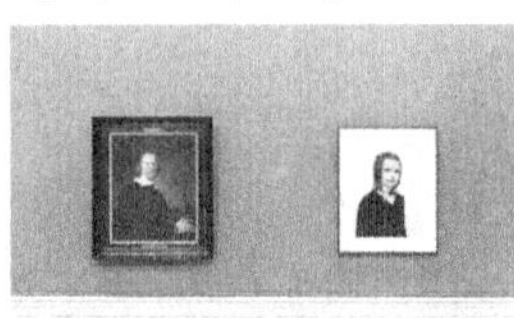

2 Cornelisz. Verspronck, *Portrait of Dr. Jacobus Akersloot*, 1654, oil on canvas; Rineke Dijkstra, *Lucy Smeets*, 2008, archival inkjet print, installation view, 'Conversation Piece VI: Rineke Dijkstra | 17th-Century Portraits', Frans Hals Museum, 2014. Courtesy Frans Hals Museum | De Hallen Haarlem. Photo: Gert Jan van Rooij, 2014.

Acclaimed Nigerian-British poet Ben Okri once stated that 'our future is greater than our past'.[1] As museums that harbour and host collections that are both historical and contemporary, we beg to differ. In the (visual) arts the present, future, and past are intimately connected and engaged in an ongoing polylogue of mutual enrichment. A museum that aims at being contemporary should ideally develop a contemporary perspective on art of the past and find historical moorings for art of the present by fostering an ongoing 'to-and-fro' between artworks, ideas, and artists from different time zones. Museums that think transhistorically do just that and facilitate a rendezvous between the old and the new, the artists of the past and those of the present,[2] linking heritage and tradition to contemporary art and social questions. In doing so, they try to break through the separatism that seems inherent in Western European art history with its focus on periods and movements.

As Hal Foster notes, scholarly movement across these historical fields is hardly new: for example, even before the First World War, Wilhelm Worringer connected German

Expressionism to the Northern Gothic tradition; between the wars, Meyer Schapiro moved easily between abstract painting and Romanesque sculpture; and after the Second World War, Leo Steinberg wrote with equal insight on twentieth-century innovators such as Picasso, Robert Rauschenberg, and Jasper Johns, and Old Masters such as Michelangelo, Caravaggio, and Velázquez. This traffic, as Foster explains, is busier than ever before, with art historians such as Hans Belting, Horst Bredekamp, and Georges Didi-Huberman and recently Alexander Nagel at work on various subjects from the premodern to the postmodern.[3]

Since the turn of this century, we have moreover witnessed a significant expanse in the field of transhistorical exhibition practice in and outside of (museum) institutions: a diverse range of curatorial efforts in which objects and artefacts from various periods and art-historical and cultural contexts are combined in display, in order to question and expand traditional museological notions such as chronology, linearity, and medium. Such experiments potentially result not only in fresh insights into the workings of our entrenched historical presumptions, but also provide a space to reassess interpretations of individual objects in relation to their contexts and narratives. The transhistorical museum thus offers us a way to look at the past via the present (or another historical period) and vice versa, and has the potential for new ways of interpreting and learning.[4] Such a museum believes that all artworks are essentially transhistorical, time travellers. They are 'born' or created at a particular time and in a specific context. They survive that context and are shown and read years or even centuries later in a different era, a different setting, a different cultural environment. 'They live in the present but in the company of the past', as John Berger is said to have put it. Moreover, transhistorical thinking seems to have an

3 Hal Foster, 'Preposterous Timing', review of *Medieval Modern: Art out of Time*, by Alexander Nagel and *Depositions: Scenes from the Late Medieval Church and the Modern Museum*, by Amy Knight Powell. *London Review of Books* 34, no. 21 (2012), pp. 12–14.

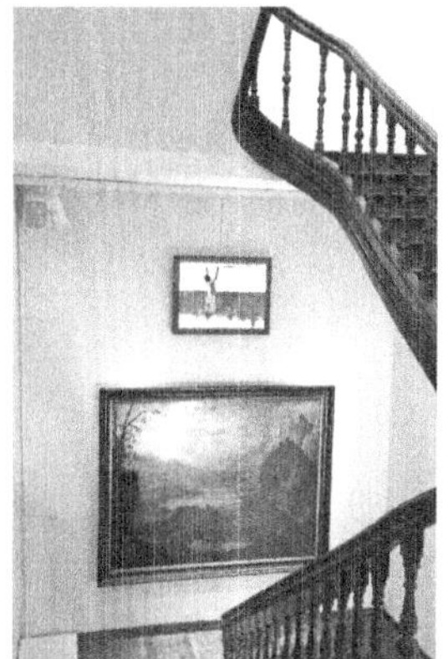

4 Mika Rottenberg, *Cheese, Squeeze & Tropical Breeze*, 2011, installation view. Courtesy M-Museum Leuven. Photo: Dirk Pauwels, 2011.

5 'Neo Rauch, in conversation with Ralph Keunig', in *Neo Rauch: Dromos Malerei 1993–2017*, ed. Harald Kunde (Ostfildern, 2018).

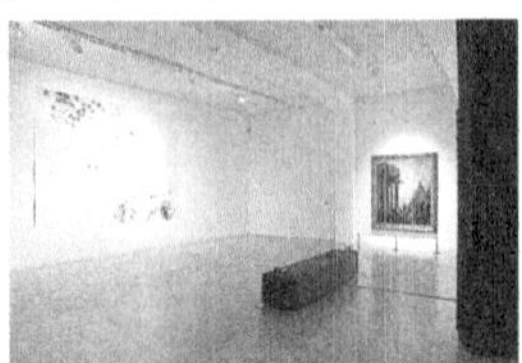

6 Cai Guo-Qiang, *Black Fireworks: Project for Hiroshima*, 2008, installation view, 'Ravaged: Art and Culture in Times of Conflict', M-Museum Leuven, 2014. Courtesy of the Hiroshima City Museum of Contemporary Art. Photo: Dirk Pauwels, 2014.

affinity with the way artists work. Very generally speaking, artists are not interested in respecting different time periods by marking them as different; nor in historic artworks by describing them as historic. On the contrary, they are concerned with what these works mean now. The artist seems to be the one, as Neo Rauch quite esoterically puts it, that has an inkling or a suspicion that everything coexists simultaneously.[5] They act from that interconnectivity between what once was and what is yet to come. The transhistorical museum, in imitation of that, complements its own museum methodology and classification system (arrangement by medium, style, and period) with an (artistic/associative) way of thinking that cuts right through the constraints of time, space, culture, and geography.

M-Museum Leuven and Frans Hals Museum—formerly known as Frans Hals Museum | De Hallen Haarlem—are proud to host 'mixed' collections and presentations. In the case of M the collection consists of more than 52,500 objects from the Middle Ages to the twentieth century, with a central focus on post-1945 Belgian art. M combines this historical collection with a varied exhibition programme of classical and contemporary art. M organizes temporary exhibitions that introduce the audiences to lesser-known pieces in the collection alongside monographic exhibitions by old masters and contemporary artists. At the same time, artists and curators are invited to explore the collection from a contemporary point of view to create new opportunities.[6]

The Frans Hals Museum is proud to work with a collection that spans from the sixteenth century till the present, characterized by two 'nodes': the Old Art collection organized around the eponymous figure of Frans Hals and Haarlem as a centre of artistic innovation in the sixteenth/seventeenth century, and the international Contemporary Art collection, which focuses on innovative (mostly 'new media') practice in the twenty-first century. Over the past years both institutions have increasingly focused on their own 'transhistoricity' (or 'cross-historicity')[7] and explored methodologies that interrogate strict periodization and foster dynamic relationships and interconnections between art from different eras and ages.[8]

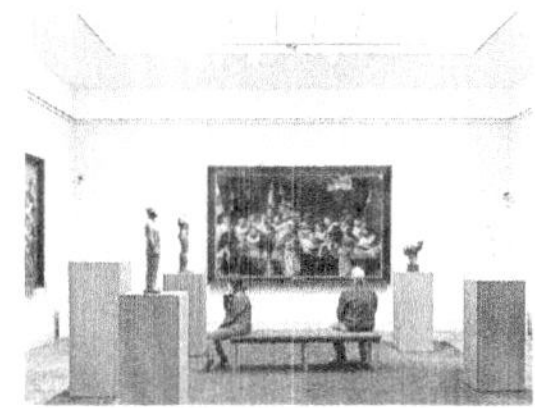

7 'Hommage Arnoud Holleman', installation view, Frans Hals Museum, 2015. Courtesy Frans Hals Museum | De Hallen Haarlem. Photo: Gert Jan van Rooij.

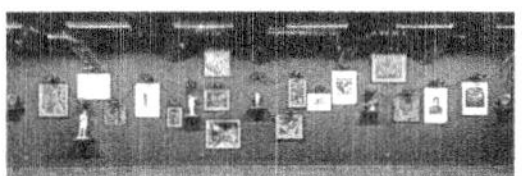

8 'Erkka Nissinen: God or térror or retro dog', installation view, De Hallen Haarlem, 2015. Courtesy Frans Hals Museum | De Hallen Haarlem. Photo: Gert Jan van Rooij.

Since 2015, this active research has resulted in a number of exhibitions, two conferences, a curatorial workshop, made possible by the Van Toorn Scholten stichting, and a lecture in collaboration with de Oude Kerk/Castrum Peregrini and Museum Van Loon bringing together different perspectives (museological, curatorial, theoretical) and producing discourse on this topical subject. As museums, we are convinced that we not only need to perform the transhistorical but think about it as well, on a meta-level that transcends our own practice. We aspire to critically map this domain and both trace its genealogies (existing theory and practice) and present new ideas with regards to questions like: Can a transhistorical approach produce relevant new insights into the specific qualities of art objects, by manoeuvring them into uncharted contexts—historically, materially, and ontologically? What can we learn from historical artworks, when we study them through the lens of contemporary artistic production—or vice versa? How do we read art history forward into the present, and use recent practice as a vantage point from which to revise the past? Can we build new educational models on these ideas, and engage our audiences in a different way?

This publication aims to do just that: it examines the ways in which curatorial, institutional and artistic practice relates to the notion of transhistoricity. The book brings together an international roster of theorists, art historians, curators, and researchers, aiming to produce more substantial discourse on this subject, and it offers a framework within which future institutional and curatorial strategies can be developed. It is a first—and not a final—attempt to trace the outlines of this enormous field of research. We hope that this book will have an offspring and lead to many others.

This anthology is divided into three sections. The first deals with the transhistorical as a concept as it has emerged as a counter dynamic to a particular tradition of art history, exhibition practices, and scholarly thinking. This first part aims to set the stage for the remainder of the book by clarifying the theoretical and disciplinary background that the transhistorical relates to and positions itself against. Nicola Setari's opening essay makes an important and useful distinction here, in—what he calls—a negative and a positive concept of transhistoricity. The positive attests the artwork with a surplus value that allows it to form relations across time, whereas the negative is based on the idea that historical artworks need to be activated to become meaningful for an audience. This is most often achieved by way of a juxtaposition with contemporary art. Whereas the positive is attributed to the artwork as such, the negative unfolds in relation to an audience and results in a curatorial project—the histories we tell about an artwork. The contributions that follow hone in on this context. Hanneke Grootenboer explains how the transhistorical can be understood in relation to art history and what kind of approach to artworks a transhistorical methodology implies. One, as Grootenboer explains, that always takes the viewer in the here and now into account, since an artwork is always completed by a viewer. The pioneering cultural theorist Mieke Bal then takes a critical stab at the term 'transhistorical' itself. While she agrees that artworks can form meaningful relations across time and that indeed this can be accomplished in curatorial and scholarly projects, to her, the prefix 'trans-' seems inappropriate, as it implies an engagement that wants to penetrate rather than relate. Consequently, Bal advocates replacing the prefix with 'inter-' and to emphasize a layered relationality between artworks. The fourth contribution in this section further broadens the scope of the 'transhistorical' by relating it to postcolonial theory. How has the transhistorical been connected to the ways in which colonial histories are told in the context of the art museum? This is the question María Íñigo Clavo and Olga Fernández López raise in their contribution.

The contributions in the second part of the publication shift the focus to the work of art, and its relationship to time. This is the field of the art historian Alexander Nagel whose work is concerned with the complex relationships between artworks and time. To him, artworks can have the capacity to be anachronistic: to fall out of time, even undo it. Penelope Curtis' curatorial practice might be seen as an exercise in precisely that: to find ways to stage different temporal relations between artworks and to test what kind of temporalities can be evoked between and with them. Her contribution 'In & Out of Time' contextualizes her many exhibition projects that connect to these questions. Confronted with the paradox that artworks continue to fascinate us even if we cannot access their meaning, Peter Carpreau finds the solution in the viewer. To him, each present creates a new temporal zone, a new cultural field that a historic work can connect to. In that sense, meaning arises transhistorically, as it is always bound to the specificity of the time that constitutes a viewer's context. Christa-Maria Lerm Hayes then further zooms in on transhistorical projects by individual artists, projects that take their relationship to time seriously by thinking in cycles, rather than quick results, and care for the old, instead of engaging with the ever new. To Lerm Hayes then, these projects are examples of an ethical engagement with and through time.

The third part of the book brings together the voices of six curators from different generations, each of whom presents one project that is linked to a specific approach of the transhistorical. Jasper Sharp, curator at Kunsthistorisches Museum in Vienna, presents the format of the artist intervention—artists are given a carte blanche to engage with the historic collection of the museum. Jean-Hubert Martin, the curator of such seminal exhibitions as 'Magiciens de la terre' (1989) and 'Théâtre du Monde' (2014) presents his most recent exhibition 'Carambolages' (2016) at Grand Palais in Paris. Here, Hubert aimed to stimulate an associative, visual thinking, one that arises from the relations between artworks and doesn't rely on a concept, theme, or narrative. On the example 'Deftig Barock/Riotous Baroque' at Kunsthaus Zürich (2012) Bice Curiger then introduces the concept of montage as a format to bring together old and new, instigating a play of contrasts and affinities alike. Next, and based on her curatorial concept for documenta 12 (2007), Ruth Noack introduces her take on the transhistorical that manifests itself in 'the migration of forms': through resonances between artworks that playfully reach across geography and history, aiming at a more inclusive and open form of display, one that engages the viewer in non-discursive ways. The publication concludes with two more recent examples. By way of a rereading of seventeenth-century still-life paintings, and the food presented in them, Abigail Winograd was able to create a new context for these works, a context that brings crucial aspects of the Dutch colonial history into a critical focus by way of presenting them with contemporary artworks. The theme of food acts as a transhistorical medium in this exhibition organized at the Frans Hals Museum | De Hallen Haarlem in 2017–2018. Finally, Hendrik Folkerts, one of the curators of documenta 14 (2017), describes how the past has formed a net of relations between Greece and Germany and Athens and Kassel in particular. This relational field initiated a process to think about history as a complex fabric with manifold relations to the present, that continues to inform our lives today and as such also provides the opportunity to critically and artistically interfering with it.

We sincerely hope you will appreciate this book, which starts in the now, explores yesterday, and will hopefully find continuation in tomorrow.

Eva Wittocx
Ann Demeester
Peter Carpreau
Melanie Bühler
Xander Karskens

Part 1

Terminology & Theoretical Horizon

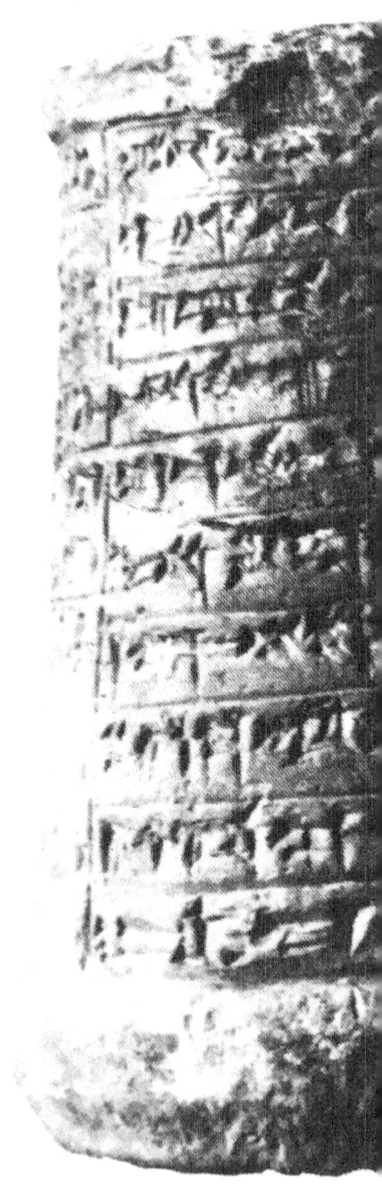

*A baked clay drum-shaped object with copies of
when Sinbalassuiqbi was searching for the anc
found in a Neo-Babylonian building by W*

scriptions on bricks of Amar-Sin found round-plan of Egishnugal. *This was y, who called it a 'Museum label'*

First museum label found in Princess Ennigaldi-Nanna's Museum and dating from around 530 BC. The description is in three languages. From Leonard Woolley, *Ur 'of the Chaldees'*, p. 253.

Notes on Transhistoricity

Between Art Theory and Curatorial Practice

Nicola Setari

Preamble
Digging up Transhistoricity: Ennigaldi-Nanna's Museum

The first museum curator was a woman. Such a claim can be made when one accepts the idea that Princess Ennigaldi-Nanna of the Neo-Babylonian empire created a museum around 530 BC in her palace in the city of Ur. Her museum predates the cabinet of curiosities of the seventeenth century, which is usually considered the forerunner of modern museums, by more than 2000 years. She was the daughter of Nabonidus, the last king of the Neo-Babylonian empire, known to have led several important archaeological excavations in the course of his reign. The British archaeologist Leonard Woolley discovered Princess Ennigaldi-Nanna's Museum in 1922 on an expedition for the British Museum.

In *Ur of the Chaldees* Woolley reworked his original notes about his excavations and described the site of the 'museum' in these terms:

> Suddenly the workmen brought to light a large oval-topped black stone whose top was covered with carvings in relief and its sides with inscriptions; ... Now, this stone belonged to the Kassite period of about 1400 BC. Almost touching it was a fragment of a statue, ... that had been carefully trimmed so as to make it look neat and to preserve the writing; and the name on the statue was that of Dungi, who was king of Ur in 2058 BC. Then came a clay foundation-cone of a Larsa king of about 1700 BC, ... and a large votive stone mace-head which was uninscribed but may well have been more ancient by five hundred years. What were we to think? Here were half a dozen diverse objects found lying on an unbroken brick pavement of the sixth century BC, yet the newest of them was seven hundred years older than the pavement and the earliest perhaps sixteen hundred.[1]

Here is Woolley's conclusion:

> The room was a museum of local antiquities ... and in the collection was this clay drum, the earliest museum label known, drawn up a hundred years before and kept, presumably together with the original bricks, as a record of the first scientific excavations at Ur.[2]

What are the clues that led Woolley to conclude he found a museum and not a temple or some other public space? 1) The objects in the room are out of context and useless in terms of practical activities; 2) They are treated as objects to be displayed: one was polished to look better even though it had been broken; 3) They belong to very distant historical periods and, finally, 4) There is a label (the clay drum) explaining in different languages what the exhibit is.

1 Woolley, *Ur 'of the Chaldees'*, pp. 251–252.

2 Ibid., p. 252.

But can one also conclude that the room and the objects inside it were actually a museum? Or is this just the fantasy or projection of an archaeologist working for the British Museum? Even though this is an impossible question to answer, Woolley's story can help us to become aware of the arrogance in assuming that the museum—as a place of conservation and display of artefacts—could only come about in the modern era and in Western European culture.[3] The story also provides an additional 'morale' about museums. If the room Woolley discovered had been filled with objects coming from the same period, it is unlikely that the archaeologist would have suspected it to be a museum: it is precisely and paradoxically the transhistorical character of the display that made him conclude this.

There is one more paradox in the story worth noting: the objects in Ennigaldi-Nanna's museum were not the artistic masterpieces found in other rooms of the palace and that visitors today can admire in the British Museum: because these—more valuable—objects continued to be used for private purposes in Ennigaldi-Nanna's time. The objects displayed in her museum served an educational function of telling the story of the dynasty.

This intersection between the cultural, archaeological and 'museological' practice of an ancient civilization and of one closer to us, the British Empire, points to the final question that serves as preamble to this text: The British Museum legitimates its possession of the cultural heritage of other civilizations—and often refuses to return artefacts—with the argument that as a museum it does not represent and serve a country, but instead it is a museum in the service of humanity, with a universal mission to preserve the memory of lost civilizations, also implying or explicitly stating that it guarantees better material and intellectual conditions for their

3 The word museum has classical origins. In its Greek form, *mouseion*, it meant 'seat of the Muses' and designated a philosophical institution or a place of contemplation. Use of the Latin derivation, museum, appears to have been restricted in Roman times mainly to places of philosophical discussion. Thus the great Museum at Alexandria, founded by Ptolemy I early in the third century BC, with its college of scholars and its library, was more a prototype university than an institution to preserve and interpret material aspects of heritage.

display. Is there a concept of transhistoricity implied here and is this not the same reasoning that many ethnographic museums across Europe also employ? Or, asked differently, can we establish a difference between universalism and transhistoricity?

Two Concepts of Transhistoricity

My premise is that there is a dialectical tension between, what I propose to call, the positive and the negative concepts of transhistoricity, which are respectively in play in certain positions in art theory and in curatorial practice. The terms positive and negative here are not attached to value judgements. Instead, they could be compared to Isaiah Berlin's positive and negative concepts of liberty,[4] where the negative concept refers to the freedom of acting without constraints, while the positive refers to the freedom to self-impose constraints in order to pursue or fulfil oneself. Transhistoricity when engaged in curatorial practice often embodies the negative concept and refers to what we can do with artworks, or how we can free artworks from certain historiographical concerns in favour of thematic or formal ones, defined by the taste and research of curators. Understood theoretically, transhistoricity embodies the positive concept and relates to the purpose of art, to what it can achieve or fulfil beyond, or better, through its historical determinations. In other words, in the first case, transhistoricity is often limited to a strategy to reanimate or activate artworks from the past that are perceived as having been buried by history or that run this risk, by associating them with contemporary artworks or projects, while in the second, transhistoricity is a kind of intrinsic quality of certain artworks or objects of interest,

4 Berlin, 'Two Concepts of Liberty'.

which through their historical determination overcome their historicity.

Again, it is important to reiterate that there is no superiority of the positive concept of transhistoricity over the negative one. The positive concept does tend to receive less attention because it is informed by humanistic values that do not seem to have much currency in the contemporary art world, or, better, in the dominant discursive formations that inform it. This is why this text largely focuses on the positive concept and not on the negative one. The humanistic values underlying the notion of transhistoricity need to be brought to the foreground to understand what exactly we are dealing with.

The three thinkers to whom I resort to introduce the positive concept of transhistoricity are: Paul Ricoeur, Charles Martindale, and Paul Crowther. I will then briefly look at and compare two examples of what can be understood as transhistorical curatorial practice through the lens of these ideas.

In an interview[5] from 1996, Ricoeur answered a question on aesthetic relativism by turning to Kant to understand in what ways an artwork can be transhistorical:

> At first glance, one might say that sociology shows that Kant is wrong, because there is … the history of styles and tastes that demonstrates that he is wrong. In a second analysis, however, this latter proves him right, because in the long view, as this would appear in Malraux's works,[6] there is revealed a dimension of transhistoricity. And this transhistoricity consists in sum in the permanence, or better the perdurance, of works of art in escaping the history of their constitution. One could say that the work of art escapes the history of its

5 Sweeney, 'Arts, Language and Hermeneutical Aesthetics'.

6 Malraux's *Le Musée imaginaire* (or *Museum Without Walls*), a book first published in French in 1947, expresses the idea of bringing together the works of art that generate universal consensus. The book also exposed the for the time revolutionary idea that artworks should no longer be presented according to the traditional museum groupings of periodization and country of provenance. Malraux can therefore be seen as an anticipator of transhistorical museums. The word transhistorical began to circulate in France in fact in the 1940s and in the Anglo-Saxon world only from the early 1960s.

> constitution, and it is this temporality of a second degree which constitutes the temporality of communicability. This transhistorical communicability is the rational equivalent of objectivity, as much in the beautiful as in the sublime.[7]

Here we have a concept of transhistoricity or temporal transcendence of art, which has to do with the reception of art by publics that are diverse in time and in space.

Returning to Ricoeur's reference to Kant, it is worth recalling that the universality of the judgement of taste is intersubjective and never objective, meaning that the judgement of beauty (or of the sublime) in a subject is always accompanied by the aspiration that this judgement be shared by all other subjects. Transhistoricity in other words can be understood as a form of aspired intersubjective consensus across history that certain artworks are able to generate, making us feel close to something from a thousand years ago. This is of course an assumption that the reality of many historical museums contradicts, in the sense that audiences grow increasingly disconnected from artworks of the past and this is one of the reasons why museum curators take action to reactivate them with transhistorical exhibitions. In the interview, Ricoeur goes on to explain how hermeneutics have both an archaeological reductive dynamic, and a teleological one, one that is attentive to the surplus of meaning: 'Such would be the persistence of the work of art [Ricoeur calls this persistence also transhistoricity], capable each time of engendering a surpassing of archaeology into teleology.'[8] This is a fascinating statement, it points us towards the ways in which art can give a sense of purpose to human beings, and according to Ricoeur it is precisely this movement, the surpassing of archaeology into new meaning, the transformation from

7 Sweeney, 'Arts, Language and Hermeneutical Aesthetics', p. 936.

8 Ibid., p. 939.

9 Martindale, *Redeeming the Text*.

10 Martindale, 'Reception'.

11 Ibid., p. 173.

documentation of the past to possibility for the future, that is transhistoricity.

The second voice that formulates a positive concept of transhistoricity is that of the Classics scholar Charles Martindale. Bringing him into the picture means shifting our attention to the study of literature and how transhistoricity functions in this context, to see what 'lessons' we can learn from this. In the nineties, Martindale introduced the hermeneutics of reception as a key methodology in the study of Classics in his book *Redeeming the Text: Latin Poetry and the Hermeneutics of Reception*.[9] In a more recent article[10] addressing reception and the transhistorical he writes:

> The transhistorical [in *Redeeming the Text*] was also perhaps tainted by association with universalism (a view of things seen as designed to enforce undesired uniformities), and complicit with the kind of 'grand narratives' of which postmodern critique was so suspicious. However, if I were writing an introduction to reception studies today, I would want to theorize the role of 'the transhistorical' much more explicitly, as indeed a crucial part of the experience of being human as well as necessary to the understanding of the great texts of the past. By the transhistorical I do not intend what is usually meant by 'universal human nature' or any crude version of 'universalism' but rather the seeking out of often fugitive human communalities across history, communalities that emerge only in the processes we may term 'reception'.[11]

Martindale also works against collapsing transhistoricity and universality into the same concept, by stressing the idea of fragile and fugitive communalities that texts/artworks can establish between each other across time. What is also worth noting in Martindale's approach is that it advocates a new humanism, one that does not put the stress on the pedagogical importance of studying the past, but instead on engaging selectively with it to show its actuality in the present. In other words, transhistoricity is grounded on the idea that the ancient and the modern can dialogue and respectively illuminate each other on the basis of specific questions and that the movement does not necessarily have to follow only one direction.

Paul Crowther in his book *The Transhistorical Image*[12] from 2002 takes on the challenge of arguing in favour of a formalist understanding of images, which he frames as transhistorical. In his introduction, he claims that poststructuralism's critique against formalist approaches to art and in favour of the social history of art produces a sceptical art history that ultimately makes 'artistic production a means to curatorial production'.[13] Art loses its intrinsic value. Crowther's formalist approach and belief in the intrinsic value of art is according to him 'not based on formal properties per se, but rather on the pictorial image understood as a formative power that expresses constant factors in human experience and cognition'.[14] One must transcend the documentary or denunciatory functions of an artwork to see the distinctive individual features of the artwork and how these enlarge or develop the scope of pictorial imaging as a formative power. The distinctive individual features of an artwork should not be confused with the notion of style and its history, something that classical art history is traditionally focused on; instead it refers to the phenomenological quality of the visual representation, its empowering of cognition, in terms of spatial and temporal conceptualizations. According to Crowther this allows us to overcome the dualism between historical and ahistorical understandings of an artwork, and instead invest it with transhistorical significance.

12 Crawford, *The Transhistorical Image*.

13 Ibid., p. 2.

14 Ibid., pp. 2–3.

To attempt a synthesis of these three positions, one could say that the positive concept of transhistoricity or the transhistorical in relation to art can be defined as art's intrinsic ability to communicate across time. As a phenomenon of human production that escapes the conditions of its production, it establishes fragile human communalities between artists and between artists and an audience. These communalities are grounded on the ontological capacity of certain images to expand our imagination and our conscience of time and space. If one translates this synthesis in the context of museums, then the transhistorical museum is the museum that focuses on the transhistorical surplus of artworks. How this focus is translated into display, is a matter that none of the three authors addresses. My sense is that it is a question of finding the right conditions for an aesthetic experience of the artwork to occur. To ask the question what these conditions might be, is to acknowledge that there are disturbing factors that do not allow them to appear and these have to do with the workings of the museum as well as with the economic and social dynamics that are in play within its setting. In other words, the positive concept of transhistoricity directs us towards asking ourselves what should we, as curators and museum directors, restrain ourselves from doing in order to allow aesthetic experience to occur.

The negative concept of transhistoricity instead could be translated as experimenting freely with associations between artworks within a museum display to bring to light transhistorical dialogues between them. These are not conflicting drives, but it is possible that the focus on one, can diminish the focus on the other. Can curatorial practice enhance the positive concept of transhistoricity in relation to artworks and can it be achieved by exhibitions that are organized transhistorically following the negative concept of the term? In trying to establish a dialogue between objects of different temporal periods, or by asking artists to make new works in relation to objects/artworks of the past? These are the questions that this essay can only provide a conceptual framing for.

Epilogue: A Thought Experiment

As already mentioned, I would like to briefly refer to two examples of practical applications of transhistorical curating, which I think can be positioned on the extremes of the spectrum and hopefully can provide a practical frame of reference: the Louvre Museum's programme of inviting contemporary artists to enter into a dialogue with its collection, that ran from 2003–2013 and dOCUMENTA (13)'s 'Brain',[15] presented in the rotunda of the Fridericianum in 2012.

15 dOCUMENTA (13)'s artistic director was Carolyn Christov-Bakargiev. For an interesting email discussion thread around how the rotunda should be titled, see *dOCUMENTA (13)*, pp. 86–87 and pp. 288–289.

What is key to this first strategy, the Louvre Museum's, is that artworks from the past are defined as in need of being reactivated, of receiving new life through a visual dialogue with contemporary artworks. The guiding principle is that the masterpieces from the past need to be freed from the dust and incrustations of history and from codified forms of spectatorship and that contemporary art has the power to achieve this.

This logic of reactivation of artworks from the past in the course of the twentieth century can be associated with iconoclastic practices within artistic movements such as Surrealism and Dadaism. The classic example is Marcel Duchamp's, *L.H.O.O.Q.* from 1917, in which the artist with the simple gesture of ascribing a new name to the work and ironically shifting the gender of the portrayed person reanimates, and, in this case, eroticizes the work. It should come as no surprise that institutionalized forms of reactivation or reanimation, to

16 The historian Marc Fumaroli was the most severe critic of Jan Fabre's exhibition in the Louvre. See: Lequeux, 'Polémique Jan Fabre au Louvre' or Larceneux, Caro and Krebs, *De l'art contemporain dans les musées d'art classique?*

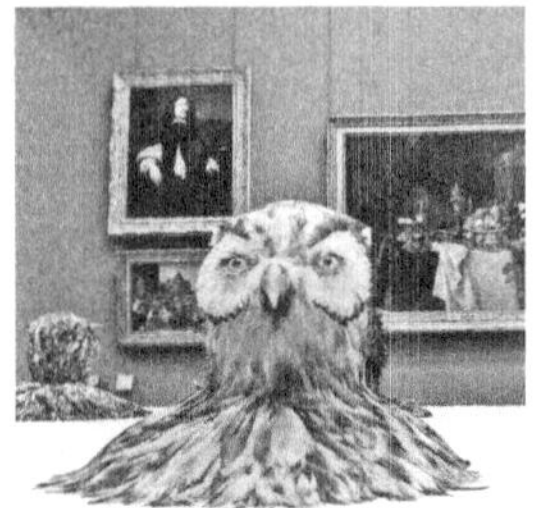

17 Jan Fabre, 'The Angel of Metamorphosis', installation view, Louvre, Paris, 2008. Photo: Pascal Berger, Paris.

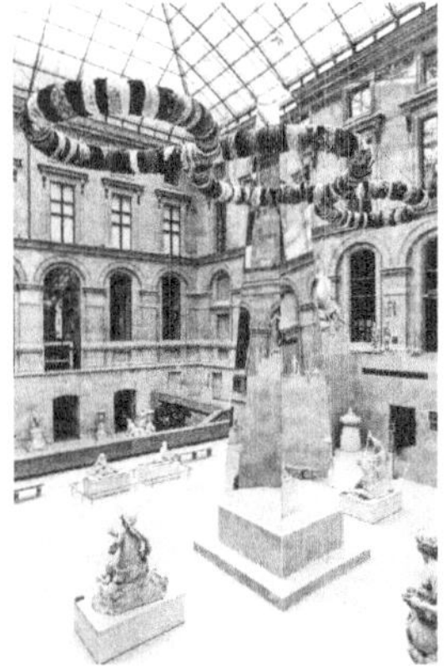

18 Michelangelo Pistoletto, *Obelisco e Terzo Paradiso*, 1976–2013, wood, metal, mirror, polystyrene, fabric, installation view, 'Year One: Paradise on Earth', Louvre, Paris, 2013. Photo: Aurélien Mole, Paris.

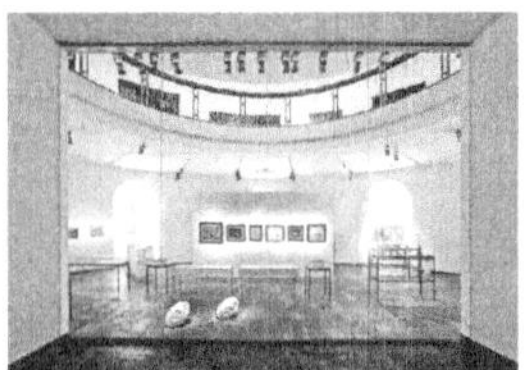

19 'Brain', installation view, dOCUMENTA (13), Kassel, 2012. Photo: Roman März, Kassel.

use another popular notion, such as the ones proposed by the Louvre Museum are often perceived as iconoclastic by historians and art historians.[16] The iconoclastic character lies in the underlying and often not concealed idea that reanimating art from the past is a successful marketing strategy for museums attempting to attract new audiences. In particular, in the case of the Louvre, the explicit and achieved target was to bring in young people from age 18 to 30, who otherwise never would visit the museum.

There is no doubt that the invitations by the Louvre, for example to Jan Fabre[17] in 2008 and to Michelangelo Pistoletto[18] in 2013, yielded spectacular results. The value of those exhibitions cannot be measured in terms of the advancement of art-historical or transhistorical knowledge and awareness, instead they reflect the societal shift that has brought contemporary art from a position of marginality to one of dominance over artworks of the past, something that can also be observed by comparing market values. The Louvre transhistorical exhibitions series clearly engages the negative concept of transhistoricity, with contemporary artworks playing the key role.

If we look at DOCUMENTA (13)'s section 'Brain',[19] which was installed in the rotunda of the Fridericianum, the strategy in play is the opposite: a transhistorical and transcultural display of objects and artworks, with no hierarchy, spanning from the Afghan Bactrian Princesses sculptures dating from four thousand years ago to Sam Durant's work *Calcium Carbonate (ideas spring from deeds not the other way around)*, from 2011, meant to bring together the various thematic strands of that edition of documenta. If a sense of direction can be identified, it goes outwards, from *the middle of the middle of the middle* of the exhibition, to use the title of Lawrence Weiner's work that one could read on the inside of the glass separating the rotunda from the rest of the exhibition. It is in the associations between diverse objects from the past and more recent artworks, ranging from modern to contemporary, through which one finds the keys to understand the contemporary artworks and the themes on display across the overall exhibition, so one could say that the approach is inverted, compared with the Louvre.

A thought experiment might be a good way to conclude these notes: let's say that a meteorite had crashed in Kassel at the time of dOCUMENTA (13)[20] and had covered the Fridericianum with layers of earth and dust, and something similar happened in Paris during one of the transhistorical exhibitions at the Louvre, and shortly after our civilizations had come to an end. And let's say some future humans dug up both sites. Which one would they call a museum, a transhistorical museum?

20 A meteorite was actually supposed to land in front of the Fridericianum as part of the artistic project of Faivovich & Goldberg for dOCUMENTA (13), as part of a project that shed light on the expropriation of heritage of indigenous people in Latin America.

This text was delivered in a different form at the two-day symposium 'The Transhistorical Museum' at M-Museum in Leuven on 12 May 2016.

Literature

Berlin, Isaiah. 'Two Concepts of Liberty.' In *Four Essays on Liberty*, pp. 15–53. Oxford, 1969.

Crawford, Paul. *The Transhistorical Image: Philosophizing Art and its History*. Cambridge, 2012.

dOCUMENTA (13) Catalog 2/3: The Logbook. Edited by Carolyn Christov-Bakargiev, Bettina Funcke and Nicola Setari. Ostfildern, 2012.

Larceneux, Fabrice, Florence Caro and Anne Krebs. *De l'art contemporain dans les musées d'art classique? Une analyse de la perception des visiteurs*. Cahier de Recherche de DRM no. 2010–15. Université de Paris, 2010.

Lequeux, Emmanuelle. 'Polémique Jan Fabre au Louvre.' *Beaux-arts magazine* no. 288 (2008), pp. 76–79.

Martindale, Charles. *Redeeming the Text: Latin Poetry and the Hermeneutics of Reception*. Cambridge, 1993.

———. 'Reception: A New Humanism? Receptivity, Pedagogy, the Transhistorical.' *Classical Receptions Journal* 5, no. 2 (2013), pp. 169–183.

Sweeney, R.D. 'Arts, Language and Hermeneutical Aesthetics: Interview with Paul Ricoeur.' *Philosophy and Social Criticism* 36, no. 8 (October 2010), pp. 935–951.

Woolley, Leonard. *Ur 'of the Chaldees': A Revised and Updated Edition of Sir Leonard Woolley's Excavations at Ur.* Edited by P.R.S. Moorey. Ithaca, 1982.

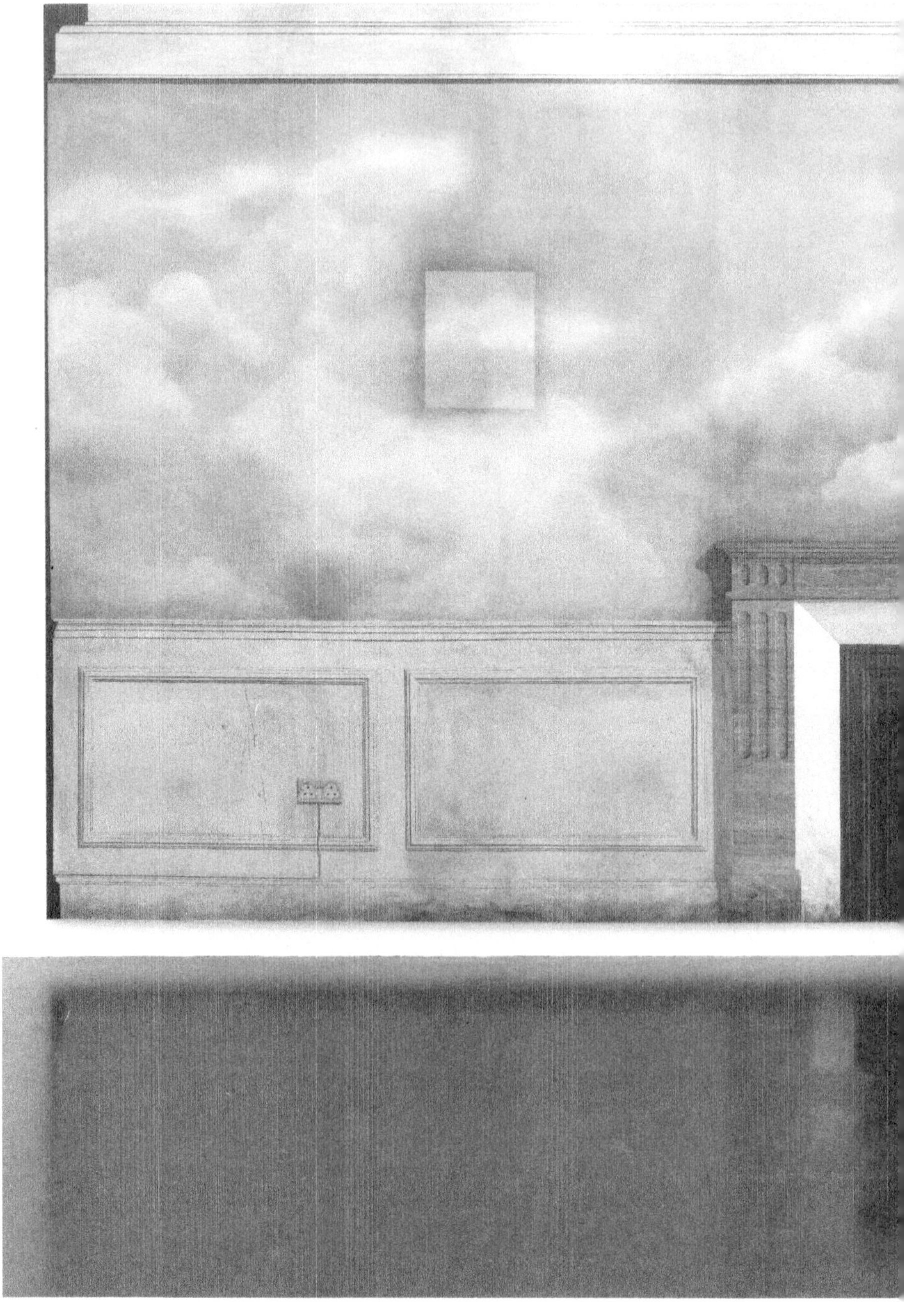

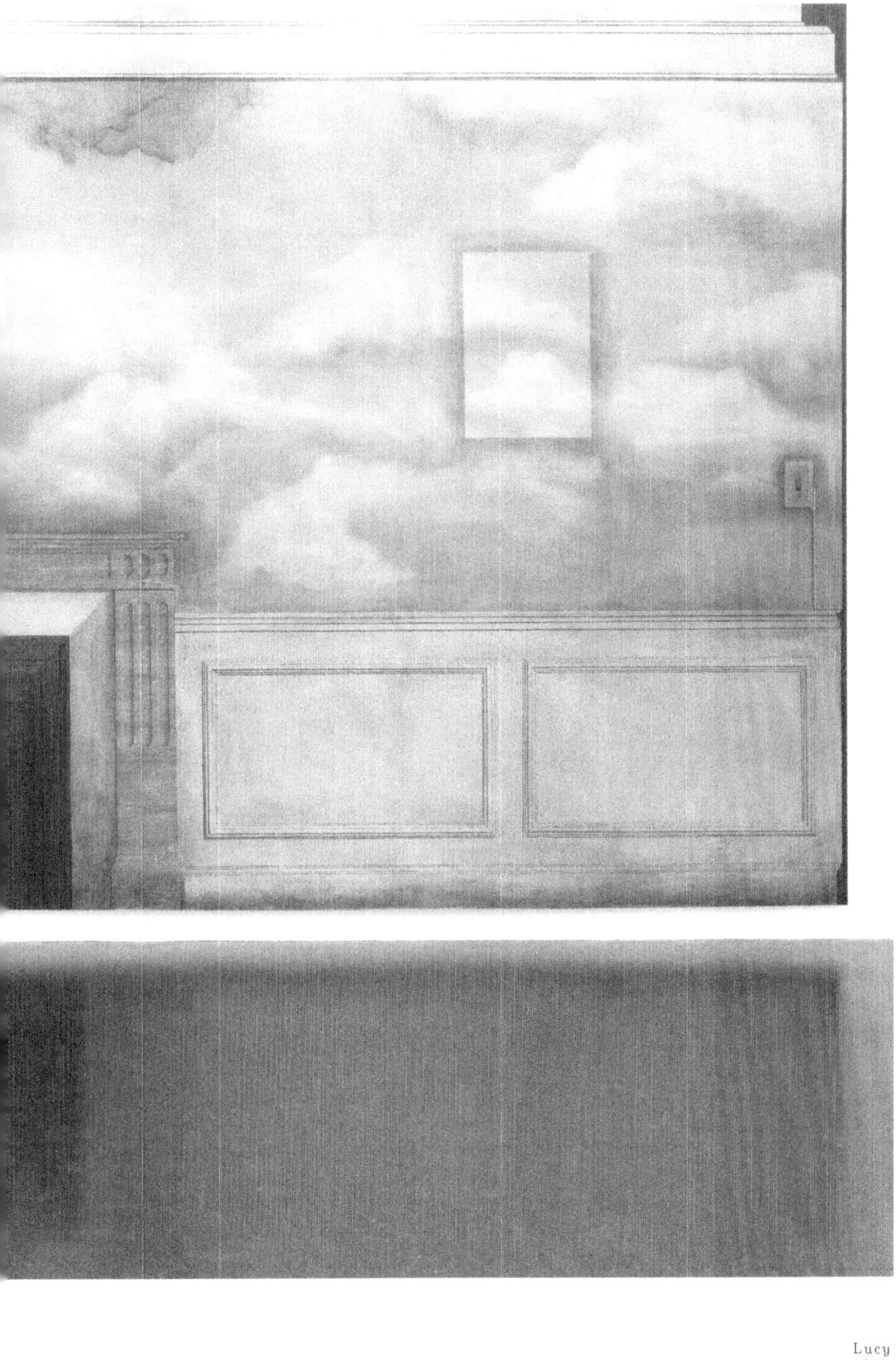

Lucy McKenzie, *May of Teck*, 2010, oil on canvas 2 parts, each 290 × 300 cm, installation view, Galerie Buchholz, Cologne, 2010. Courtesy Galerie Buchholz, Berlin/Cologne/New York.

(Re)Discovering Art History's Philosophical Foundations

An Interview with Hanneke Grootenboer

Melanie Bühler

MELANIE BÜHLER Why is it justified to apply an interpretation to a work of art that goes beyond its historical context?

HANNEKE GROOTENBOER Artworks do not belong to the period in which they were produced, but live a life in front of constantly changing audiences. This life is something that we, as art historians, should study as much as the historical context that produced it. In light of its biography, an artwork it is as much part of history as it is of our present day.

MB Your profile on the website of the University of Oxford describes you as follows: 'She insists that early modern art [which is your field] be viewed through the lens of contemporary art and theory.' Could you explain this?

HG I use twentieth- and twenty-first-century critical theory and philosophy to interpret early modern art. I explore the ways in which historical objects function as theoretical objects: as offering ideas or raising issues that are still urgent today. In my work, I attempt to (re)discover art history's philosophical foundations.

MB Would you call this transhistorical?

HG It is, in a way, because my approach goes beyond the idea that a historical paradigm is the one and true way for approaching historical objects. Rather than explaining a work of art by placing it back in its historical context, and asking what meaning it had when it was produced, I am interested in what philosophical or theoretical issues artworks raise, how they shape thought, and how they might be able to contribute to contemporary debates, on meaning making, for instance, or on issues related to medium and materiality.

MB There have been art historians who have been working with these kinds of questions since the beginning of the last century. In the texts that I have gathered for this publication, one art historian in particular is mentioned often: Aby Warburg. Could you talk a little bit about the art historical tradition that has inspired transhistorical thinking?

HG Aby Warburg is an interesting case. He believed that visual forms and particular motifs had a life of their own that corresponded to one another within a larger history, and that those forms had their own memories, so to speak. He was looking for visual rhymes and similarities, traces that would us lead to these memories on purely visual terms. His essentially visual approach was rather different from that of other art historians who participated in founding the discipline, for instance Erwin Panofsky, whose method to determine the meaning of a work of art (that he saw as inherent to the work) involved mostly textual sources. Warburg reasoned differently. His *Bilderatlas* is a constellation of images (photos, postcards) attached to sixty wooden panels, through which Renaissance art could be traced back to the visual language of the antique period. He called this project his *Mnemosyne Atlas*, after the Greek goddess of memory who, very aptly for his project, is also the mother of the nine muses. His *Atlas* is a wild assemblage of images that all seem to correspond to one another. Looking at these images, one would be able to become aware of visual links and resonances: the afterlife of antique forms. It was an amazing project that no one has ever followed after him. He could be called the father of visual culture who presented visual art in a fundamental transhistorical perspective. Our looking at art is comparable to Warburg's *Bilderatlas*, as we produce associations and set up dialogues between works of art from significantly different periods. We constantly look for similarities and differences between objects of different time periods.

I agree with Amy Powell (who teaches at UC Irvine, US) who proposes that artworks do not so much transcend time as transgress our linear conception of it. She argues that medieval art prefigures, upsets, and repeats its own historical course. In my work, I suggest that art, past and present, offers us a thought (rather than a meaning, or a narrative), and that it is capable of articulating thought in visual terms. As such, it invites us to think. Semiotics is a mode of interpretation whereby meaning is not located *in* a work of art, but is produced through the viewer. Meaning is only created at the moment a viewer comes on the spot and interacts with the work of art. Artworks are made to be looked at, they are made *for* viewers, and we could say, with Alois Riegl, that an artwork is waiting for us, as viewers, to come and see it, and to complete it, so to speak. A semiotic paradigm allows us to make transhistorical connections and approach early modern art from a twenty-first-century perspective.

In fact, we have seen this transhistorical perspective before. If we look at seventeenth-century Kunstkammer and cabinets of curiosities,[1] filled with all kinds of precious objects from the four corners of the world, small paintings, butterflies, and other specimen and so on, such collections were in fact a chaotic mess in which viewers brought order by looking around and reflecting on how these objects contained knowledge about the world, and what they were able to tell about history or time.

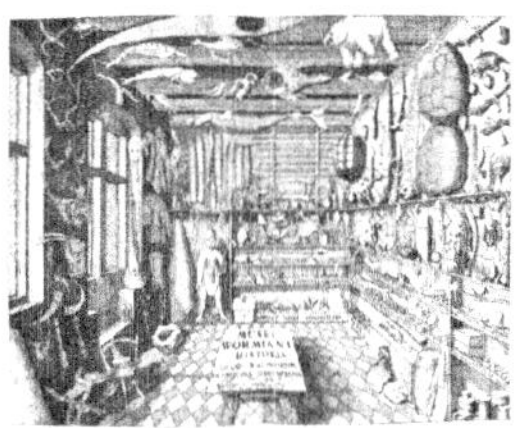

1 Cabinet of rarities (curiosity cabinet) of the museum of Ole Worm in Copenhagen, with natural history specimens on shelves against the walls, antlers on the left wall, fish and other animals hanging from the ceiling, spears and other weapons against the back wall; frontispiece to Ole Worm's 'Museum Wormianum' (Leiden, 1655), engraving, British Museum, London.

MB But then, between the seventeenth and the twenty-first century something happened: art history. So what happened that made this kind of context of looking and chaos a different one?

HG A lot happened: Enlightenment brought systematic thinking, Romanticism brought us the myth of the (male) genius. However, particularly for the discipline of art history, I think that Hegel's *Phenomenology of Spirit* was immensely influential on the foundation of the discipline. The idea of history as progress, of time unfolding in a direction and with an aim, and specifically his theory on art as developing towards an ideal form has become a part of the major art historical narrative, or at least for prominent, early art historians such as Alois Riegl. Ernst Gombrich's idea that art, in particular painting, is on a trajectory towards the ultimate copy or reality also echoes Hegel's thought. What does not quite fit within his concept of art's story is the invention of photography, and non-figurative art.

MB Did this kind of traditional art history that is connected to a linear conception of time persist, even after the

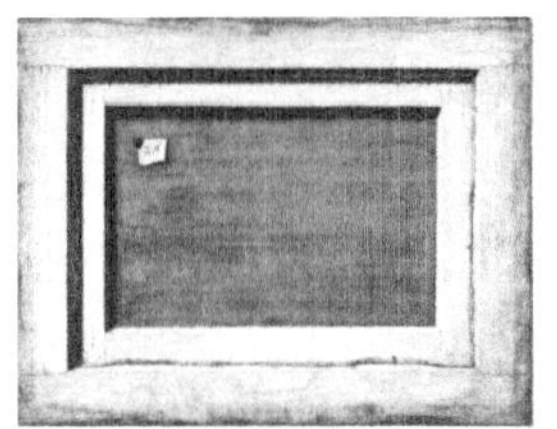

2 Cornelius Norbertus Gijsbrechts, *Trompe l'oeil. The Reverse of a Framed Painting*, 1670, oil on canvas, 66.4 × 87 cm, National Gallery of Denmark, Copenhagen.

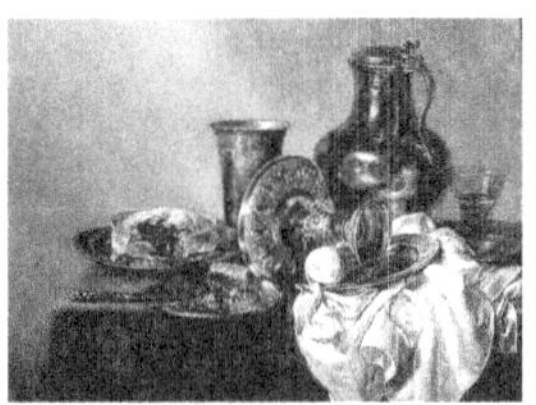

3 Willem Claesz. Heda, *Still Life with Pasty*, 1633, oil on panel, 58.6 × 79 cm, Frans Hals Museum. Photo: Tom Haartsen.

invention of photography? Or was modernism linked to a different kind of history?

HG We need to make a distinction between art historical writing and art making. Modernist artists were consciously breaking with the tradition of realistic representation, and keen to develop a new narrative that was intensely self-reflexive. The historical avant-garde proposed a different conception of time and of history whereby history could start anew. The point I make in my work is that early modern art is as self-reflexive, and as complex in its theoretical conception as modernist or contemporary art. For instance, if we look at early modern trompe-l'oeil painting we see a form of art that was profoundly self-aware, very much 'thinking' about the possibilities and limitations of itself as medium.[2] If you look at the work of Lucy McKenzie, or photorealism, you see how essential a sound conception of the history of illusionism is for our contemporary debates. Another obvious example is the way in which still-life painting contemplates different shapes and modulations of time, trying to come to terms with the tension between biographical time, and outliving. Not so much the represented objects in still lifes, but the representation as such, will outlive its maker as well as its owner and its viewers.[3] Such images are essentially painted philosophies, and they should not be seen as mere as historical objects, but as statements that are still relevant today. My work is driven by the idea that we should not only theorize history but also historicize theory.

MB You said that artworks invite us to look at them. Do artworks also invite other artworks to be compared with them?

HG If there is such a thing as a life of forms in art (as Henri Focillon would have it), and if forms have a memory, as Warburg suggests, then artworks are embedded in an ever expanding network of shapes and forms. Art practice exists as a result of a shaping and reshaping of these forms, and as a consequence are constantly resonating with other artworks through their very materiality. Every act of viewing an artwork is an act of interpretation, of making sense of these shapes and forms, comparing them with what is around them (in a museum context) or associating them with other works. Their shapes per definition recall previous shapes and anticipate future ones. So, yes, artworks are part of a larger network that museum curators and us art historians can further activate.

MB So, the activation always happens through the present because we are in the present, but it can actually configure a network of references that go to different parts in a time line.

HG Yes.

MB I was wondering if transhistorical relationships can also be formed within the past?

HG Renaissance art exists per definition as an answer to Antique art and thought. The revival of Antiquity, or the Gothic revival in the nineteenth century are both movements that self-consciously make transhistorical connections. The same holds for instance in which we see a clear break with the past, and the attempt to find a new language of forms. Another example of transhistorical relations that are formed in the past but spill over in the present time is a work of art that has continued to spark theoretical debates, such as Velázquez'

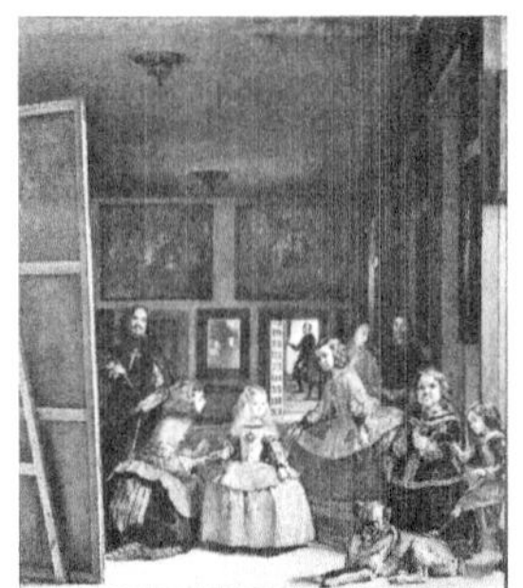

4 Diego Velázquez, *Las Meninas*, 1656, oil on canvas, 318 × 276 cm, Museo Nacional del Prado, Madrid.

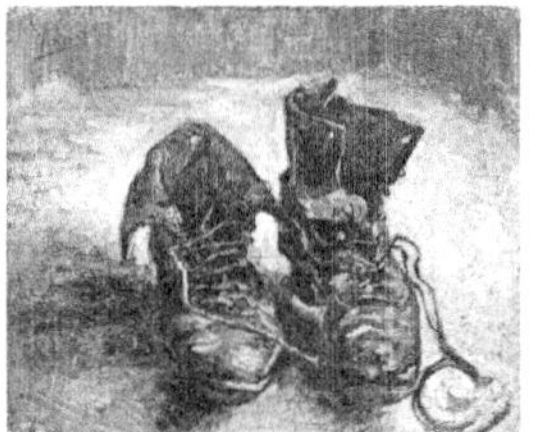

5 Vincent van Gogh, *Shoes*, 1886, oil on canvas, 38.1 cm × 45.3 cm, Van Gogh Museum, Amsterdam (Vincent van Gogh Foundation).

Las Meninas[4] or Van Gogh's *Shoes.*[5] Major reference points in the past, such works have continued to shape our modes of looking and thinking. Issues raised in contemporary art may not be incidental or contemporary, but often have deep roots in art's history. From a transhistorical perspective, it becomes clear that early modern or antique art is as theoretically complex as contemporary art practice.

MB Are we allowed to ask the same kind of questions that we ask ourselves in front of a contemporary artwork?

HG We could, but I think that artworks also ask things of us.

MB In a traditional art-historical sense, one would say that this is problematic because certain questions do not belong to a certain time; there is a certain horizon of possibility and if you go beyond that you are being ahistorical. Is there such a thing as being ahistorical?

HG Limitations of traditional historical research are the product of disciplinary institutions and present-day historians. The horizon of possibilities is not shaped by the past but drawn up by us in the present. I wrote a book on so-called eye-miniatures, a short-lived subgenre of portrait miniatures around 1800 of which hardly anything was known. Obviously, this project involved a lot of historical research but the amazing material of portraits of staring eyes also evoked a distinct theory of eighteenth-century gazing that sharpened the current art historical debates on the (Lacanian) gaze, and it presented a blue print for idea that artworks somehow 'look back' at their viewers. Our vision of the past is always through the lens of the present, per definition conditioned by present-day media and technology, and our viewing of artworks is always an encounter, a clash of gazes.

MB You described how in your own methodology, you confront artworks from the past with contemporary discourse and questions. A transhistorical display often places contemporary artworks next to historical artworks. Would you say that this is the same kind of thought but then just visually executed, or would you say this is different?

HG The approach is very similar, and similarly thought-provoking. Interventions of contemporary artists in art galleries, for instance, always bring with them the unexpected, a moment of surprise, with the result that they create a situation in which both past and present object are suddenly placed in a different light. They are brought into dialogue, not just with one another, but also with us. Through this unexpected encounter, the objects challenge us, tease us for a response, and push us to question our being there, our mode of looking. They invite us to think.

Literature

Grootenboer, Hanneke. *Treasuring the Gaze: Intimate Vision in Late Eighteenth-Century Eye Miniatures*. Chicago, 2014.

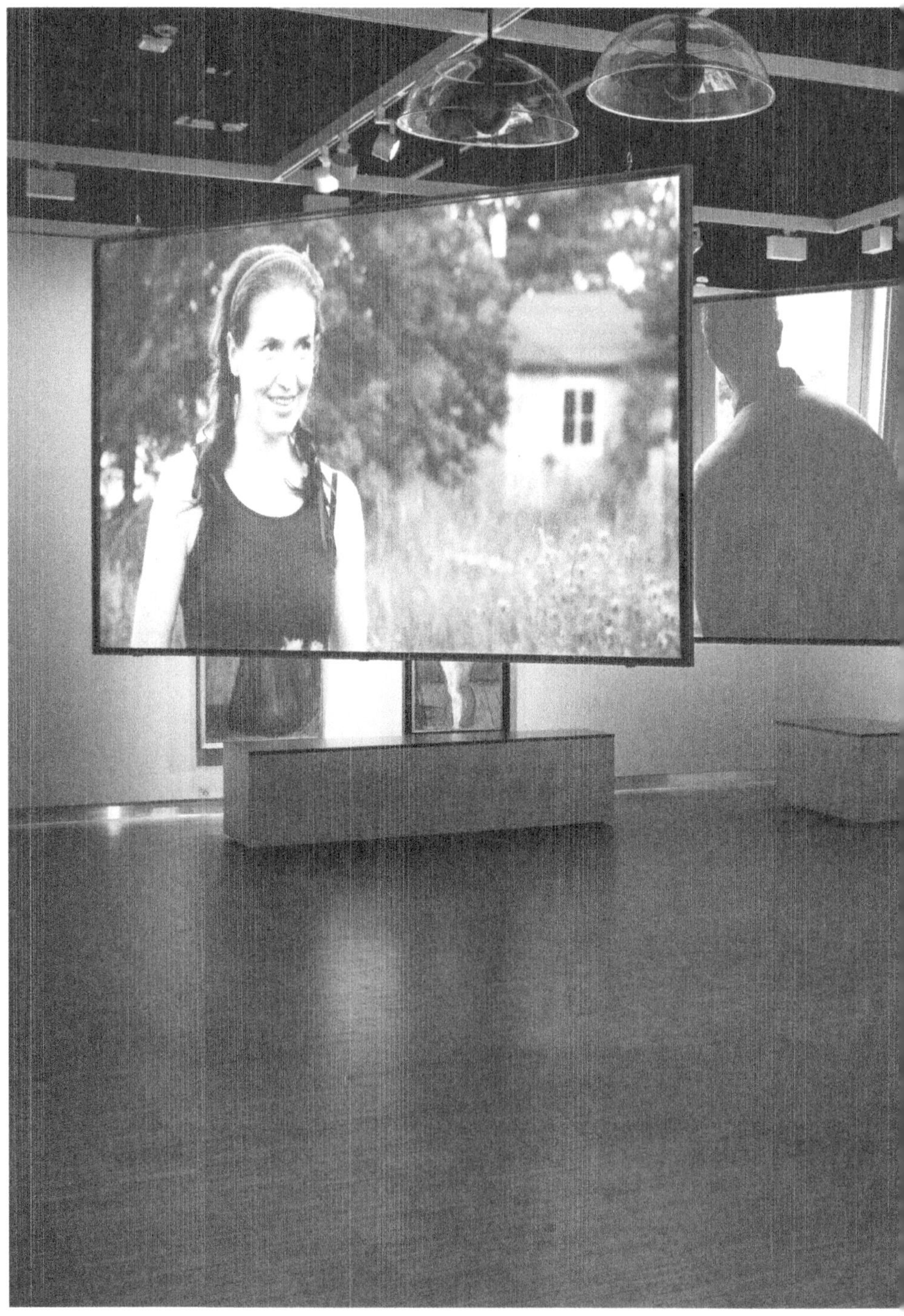

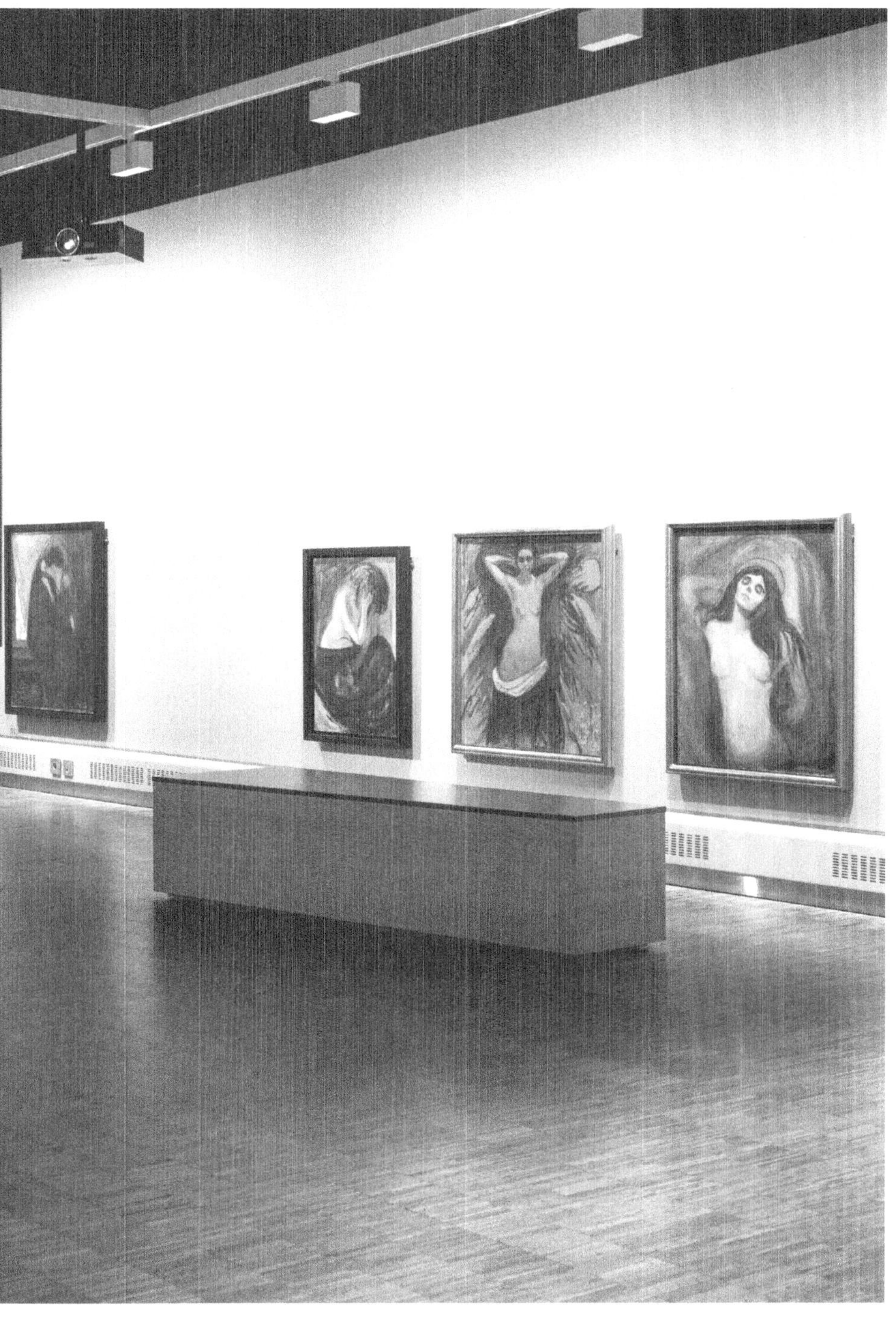

'Emma & Edvard: Love in the Time of Loneliness at the Munch Museum', curated by Mieke Bal, installation view, Munch Museum, Oslo, 2017. Courtesy Munch Museum.

Towards a Relational Inter-Temporality

Mieke Bal

Countering Historicism

This volume is devoted to a practice that counters a dogmatic historicism. With 'countering' I don't mean rejecting. The nuanced difference between 'counter-' and 'anti-' lies therein, that countering recognizes and engages history critically, whereas opposing it and simply rejecting it would be a case of throwing away the baby with the bathwater. Hayden White is the historian who shook up the complacency, arrogance, and certainty of history as an academic discipline. White did not write about art, although he did touch upon literature, but his views have had a lasting impact, not only on the historical discipline itself but also on art history. His view served as a deliverance, of the kind that stimulated thinking.[1]

When it comes to bringing this doubt cast on linear chronology to bear on museums and exhibitions—the subject of this book—I consider myself very lucky: I had the opportunity to visit, revisit, and visit again, both exhibitions Jean-Hubert Martin mentions in his contribution. He describes 'Carambolages' as a guideline for his views on exhibiting more in

1 White, *Metahistory*. I wrote an article about White's work: 'Deliver Us from A-Historicism: Metahistory for Non-Historians'.

general. The avoidance of all categories we are used to opened up the space for the experience of a different kind of relationships between the objects and between each object and the viewer. Briefly, visiting, or 'being inside' 'Carambolages' was an experience of recognition of the objects as subjects—as genuine interlocutors. Suddenly, a relatively small exhibition became too large to see it in a single visit, since each artwork now needed my time to say all it had to say, and to point out things about its neighbours. Although the material spatiality of the exhibition was more or less linear, the selection and display made it an immersive show—not in the old sense of drowning and becoming passive, but in the sense of completely going into a fictional universe where things happen.[2]

The other exhibition he only mentions briefly, 'Theatre of the World', I saw several times in La Maison Rouge in Paris, in 2013–2014. It had sections that created scenes, or phases of an unnarratable story of 'life'. No chronology, no coherent story, but still, each space made for the kind of intimacy that awakens the objects from their sleep. Throughout, there were no distinctions based on provenance, nor on art-artefact systems of knowledge and value hierarchies; no chronology. Antoine de Galbert, the owner and founder of La Maison Rouge, and in the catalogue for 'Theatre' Martin too, calls it 'décloisonnement'—clumsily translatable as 'decompartmentalization', removing the walls between categories. This is a negative epistemology in the constructive sense in which Nicola Setari discusses negative transhistoricity as liberating. This is the concept of literally 'removing walls' that I want to retain for the problematic discussed in this volume. Martin's opening article in the catalogue of 'Theatre' is subtitled 'The Museum of Enchantments versus the Docile Museum'. He refers to the theatre in the sixteenth century, in particular Shakespeare, and to the Renaissance idea of

2 See the illuminating catalogue, Jean-Hubert Martin, *Carambolages* (Paris, 2016). For White's views including their relevance for visual art, see my article, 'Deliver Us from A-Historicism'.

'theatre of memory' put forward by Giulio Camillo (1480–1544) as a tool to achieve universal knowledge, to offer (contestable) associations for the exhibition's title. He also mentions the association with cabinets of curiosity. But these references to historical objects and situations are not ways to sneak in a chronology, on the contrary.[3]

Offering enchantment as an alternative to docility is implying something for which I have myself often felt the need when visiting more traditional exhibitions: by ordering works in chronology, for example, the visitor is encouraged to be docile, following under the guise of allegedly objective knowledge a development that implies fixed values, from youth (not yet good enough but promising) to maturity (the best) and decline (alas, the work gets worse). It makes visitors into obedient students, followers. Enchantment, instead, is like the Romantic poet Samuel Taylor Coleridge's 'willing suspension of disbelief' as a definition of fiction. This is not a manipulative seduction, because the suspension is willing. But it allows letting go, if only provisionally—'suspension' is not 'abolition'—of the restrictions that rule our practical lives, and opening up to new experiences. As a consequence, when leaving the fictional space and time, we feel enriched, and are therefore better able to negotiate said restrictions creatively. This makes art an important player in the (utopian) impulse to change the world. Such an interpretation brings enchantment and magicians closer together, and takes away some of the controversial connotations that had been attached critically to the title of Martin's 1989 ground-breaking, yet hotly debated and criticised exhibition, 'Magiciens de la terre'.[4]

One gallery of 'Theatre,' a bit isolated from the others and lined with fabrics that muted sound—a practical as well as aesthetically relevant consequence of the curation—was especially significant. A Giacometti sculpture, one foot

3 De Galbert mentions the concept in *La Maison Rouge*. Martin's article is in the bilingual catalogue to his exhibition, English: 'Theatre of the World: The Museum of Enchantment Versus the Docile Museum', pp. 191–203.

4 This paragraph and the next are condensations from an article I published in 2015 on La Maison Rouge, 'Eccentricity in Order to Re-centre', which contains some images. This was before the devastating news, published in 2017, that De Galbert has decided to close this fabulous exhibition space, which has had such a ground-breaking impact on the Parisian art scene.

forward to indicate walking towards, all alone, faced a larger figure: a standing ancient Egyptian sarcophagus, towards which the Giacometti seemed to be on its way, as if for a conversation. Giacometti's figure seemed fearless, bold, yet modest, because the tall sculpture appeared so small and slim in comparison to the bulky sarcophagus. The sculptural objects were surrounded by a dazzling collection of bark cloths from different cultures. These are mostly abstract pieces of fabric most often used for ceremonial purposes. The section of this gallery was titled 'Majesté', a title that enhanced the sense that the sculpture was paying homage to, even venerating, the North-African object-subject, the 'Majesty' of the sarcophagus.[5] The lone sculpture from Western modernism is placed so as to represent the opposite of the traditional Euro-centric arrogance. Here, there is not a single, token African inclusion in an otherwise Western display, but the opposite. And this brings the entire gallery into movement, letting visitors imagine what it means to be alone immersed in difference, as visitors are, in fact, when they stand or walk in this large gallery. I expect this would mitigate Alexander Nagel's reservations about the alleged 'timelessness' of anachronistic exhibitions. The display was neither timeless nor geographically arbitrary; on the contrary.

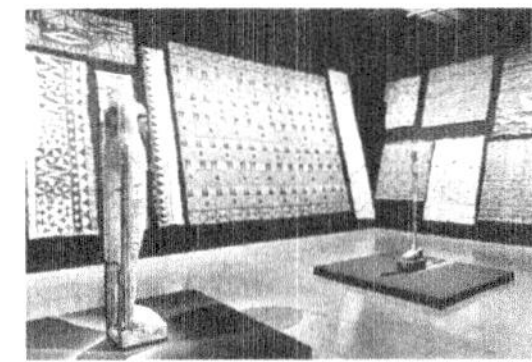

5 Majesté', installation view part of 'Théâtre du Monde', La Maison Rouge, Paris, 2013. Courtesy the artists, La Maison Rouge, Paris; MONA Museum of Old and New Art, Hobart. Photo: Marc Domage, 2013.

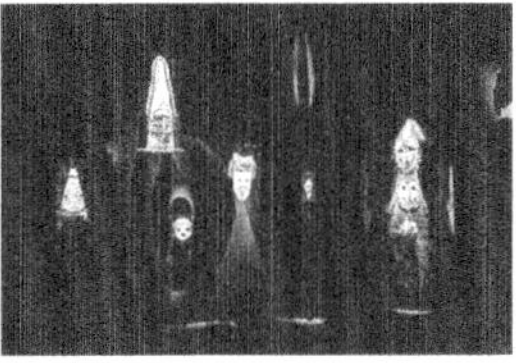

6 'Apparition', installation view as part of 'Théâtre du Monde', La Maison Rouge, Paris, 2013. Courtesy the artists, La Maison Rouge, Paris, MONA Museum of Old and New Art, Hobart. Photo: Marc Domage, 2013.

My other favourite in 'Theatre' was a small, transitory, very dark gallery where about 15 masks were hung on a rather wide, dark wall in front of which a bench invited seating.[6] This set-up, it turned out, was highly performative, and not only for me, as conversations with other visitors taught me. I learned in that moment something I knew but didn't realize: *seating means time.* And time, in its heterogeneous duration and subjective nature, is key to the experience of art. By making time easy, seating increases the willingness to stay; it encourages a durative immersion that gives the artworks the chance to have an impact. And indeed, time was needed, and spending time sitting on the bench was the tool to make that need felt. For, the masks were illuminated one by one, in random order and for an unpredictable duration. As a result, for the viewer sitting did not mean relaxing but, on the contrary, a condition to exercise active agency. One was sitting, but on (the) edge. The active agency, in turn, was indispensable to be able to *see*, and experience seeing as an activity requiring mobility, alertness, as well as trust that the work of the display will continue to be worthwhile; an acceptance that connects the mind and the body, and demonstrates their inseparability, in an active surrender, to use a paradox. Martin had transformed inert objects, often put away as 'artefacts', into a *moving* image—and feel free to give that qualifier as many meanings as you like ranging from cinematic to affective.[7]

Each object became singular, and the durational experience was both activating and humbling the viewers, since the possibility to see was out of their hands, yet also dependent on them. Different from sitting in a movie theatre, there was no sitting back and relax—no passive immersion as giving oneself over to the film. And different from being in a gallery, there was no way to hasten, walk through, and decide yourself how much time you spend there. This was a practical theorization of how *not* to make this display ethnographic, in other words an outside view displayed for consumption.[8]

Thus, I learned from Martin a lesson I had soon after an opportunity to bring into practice, in an exhibition I had the profound joy to be invited to curate in the Munch Museum in Oslo. This monographic museum devoted to the legacy of Norway's most important artist—and in my view modernism's most radical one—expressed the wish to change and update itself. I had three wishes for such an update, not only to adapt it to our time, but more importantly, to do better

7 Affective as that mind-body interaction that makes viewers *feel* the beauty. On affect as a concept in cultural analysis, see Van Alphen and Jirsa, *How to Do Things With Affect* (forthcoming).

8 See Heathfield, *Out of Now*, esp. pp. 17–23, 30–36 for an analysis of time in art.

justice to the art it houses, preserves, and shows. All three are attempts to innovate from within, to produce a kind of shock effect through inappropriate mixing. Mixing up chronology, as I had been advocating for a long time; mixing artists and media, as the director of exhibitions invited me to include our video installation *Madame B*, and—my lesson from Martin—radically change museum culture in the very practical sense of display: height of hanging, wall texts and captions, and, most crucially, seating.[9]

Mixing modes of being with art, that is. The latter is not only for visitors' convenience, but also to make them engage with the art, give it time, as the phrase has it, and make good on the fact that viewing, no matter when an artwork was made, occurs *in the present tense*. This does not reject a relationship with history, with the past; on the contrary. But that relationship can only occur if the present is endorsed as the time of viewing, hence, the viewer's responsibility is also necessarily endorsed. Only then can the 'middle voice' Mia Lerm Hayes cites from Maria Boletsi, emerge, and can the visitor and the artwork speak in a merging of affective, aesthetic and political discourses that is a true middle voice between active and passive, or better, emission and reception. This, in turn, dissolves the binary oppositions Penelope Curtis is rightly contending with in her contribution to this volume. So, do we all agree? Not really, fortunately. For, discussion, including disagreement, is necessary for culture to stay alive.[10]

9 For an extensive argumentation of these points, see my book that was published with the exhibition (not a catalogue), *Emma & Edvard Looking Sideways*. For a video tour and more information on the exhibition, see <www.miekebal.org/artworks/exhibitions/emma-edvard-love-in-the-time-of-loneliness/>. *Madame B* is a 19-screen video installation (Mieke Bal & Michelle Williams Gamaker, 2014); an inter-historical work based on Flaubert's novel *Madame Bovary*, made relevant for the present.

10 The invitation from Jon-Ove Steihaug, director of collections and exhibitions, included the idea to bring *Madame B* to the museum. In chapter 10 of *Emma & Edvard Looking Sideways* I develop the argument that Munch, without rejecting figuration, was not less but more radical in his modernism that his French colleagues. On the middle voice, see the fabulous article by Boletsi, 'From the Subject of the Crisis to the Subject in Crisis'.

Against Trans-, 'Post-', 'Beyond', and Other Problematic Terms

For me, the problem is in the term, and I contend that terms are not innocuous. It seems the authors of the articles in this volume converge on the need to break with chronological and spatial linearity. None of us have quarrels with that, even if Nagel has (justified, in my view) reservations on the ongoing practice of a mode of display that, as many of the other contributors also notice, has little innovation to boast about. Juxtaposing works across times of production may indeed even get as boring as the dogmatically chronological displays have become. The danger is that the idea can be positive in the sense of stimulating and negative in the sense of predictable alike. The authors would all probably underwrite what I wrote at the beginning of my 1999 book *Quoting Caravaggio*—which I quote here, with apologies for the impression of narcissistic self-indulgence:

> Quoting Caravaggio changes his work forever. Like any form of representation, art is inevitably engaged with what came before it, and that engagement is an active reworking. It specifies what and how our gaze sees. Hence, the work performed by later images obliterates the older images as they were before that intervention and creates new versions of old images instead. This process is exemplified by an engagement of contemporary culture with the past that has important implications for the ways we conceive of both history and culture in the present.

The reason I must quote it is that, in spite of the consensus that contemporary art, with the visions that feed it, and art from the past, are connected, is not enough. For, what is erased in the currently wide-spread term of 'transhistoricity' is precisely that connection: engagement. In other words, the relationship. And in my view, forgetting relationship can easily lead to an arbirary formalist, or repetitive thematic grouping of artworks. It is this that most contributors seem to have doubts about. I am not saying that what is called transhistoricity is wrong in itself, on the contrary. But a more focused attention to words and their implications would necessarily entail a rethinking of the choice of preposition. 'Trans-' means 'through', as in going through, without stopping, or changing one's own view, or being affected by what one traverses; without relating.[11]

Some time ago, when I was invited to give a lecture at a conference on 'Narrating Beyond Narration', I was irritated enough by the easy dismissal implied in 'beyond' to devote the entire lecture to the risks of the use of the preposition 'post-': the way it erases any relationship to what comes before, the subsequent claim to originality and superiority, based on the denial of the pernicious continuation of what was so wrong in that past, yet persists in the present. Denying that makes it again invisible; as invisible as it was when it was too self-evident to be noticed. 'Postcolonial' is the most blatant example. So, after bracketing that preposition I went on to defend narrative, and dismiss the implied dismissal—as, in fact, all the other speakers also did. No one really left narrative behind. But many still used the term 'post-' because of its hip connotations.

With this in mind, it seems timely to recall what I distinguished in 1988, relatively early on in the attempt to make disciplines less rigidly divided, when discussing different models according to which disciplines were trying to connect, merge, or otherwise collaborate. With 'transdisciplinarity' academics indicated thematic explorations that would bring together literary, folkloristic, anthropological, and visual 'versions' of a story that, according to early structuralist thinking, could be considered basically the same at heart. The influence of Vladimir Propp's *Morphology of the Folktale,* published in English in 1966, which proposed a grammar of

11 My first extensive statement in favour of what has later regrettably become 'anachronism' and I had termed 'preposterous history' can be found in that 1999 book, *Quoting Caravaggio*. Two extensive review articles on that book are worth consulting: Andersen, 'Mieke Bal's Preposterous Art History', and Salwa, 'The Space of Art History'. I further developed the concept and related issues in *Louise Bourgeois' Spider*.

stories entirely based on thematic categories, is evident here. This was soon followed by Roland Barthes' elaboration of it into a structuralist theory of narrative in an article from 1975, which made a great impact and attracted as many fierce critics. The key concepts in structuralism, such as similarity, repetition, and abstraction soon made the structuralist theory irrelevant for the study of literature. With the sense that nuances got lost, the transdisciplinarity lost any critical edge it might have had. Multi-disciplinarity was conceived as an 'umbrella' under which people from different disciplines studied similar objects, in projects like 'musical instruments in painting and literature'. I believed, and still believe that only *inter*disciplinarity led to new visions that affected the participating disciplines themselves.[12]

Since then I have tried to advocate the concept of interdisciplinarity, along with inter-historicity and many other forms of 'inter-ships'. The latter noun brings together all forms of activity named with the help of the preposition inter-, from interdisciplinary to intertextual, international, intermedial, intercultural to interdiscursive. Inter- means *between*. It denotes a willingness to exchange on an equal basis. To no avail: although many are involved in such endeavours, the terminological victory of the preposition 'trans-' seems irreversible. Which hurts my linguistic as well as my political and artistic feelings. The meaning of 'trans-' is 'going through'. This is why 'trans-' so often comes with 'across'.

12 Propp, *Morphology of the Folktale*; Barthes, 'An Introduction to the Structural Analysis of Narrative'. I made this distinction in *Murder and Difference*. In spite of the dismissal of structuralism implied in the term 'poststructuralism', more recent movements such as 'cognitive narratology' deploy similar structures, now called 'story logic'. See, for example, Herman, *Story Logic*.

In Praise of Inter-Ship

We know from translation, however, that such a movement does not mean that there is no impact of the original on the translations. And if we think that should be avoided, we ought to rethink Walter Benjamin's brilliant, perhaps disillusioning but linguistically and philosophically loyal view of language and translation. According to Benjamin, history, including the history of art, is neither a reconstruction of nor an identification with the past; it is a form of translation. Yes, here the preposition 'trans-' makes enough sense, and has become common enough, to maintain it, as long as we heed Benjamin's multiple qualifications. And these are more than relevant for our concern with the museum as temporally heterogeneous or, as we can also call it, 'heterochronic'. That relevance comes from the impossibility of trans-, as a non-affecting going-through; an indifferent traversal.[13]

Translation: *tra-ducere*. To conduct through, pass beyond, to the other side of a division or difference. If this etymology of translation is acceptable, it can be recognized in Benjamin's celebration of translation as liberation (p. 80), transformation, and renewal (p. 73), as a supplementation that produces the original rather than being subservient to it. The philosopher's view of translation becomes relevant when we consider it as a backdrop to his crucial remark in the fifth of the 'Theses on the Philosophy of History', where he warns, in one statement, against both the neglect and *fetishization* of the past, while foregrounding both visuality and the imagination:

> The past can be seized only as an image which flashes up at the instant when it can be recognized and is never to be seen again. ... For every image of the past that is not recognized by the present as one of its own concerns threatens to disappear irretrievably.[14]

The past rejected by 'anti-historical' thought disappears, forever. The past made irrelevant for the present deprives past

13 For a discussion of heterochrony, see the catalogue for the exhibition I co-curated: *2MOVE*. There the issue was especially discussed in view of 'migratory aesthetics'.

14 Benjamin, 'Theses on the Philosophy of History', p. 255.

art of its political agency, and nurtures indifference. The preposition 'trans-', premised on the traversal without stopping and engaging, risks neglecting the awareness that the past does not need to be fetishized, precisely because it is inevitably with us. And this is the case because older art has its own contemporaneity. Artists from the past made their work as contemporary—inevitably. It is that contemporaneity that needs to be kept in view. If artworks still have so much to say to us, it is not because of some concept of beauty, since such concepts, and the taste that sustains them, change with time. Nor can coherence, plausibility, or depth of ideas, narratives, or figures be considered transhistorical or universal criteria. If there ever was an unreflected anachronism, it is such judgments presented as universal, as all contributors to this volume caution. This entails a careful generalization concerning inter- and hence, 'intership' that, in turn, serves as a frame for my plea for anachronism as a guide for assessing the loyalty, or friendship, and debate between contemporary art and its predecessors, whether or not these can be considered 'sources'.

The need of relationality and the acknowledgement of the past's presence in our present makes a distinction between 'good' and 'bad' anachronism so necessary that the term 'preposterous' that brackets the more common term while alluding to the common rejection, seems to serve the purpose better. Indeed, historians tend to think of anachronism as the worst mistake, and they are not altogether wrong. It implies projecting a contemporary vision on a past for which that vision could not yet exist, and hence, cannot be relevant. Thus, it is historically naïve and it hampers insight into that past one seeks to understand. Anachronism, one might think, flattens time, makes everything resemble the present, and thus clouds the historical artworks with irrelevant considerations. Often, such criticisms are justified. I want to argue, however, how a strengthening of anachronism brings us closer to older artworks, not as a heritage from the past but as partners in a discussion of what matters in contemporary culture. This approximation does not come at the cost of historical difference; on the contrary, it enhances it, deploys it as a tool to sharpen how and what we can see. Anachronisms can invigorate our interactions with historical objects. They can achieve this revitalizing by means of different responses to the past in relation to the present.

In an installation at the Guggenheim Bilbao Museum, Michelle Williams Gamaker and myself once had the opportunity to show visually how a strengthening of anachronism can be very productive in this sense. Anachronisms can achieve this revitalizing by means of at least four different responses to the past in relation to the present: *clash*, *continuity*, *projection*, or *reversal*. Provided we refrain from a-historical presentism, anachronism allows us to be more, rather than less, loyal to the moment in time with which it establishes a *discordant dialogue*. If history is accounting for, explaining and giving meaning to, *change over time*, then anachronism is key to history. It is indeed the *conditio sine qua non* of recording, noticing, *seeing* change. I would contend that this is, in fact, what our time has in common with the Baroque. That period shares with ours a keen awareness of the fact that time is not linear, and that past and present are co-temporal. Both are part of a present that does not flatten time but, on the contrary, multiplies and enlivens it.[15]

This must suffice to make the case for the need for relationality that, I would like to propose, is the point of what is called, but problematically so, the 'transhistorical museum'. 'Inter-', instead, makes such indifference to the past impossible. Clumsy as the term may sound, I propose to speak of

15 The installation titled 'Anacronismos' was commissioned as a commentary to the exhibition 'The Golden Age of Dutch and Flemish Painting from the Städel Museum' curated by Jochen Sander, then acting director of the Städel, in 2010. It was to make sense of the exhibition of such a classical body of painting in Frank Gehry's exuberantly 'postmodern' building that houses the Guggenheim Bilbao Museum.

the inter-historical museum. This would keep us alert to the need to establish relationships, in the way Martin did so brilliantly in 'Carambolages'. In spite of its common use in the term 'translation,' where it does enough damage by suggesting the possibility and ideal of literally adequate translation, the preposition 'trans-' is best replaced by 'inter-'. And if 'intership' as a term is so close to internship, that may be for a good reason. For the relationality of 'inter-' keeps us all learning—avoiding self-satisfaction and arrogance. So much the better; learning is the most dynamic way of life, in contemporaneity.

Literature

Alphen, Ernst van, and Tomáš Jirsa, eds., *How to Do Things With Affect: Affective Operations in Art, Literature, and New Media*. Leiden, forthcoming.

Andersen, Wayne. 'Mieke Bal's Preposterous Art History.' *The European Legacy* 6, no. 3 (2001), pp. 353–362.

Bal, Mieke. *Murder and Difference: Gender, Genre and Scholarship on Sisera's Death*. Bloomington and Indianapolis, 1988.

———. *Quoting Caravaggio: Contemporary Art, Preposterous History*. Chicago, 1999.

———. *Louise Bourgeois' Spider: The Architecture of Art-writing*. Chicago, 2001.

———, and Miguel Á. Hernández-Navarro. *2MOVE: Video, Art, Migration*. Exh. cat. Murcia [etc.], 2008.

———. 'Deliver Us from A-Historicism: Metahistory for Non-Historians.' In *Philosophy of History After Hayden White*. Edited by Robert Doran, pp. 67–88. London, 2013.

———. 'Eccentricity in Order to Re-centre: La Maison Rouge.' *Journal of Curatorial Studies* 4 (2015), pp. 214–236.

———. *Emma & Edvard Looking Sideways: Loneliness and the Cinematic*. Oslo and Brussels, 2017.

Barthes, Roland. 'An Introduction to the Structural Analysis of Narrative.' *New Literary History* 6, no. 2 (Winter 1975), pp. 237–272.

Benjamin, Walter. 'Theses on the Philosophy of History.' In *Illuminations*. Edited by and with an introduction by Hannah Arendt. Trans. Harry Zohn, pp. 253–264, New York, 1968.

Boletsi, Maria. 'From the Subject of the Crisis to the Subject in Crisis: Middle Voice on Greek Walls.' *The documenta 14 Reader*. Edited by Quinn Latimer and Adam Szymczyk, pp. 431–468. Munich, London and New York, 2017.

Heathfield, Adrian. *Out of Now: The Lifeworks of Tehching Hsieh*. Cambridge, 2008.

Herman, David. *Story Logic: Problems and Possibilities of Narrative*. Lincoln and London, 2002.

La Maison Rouge: 2004–2009. Edited by *La Maison Rouge*. Paris, 2009.

Martin, Jean-Hubert. *Carambolages*. Paris, 2016.

Propp, Vladimir. *Morphology of the Folktale*. Austin, 1966.

Salwa, Mateusz. 'The Space of Art History: Mieke Bal's "Preposterousness".' *Art Inquiry* 11 (2009), pp. 159–173.

White, Hayden. *Metahistory: The Historical Imagination in Nineteenth-Century Europe*. Baltimore, 1973.

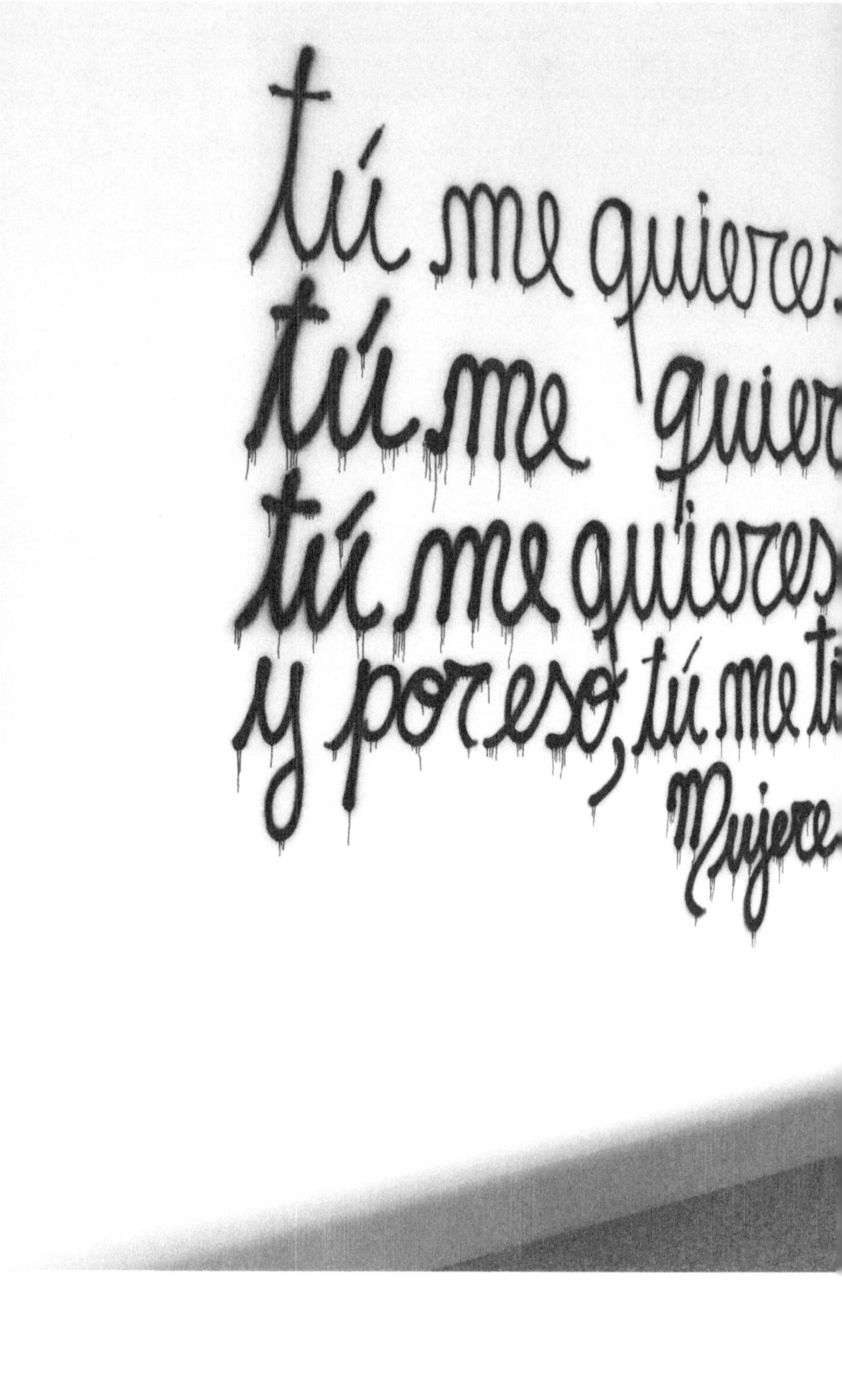
tú me
tú me
tú me quieres
y por eso, tú me

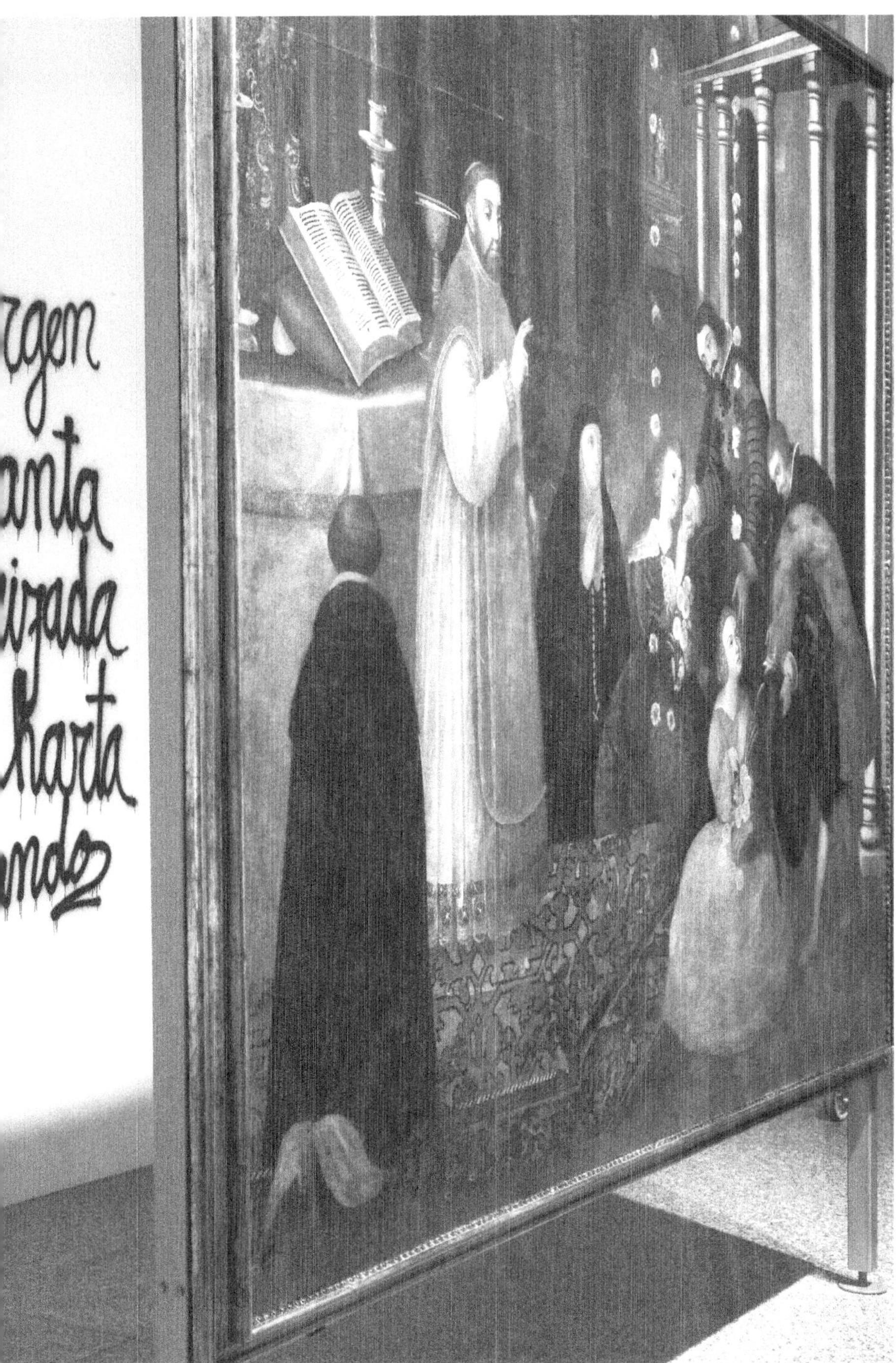

María Galindo and Mujeres Creando, *Ave Maria, full of rebellion*, 2010, installation; anonymous, *The beginners*, seventeenth century, School of Potosí, oil on canvas, installation view, 'The Potosí Principle', Museo Nacional Centro de Arte Reina Sofía, Madrid, 2010.

Transhistoric Display and Colonial (Dis)Encounters

María Íñigo Clavo
and Olga Fernández López

To hold alternative histories is to hold alternative knowledges.[1]
—Linda Tuhiwai Smith

Disciplinary (Dis)Encounters

1 Tuhiwa Smith, *Decolonizing Methodologies*, p. 34.

During the last decade, the evolving fields of museum and curatorial studies have intersected with concurrent conversations that have put forward new terms, such as performativity or transhistoricity. In the context of a transdisciplinary repositioning of the humanities, the abundance of the 'post' prefix in cultural analysis has shifted into a wider use of 'inter' or 'trans', which implies the introduction of multiple temporalities, a cross-pollination between disciplines and a decentring of methodologies. Among other encounters, the postcolonial theoretical corpus has played a crucial role in challenging the colonial nature of Western national narrations in museums, drawing new cartographies that conveyed the complex interactions between geography and history.

The fragmentation of the grand historical narratives that took place throughout the 1980s did not necessarily result in the end of history or in cultural relativism, but in a new interest in the writing and representation of the past, as well as a major critique of the national narratives and the institutions that gave shape to their ideologies. As part of this thinking modernity, capitalism and coloniality have been considered associated experiences, unfolding over time and space, emphasizing long-term processes that go beyond the traditional Western historical and geographical divisions, introducing notions such as transmodernity. This term was put forward by Enrique Dussel and expresses the need to resituate modernity in a larger map, considering the reciprocal influences that Western and non-Western cultures have had on each other. This approach questions the unidirectionality of the way the modern project has been discursively configured and tries to supersede classical positions of subalternization, violence, guilt or atemporality.[2] Postcolonial theories were not alone in this endeavour. Contemporary artists and curators were simultaneously, and in dialogue with postcolonial perspectives, dealing with the same issues, creating productive intersections between museology, history writing, and colonial histories.

2 Dussel, 'Eurocentrism and Modernity'.

It is obvious that museums and exhibitions are two of the most powerful dispositives for conveying colonial and national ideologies. Therefore it is inevitable that the naturalization they provoked has been a target of critical approaches in the last decades. As we shall see through various examples, the association of artworks, artefacts, and material culture belonging to different contexts, times or social spheres in a new epistemological, contemporary framework has been a key strategy to put into question the dominant narratives and to create a deepened, perhaps more complex sense of transhistoricity, in which the stakes are high. It needs to be said

3 See Íñigo Clavo, 'Statues also die, even...' and Fernández López, 'The Uncertainty of Display'.

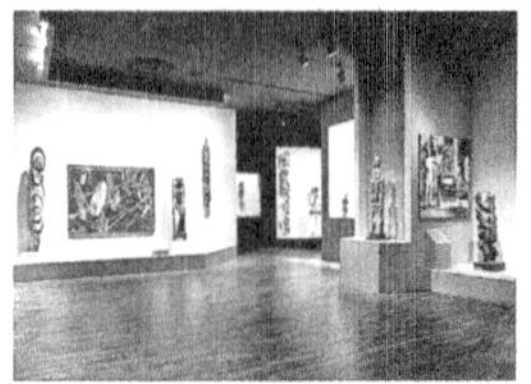

4 '"Primitivism" in 20th-Century Art: Affinity of the Tribal and the Modern', installation view, Museum of Modern Art, New York, 1984. The Museum of Modern Art Archives.

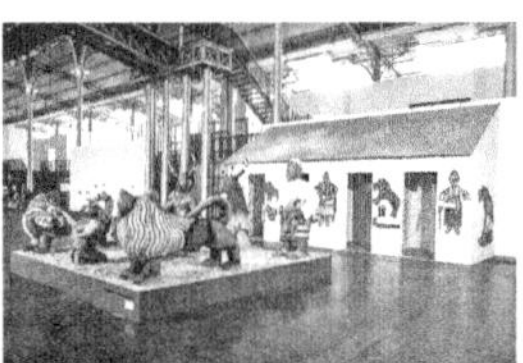

5 'Magiciens de la terre', installation view, Centre Georges Pompidou and La Grande Halle, Parc de la Villette, Paris, 1989.

that the coexistence of diverse ranges of objects was not a new curatorial strategy in the twentieth century. The juxtaposition of artworks and artefacts has been a recurrent scheme in modern art exhibiting practices since the beginning of that century. Significantly, one of the earliest modernist display trends was to assemble avant-garde works together with objects coming from non-Western cultures belonging to different historic periods, a procedure that was soon naturalized and served various agendas.[3]

Nevertheless, as we have mentioned, during the 1980s postcolonial theories had a deep impact on the ideological implications that this coexistence brought about. This was evident in the polemics generated by '"Primitivism" in 20th-Century Art',[4] an exhibition at MoMA in 1984 that addressed the formalist influences that European and US modern art received from what was then called 'primitive art' without acknowledging colonialism, or 'Magiciens de la terre',[5] a show that placed together living artists from Western and non-Western countries and that was highly criticized for its neo-exoticism and lack of contextualization. Bringing together heterogeneous objects was not sufficient. In fact, this dialogue made more explicit the latent colonialist ideology that these displays still bore. The transmodern conceptions of spatiality, temporality, modernity, and nation cannot be addressed unless curatorial projects redirect their focus, with an explicit political aim, onto the frameworks that build their discourses. The displaying together of artworks, artefacts, and material culture needs to involve not only the mere association of objects, but the encounter of disciplines that have taken these pieces as objects of study, such as art history, political, social, and economic history, anthropology, museology, and even natural sciences. The possibility of confronting disciplines through contemporary art has been one of the more useful keys to make visible the colonial nature of Western epistemology that is still at the base of most museums, especially in the way it separates human and natural sciences, human actors from passive objects of knowledge or high culture from popular culture.[6] As we will see, each discipline brings its own debates on how temporality makes these divisions effective.

6 De Sousa Santos, 'A Discourse on the Sciences', p. 39.

Art-thropology: Making the Past Part of the Same Present

The common ground of art and anthropology has been a fertile field for exploring confronting notions of time. A recurrent feature of this debate is the museological silence about the historical dimension of non-Western cultures, along with the isolation of the European narrations of its own past. During the first postcolonial momentum, an exhibition such as 'Art/Artifact' (Center for African Art, 1988) tried to confront the relationship between these two disciplines by highlighting the historicity of display systems. In the show the curator Susan Vogel reconstructed four different modes through which non-Western objects had been (re)presented in museums: cabinet of curiosities, ethnographic museums vitrines, Natural History museum dioramas, and modern art galleries.[7] This genealogy of displays re-inscribed the objects into a historical (Western) timeline and refuted the (fictive) atemporality in which non-Western material culture was suspended in museums. As Canadian First Nations art historian and curator Ruth Phillips states: 'Art historians have primarily studied the European tradition in diachronic development, while most anthropologists have studied non-European peoples synchronically.'[8] This schismatic approach was constructed on a specular negation, geographical and historical.

7 'Art/Artifact: African Art in Anthropology Collections', Center for African Art, 1988.

8 Phillips, 'The Museum of Art-thropology', p. 11.

9 Gaskell, 'Ethical Judgments in Museums', p. 229.

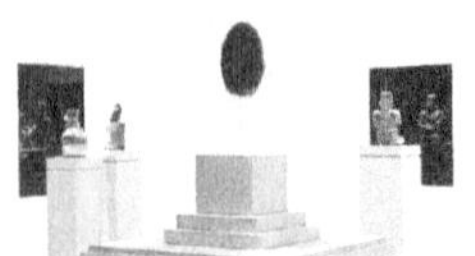

10 Pedro Lasch, 'Black Mirror/Espejo Negro', 2008, installation with dark glass sheets and works from the Nasher Museum's permanent collection. Courtesy of the artist.

11 The black mirror was commonly used in the eighteenth and nineteenth centuries by naturalists and painters to capture landscapes. Mignolo, 'Decolonial Aesthetics'.

A recent example of innovative museum curating has been that of Ivan Gaskell and his team at Harvard. In exhibitions such as 'Tangible Things' (2011), they merged the collections of the Harvard Art Museums and the Peabody Museum of Archaeology and Ethnology, considering all of the objects as artefacts, for instance a painting of Edgar Degas and an ethnographic object, in order to incite a de-hierarchization of spheres of knowledge. The kind of disciplinary destabilization that Gaskell looks for can be understood in one of his statements: 'One person's god is another's idol, which, to yet another, is an archaeological find, and to yet another, a work of art. One person's pet is another's dinner.'[9]

A similar kind of procedure was developed by the exhibition 'Black Mirror/Espejo Negro', curated by artist Pedro Lash in 2009 in the basement of the Nasher Museum of Art in North Carolina, where he re-displayed the pre-Columbian collection.[10] In the show he presented the anthropologic pieces (most of them, anthropomorphic gods and goddesses) turning their backs to the spectator and facing black mirrors in which he had printed the images of paintings from Spain from the seventeenth century. When looking at the shiny surfaces, the spectator could see at the same time the reflection of the gods and that of the Spanish kings.[11] The exhibition took place when the museum was hosting an exhibition of Diego Velázquez and El Greco in the main rooms. The symbolic location of the shows reaffirmed the discourse that placed high art pieces on the principal floors and the anthropologic pieces in the *basements* of Western history. The show triggered a double confrontation that spoke about the curatorial policies of the Museum and forced history back into the timeless ethnographic artefacts in order to re-tell the incomplete history of modernity.

The dialogue between art and anthropology underwent

broad changes in the last decades, following the postcolonial critiques and the recent indigenous questioning of the ways in which their cultures were (and still are) displayed. This has facilitated a process of reciprocal learning that may have resulted in what Ruth Phillips calls an 'art-thropology'.[12] A good example of how this notion may be materialized was the work of Clémentine Deliss at the Weltkulturen Museum in Frankfurt between 2010 and 2015. In that period she invited contemporary artists from countries whose pieces were represented in the collection for a short-term residence within the premises.[13] During their stay they would produce a piece or a show in relation to the collection that would bring certain artistic traditions to the present, challenging the assumption that there are permanent timeless world areas. Deliss works with the concept of 'remediation', an approach combining the reflection on the display medium, with a particular emphasis on translation processes, with conciliatory awareness of the origin and evolution of colonial collections.[14] Talking about her standpoints, Paul Rabinow had affirmed: 'Perhaps we say that the challenge is to make the Museum contemporary … . The registers through which the work of making a museum contemporary pass through the registers of remediation, curation and a process of contemporary assemblage.'[15] Making the museum contemporary means that the past is representable if its interpretation is done with a consciousness and explicitness of the present time, of its enunciation site and moment.

12 Philips, 'The Value of Disciplinary Difference'.

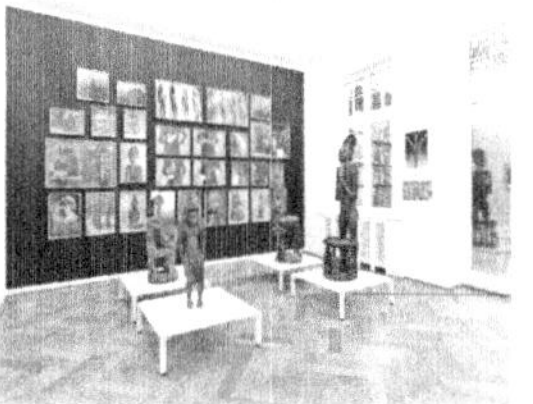

13 'Photographs of the Collection (1960–2013)' installation view with new works of Marie Angeletti, Otobong Nkanga, Benedikte Bjerre, Weltkulturen Museum, Frankfurt, 2013. Photo: Wolfgang Günzel, 2013.

14 Deliss, 'Collecting Life's Unknowns'.

15 Rabinow, 'A Contemporary Museum'.

Transmodern Entanglements: Syncing Different Histories

The possibility of giving a visual, material, and performative shape to the conflicts between disciplines through exhibition displays has also been fundamental in interrupting former

16 'Mining the Museum', Maryland Historical Society, Baltimore, 4 April 1992–28 February 1993, curated by Fred Wilson.

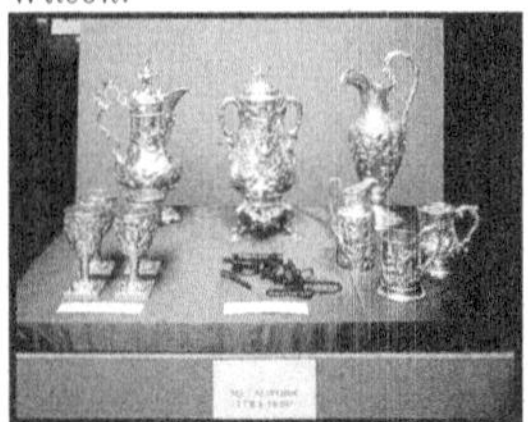

16a Fred Wilson, *Metalwork 1793–1880*, installation view, 'Mining the Museum', Maryland Historical Society, Baltimore, 1992.

17 'America: Bride of the Sun: 500 years Latin America and the Low Countries', Royal Museum of Fine Arts, Antwerp, 1992, curated by Paul Vandenbroeck and Catherine de Zegher. See also 'F(r)ictions', Reina Sofía Museum, 2011, curated by Ivo Mesquita and Adriano Pedrosa.

18 Jean Fisher, 'Conquest and the Treason of Images', at <www.jeanfisher.com/conquest-and-the-treason-of-images/> (accessed 7 February 2018).

19 'The Potosí Principle: How Can We Sing the Song of the Lord in an Alien Land?', Museo Reina Sofía, Madrid, 2010, curated by Alice Creischer, Max Jorge Hinderer, and Andreas Siekmann.

schemes of world historical narration. Two early examples of how transmodernity and the need to connect histories has been addressed through a transhistorical display were Fred Wilson's 'Mining the Museum' (1992)[16] and 'America: Bride of the Sun: 500 years Latin America and the Low Countries' (1992)[17]. In the latter, historical art and artefacts from both sides of the Atlantic were displayed in dialogue with twentieth-century Latin American artists addressing colonialism. The exhibition aimed 'to present an ambitious argument about the propaganda power of images in the historical process of conquest and religious conversion, by which it hoped to draw an analogy with the role of images in contemporary socio-political life'.[18]

If 1992 was a key year in challenging the Fifth Centennial of the Conquest of America, during the last decade the postcolonial debate has gained a growing significance in Spain. This interest has facilitated a number of transhistorical exhibition projects. One of them was 'The Potosi Principle' (Museo Reina Sofía, Madrid, 2010), an exhibition with the aim of renaming modernity from a Latin point of view, taking as a starting point the Iberian colonization instead of the Industrial Revolution, the landmark at the base of Anglo-Saxon theorizations.[19] In this project, colonial baroque paintings from the seventeenth and eighteenth centuries depicting Potosí, one of the richest mining cities of Bolivia during colonization, along with sculptures representing saints shaped after the hybrid spirituality of the indigenous population, were in conversation with contemporary art addressing contemporary capitalist exploitation in places such as Abu Dhabi or China. This parallelism speaks about the function of art in these two historical moments, suggesting that contemporary art is serving capitalism in the same way that colonial paintings were a pedagogical instrument in that period. Another example 'Apocryphal Colony' (MUSAC; León, 2014).[20] In this show, a large mixture of artworks, artefacts, and archival material ranging from the sixteenth century until the present explored how the colonial imagery had a continuity over the centuries, connecting past and present.[21] The exhibition was organized around concept-themes, such as archive, cartography, conquest, gospel, violence, and orientalism, among others, conveying how images had been and still are agents of coloniality.[22]

20 'Apocryphal Colony', MUSAC, León, 2014, curated by Juan Guardiola.

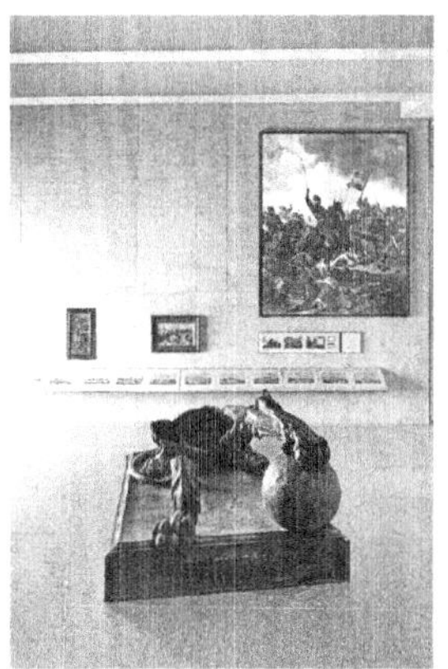

21 Fernando Sánchez Castillo, *Lion I (Anamnesis)*, 2003, installation view, 'Colonia Apócrifa', MUSAC, León, 2014.

22 Two more examples: 'Atlas of the Ruins of Europe', CentroCentro, Madrid, 2016, and 'Stimulants: Circulation and Euphoria', Tabakalera, San Sabastián, 2017. See also Vallés Vílchez, 'Desde la maraña a la araña'.

23 Phillips, 'The Museum of Art-thropology', p. 14.

Between the 1980s and the early 2000s, the transmodern argument took the Atlantic tricontinental area (Europe, Africa, Americas) as a privileged geographical and cultural space to think about the colonial long-term history. In this context, terms such as influence, hybridity, in-between, creolization, or diaspora contributed to the undermining of Western conventional classifications of objects based on typological taxonomies, genres, authors and schools, or formalist criteria. These new vocabularies designated the need to situate historical objects in the place of the transference between cultures, as negotiators of different social spheres and times. Subsequent to these, some curators have brought together postcolonial theories with renewed frameworks, such as Bruno Latour's actor network theory. Among them, Ruth B. Phillips was inspired by this theoretical background and made a link between them through the notion of translation. In her words:

> in order to reconnect that which has been severed by the modern 'work of purification', through translation we may be able better to reposition within networks of complex and apparently heterogeneous social, political, economic, and natural events.[23]

It is precisely *in* the objects where very different networks of forces and histories converge, so they need to be seen as entanglements (*imbroglios*), impure artefacts that need a political act of translation capable of making visible the threads that cross them.

However, ten years later some of these terms have begun to be insufficient to address the Western appropriationist, if not fully extractivist, condition around Southern concepts and forms. The recent development of decolonial perspectives demand a clarification of the horizons of these translations and of the goals implied in every part. In this sense, a new generation of authors, such as Jota Mombaça, have alerted to the risk of not fully acknowledging the violence imposed by colonial difference through these celebrated concepts of negotiation and to the risk of perpetuating extractivism using extra-Western concepts and instrumentalizing them in Western frames.[24] In this line of thinking, exhibitions such as 'Mestizo Histories' (Instituto Tomie Ohtake, São Paulo, 2014) have been critically appraised. This show tried to open the former Brazilian narratives by introducing non-Western religions, indigenous people, and afro-descendent material culture, in dialogue with Western objects of art and material culture, highlighting a celebratory notion of *mestizo* and also de-hierarchizating spheres of knowledge as we mentioned above. However, in spite of connecting these social spheres, the exhibition forgot to remark the political agency and the specific contributions of indigenous, slaves, and their descendants in the construction of the nation, citizenship and other political struggles. This 'oblivion' re-victimized them and ultimately, denied their participation in history.

24 See Mombaça, *Notas estratégicas quanto aos usos políticos do conceito de lugar de fala.*

In spite of some of these critiques, the clashing of artwork and historical artefacts has been an effective curatorial method to disrupt historical narrations. Another significant project was carried out by Canadian curator Richard Hill at the Art Gallery of Ontario in 2003, where he displayed objects from aboriginal cultures in the rooms of the National History section of the museum. He was explicit about the fact that those objects, if separated from the hegemonic national identity discourse, did not have the chance to challenge it. In his words: 'Our art can do much more—it can disrupt and challenge that narrative, be against it and at the same time be part of it, but not subsumed within it.'[25] However, the challenge of creating a *contemporary museum*, as Rabinow suggests, faces grand difficulties. The diachronic representation characteristic of museums of history ends up resulting in a kind of atemporality similar to the one produced in the synchronic museums of anthropology. In his book *Museum Memories*, Didi Maleuvre reflects on how the decontextualization of objects in the museum affects their temporality: 'In lifting art out of the hurly-burly of historical survival, the museum strips the artwork of its historical essence. It replaces historicity by historiography. Living historical existence turns into historiographical timelessness.'[26] The suspension of objects in a historiographical atemporality needs to be understood and challenged with the disruption of the present.

During the 1990s, authors from The Latin American Subaltern Studies Group made significant efforts to show how the Western construction of the nation is intimately linked with coloniality, pointing out that the construction of an imagined, homogenizing identity always involves the

25 Hill, 'Meeting Ground'.

26 Maleuvre, *Museum Memories*, p. 69.

27 See Rodríguez, *The Latin American Subaltern Studies Reader*.

28 They were respectively the Vice-president of the first Gran Colombian nation (1819–1827) and President of the New Granada Republic (1832 and 1837).

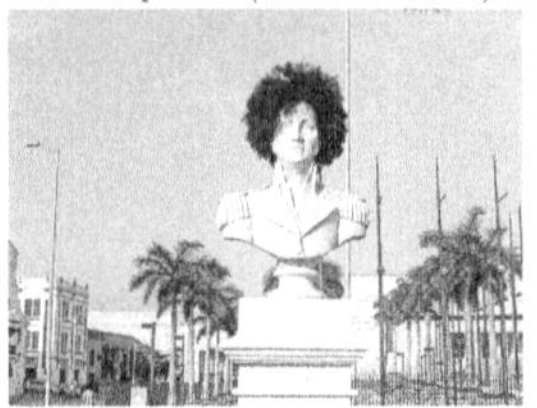

28a Nelson E. Fory Ferreira, *La Historia Nuestra, Caballero* (Our History Sir), 2008. Public intervention in the historic centre of the city of Cartagena. Courtesy of the artist.

denial of colonial difference.[27] Following from these Latin American theorizations, Cristina Lleras, curator of the exhibition 'Historia de un grito. 200 años de ser colombianos' ('The Story of a Scream. 200 Years of being Colombian') (Museo Nacional de Colombia, 2010) decided to show the rhetoric of Colombian national narration in the context of the Bicentennials Celebrations of Independence. In the nineteenth century the concept of history was developed hand in hand with the foundational moments instituted by the creation of new nations. Having that in mind, the curatorial team looked for artworks in the museum collection that depicted founders of the nation, important heroes, and emblematic battles that could make visible their politics of national identity representation and they used diverse strategies to mock, question, or contemporize these narrations, for example by writing questions on the walls of the exhibition such as: 'Do we all agree?' In the process, the exhibition succeeded in demonstrating how the memory of the nation had been administered by naming the strategies of oblivion and misrepresentation embedded in national discourses. Contemporary art was a good ally. At the entrance of the museum, presiding the exhibition, Nelson Fory Ferreira placed an afro wig on a bust of Simón Bolívar and another on Francisco de Paula Santander.[28] This simple carnivalesque gesture posed a harsh critique to the solemn objects created by the white elite that have eclipsed the stories of the noteworthy Afrocolumbian citizens.

In this text we have tried to connect various examples of the evolution of the debates on curating history and cultures in dialogue with postcolonial theory. We have written about the relationship between art and anthropology, about some attempts to display transmodernity, and about projects that focused on intervening in the national narrations. In all of them the disruption of marginalized stories through trans-historic displays had the aspiration of making evident how certain discourses have been constructed. Through a rapid overview we have seen how the questioning of the notion of Otherness in the 1980s was followed by using mediation strategies in the 1990s and, later on, by a need for destabilization that confronts our uncertainties about how to decolonize history as a discipline.[29] Recently, the demand for a more effective political action reminds us that we are far from having dismantled the colonial nature of our historical narrations. Displaying different cultures and their own sense of temporality and history necessarily involves an exercise of embracing new methodologies in our exhibition spaces. The major challenge now is to avoid what has been called epistemological counterpoint, the process of considering elements of non-Western culture under Western parameters. We need to be able to introduce not just objects from other cultures, or to reconceptualize the agency of our objects inspired in their animism, but to learn from different historical perspectives, accepting that they cannot be reduced to our parameters.

29 See Franke and Folie, *Animism*.

Literature

Deliss, Clémentine. 'Collecting Life's Unknowns.' In *Decolonising Museums*. Edited by L'Internationale Online, pp. 23–34. Ghent [etc.], 2015 ‹www.internationaleonline.org/research/decolonising_practices/27_collecting_lifes_unknowns›.

Dussel, Enrique. 'Eurocentrism and Modernity.' In *The Postmodernism Debate in Latin America*. Edited by John Beverley et al., pp. 65–77. Durham, 1995.

Fernández López, Olga. 'The Uncertainty of Display: Exhibitions In-Between Ethnography and Modernism.' In *The Ruined Archive*. Edited by Iain Chambers, Giulia Grechi and Mark Nash, pp. 145–162,

Milan, 2014.

Franke, Anselm, and Sabine Folie, eds. *Animism: Modernity through the Looking Glass*. Vienna, 2011.

Gaskell, Ivan. 'Ethical Judgments in Museums.' *Art and Ethical Criticism*. Edited by Garry L. Hagberg, pp. 229–242. Oxford and Malden, 2008.

Hill, Richard. 'Meeting Ground: The Reinstallation of the Art Gallery of Ontario's McLaughlin Gallery.' In *Making a Noise!: Aboriginal Perspectives on Art, Art History, Critical Writing and Community*. Edited by Lee-Ann Martin, pp. 50–71. Banff, 2004.

Íñigo Clavo, María. 'Statues also die, even...' *Stedelijk Studies* no. 1 (2014). ‹www.stedelijkstudies.com/journal/430/›.

Maleuvre, Didier. *Museum Memories: History Technology, Art*. Stanford, 1999.

Mignolo, Walter. 'Decolonial Aesthetics: Unlearning and Relearning the Museum through Pedro Lasch's *Black Mirror/Espejo Negro*.' In *Black Mirror/Espejo Negro*. Edited by Pedro Lasch and Jennifer A. González, pp. 86–103. Durham, 2009.

Mombaça, Jota. *Notas estratégicas quanto aos usos políticos do conceito de lugar de fala*, ‹www.buala.org/pt/corpo/notas-estrategicas-quanto-aos-usos-politicos-do-conceito-de-lugar-de-fala›.

Phillips, Ruth B. 'The Value of Disciplinary Difference.' *Anthropologies of Art*. Edited by Mariet Westermann, pp. 242–259. New Haven, 2005.

———. 'The Museum of Art-thropology: Twenty-First Century Imbroglios.' *Res: Anthropology and Aesthetics* 52 (Autumn 2007), pp. 8–19.

Rabinow, Paul. 'A Contemporary Museum.' In *Object Atlas: Fieldwork in the Museum*. Edited by Clémentine Deliss, pp. 7–10. Frankfurt, 2012.

Rodríguez, Ileana. *The Latin American Subaltern Studies Reader*. Durham, 2001.

Sousa Santos, Boaventura de. 'A Discourse on the Sciences.' *Review* 15, no. 1 (Winter 1992), pp. 9–47.

Tuhiwai Smith, Linda. *Decolonizing Methodologies: Research and Indegenous People*. London, 1999.

Vallés Vílchez, Laura. 'Desde la maraña a la araña: A propósito de *Estimulantes*: circulación y eufora.' *Concreta Magazine* 9 (2017), pp. 104–114.

Part 2

Art & Time

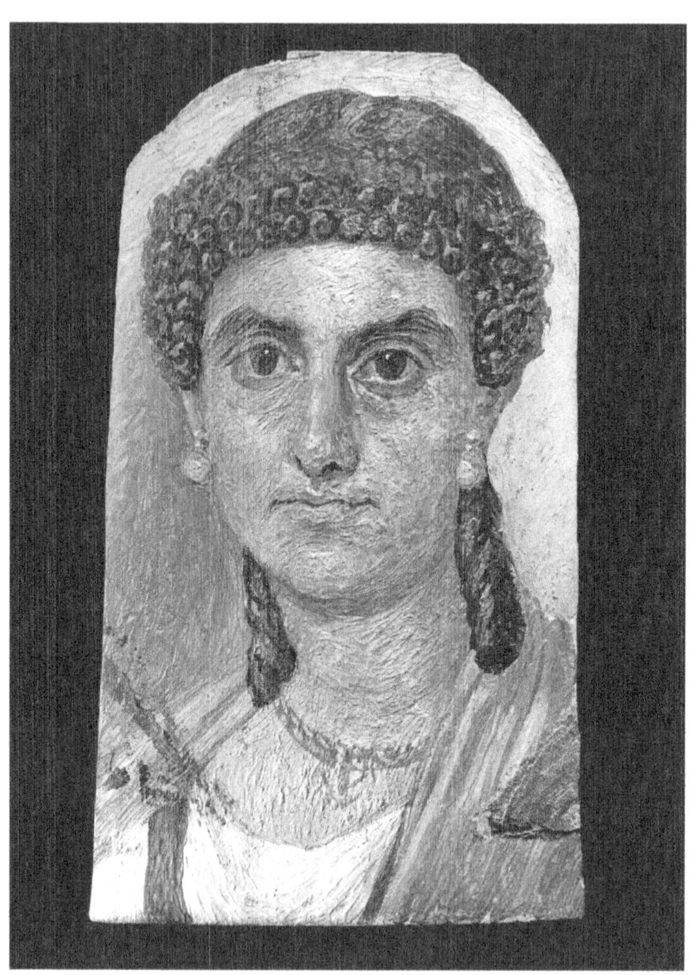

Panel painting of a woman in a blue mantle, Roman Period, A.D. 54–68, Egypt, encaustic (wax and pigments) on wood, 38 cm × 22.3 cm, Metropolitan Museum of Art, New York, Director's Fund, 2013.

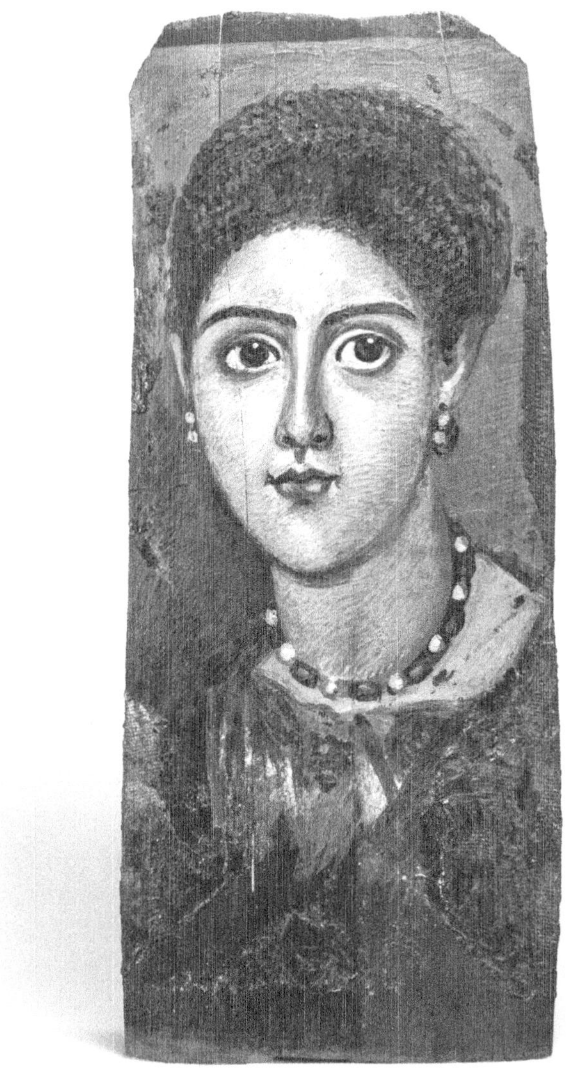

Mummy portrait of a woman, Roman Period, 2nd century A.D., Egypt, encaustic (wax and pigments) on wood, cloth, 44 × 18.9 × 1.4 cm, Walters Art Museum, Baltimore.

Undoing Time: Art's Anachronistic Capacities

An Interview with Alexander Nagel

Melanie Bühler

MELANIE BÜHLER Do you think the term transhistorical is useful?

ALEXANDER NAGEL I think the term is a relic of historicism. When you believe in historical periods, then you think about bridging them and what it means to cross those boundaries. And that may be appropriate to a certain phase in thinking that still deals with those boundaries in those configurations. So the term has a kind of symptomatic relation to the time that we're living through. I think it is interesting to imagine not needing that word. Imagine that maybe that's not a helpful term to understand the way things might have worked in the past and maybe it won't be very helpful in the future. When people think across time, either as artists creating works, or as poets or as writers—which is something that happened all the way through the history of culture—that isn't transhistorical thinking, that is poetic thinking or creative thinking. I wouldn't want to use the term transhistorical to refer to all of this because it carries the danger of imagining that this historical system, the one that we've been working with since the nineteenth century, has always been in place and that when people cross the lines that we recognize as the organizing lines of history, they are being transhistorical. I think it's important to imagine a way of proceeding that cannot simply be described as a kind of crossing of boundaries, but is its own form of thought.

MB You're an art historian and traditionally the task of an art historian is to describe how specific artworks relate to specific times. But in much of your writing you are concerned with how artworks actually fall out of their times or create temporalities that defy a clear categorization.

AN The artworks we study often make it their function, sometimes their duty, to confuse time, to, as you just put it, leave their time, and that is a challenge for an art historian. Literary scholars might say similar things about the works that they study, but I do think that works of visual art do it in particular ways. There is something about the encounter with the figurative/material configuration that is the work of art that regularly produces this effect. Another way to put this is to say that anachronism is a basic feature of the art. Anachronism means literally going against time—the prefix 'ana' means to go back or to go down, backwards, and that can mean very simply going back in time, as when a work of art represents an episode from history or myth. It can also mean going back in time at a structural level, as when a work of art reproduces an earlier work of art and participates in the time of its prototype. And it can also mean going back against the logic of time, against chronology, undoing time-keeping on a basic level. Works of art operate anachronistically on all those levels. It refers across time, it moves through time, and it throws the logic of time into question.

MB Hence it can also look into the future.

AN If it throws time into question then inevitably past, present, and future are being reconfigured.

MB Could you give an example of such a work or of such an aspect of a work?

AN For the more basic definition of an anachronism, you have the many works of art that represent other times, bringing them into the time of their first viewers and into future times. They are heterochronistic, you could say. They represent the past, they represent the future, they represent multiple times in relation to one another. This has happened so often in the history of art that the examples are almost endless. Often works of art represent contemporary phenomena, like a person, as in a portrait, but with the express intention that this portrait will outlive the person. Built into the intentionality of the work is the opening of the possibility that through the portrait the person will be able to address future people, future times, and so have a life beyond mortal life. Images of this sort are designed for time travel.

MB Would you say that certain works have a greater intensity of these anachronistic qualities and other works are more flat in that sense?

AN Yes, there is a range of, as you nicely put it, intensity of anachronism. Some works are more charged than others, if I can put it this way. Anachronism is a feature of art, whether or not it is religious, but often in a religious context; anachronism is bound up with the ideological premises of the religion in such a way as to allow contact over time and through time, such as when an image represents a saint or a sage from long ago and in producing a contemporaneity with the image's viewer, suggests an interchangeability of times in a more general sense.

MB The transhistorical—I'm using this term even if you might prefer the term anachronistic—is also often linked to a specific way of falling out of time, namely that certain values or qualities of art are universal, or timeless: that these qualities remain the same throughout time. According to this logic, a transhistorical presentation then links works from different times by tapping into these qualities. Do you believe in this kind of timelessness of art? Do you believe that certain qualities, that are essential to us as human beings, stay the same?

AN No, I don't believe in the quality of timelessness as you describe it in the way that I believe in the anachronism of art. The ideal of a kind of timelessness, of a perfect congruence of art such as to make it immune to time, is an ideal that has been promoted at various times in history. Sometimes it's called classicism, sometimes it's called idealism. I tend to see that as one of the more datable of the ambitions of art. Those efforts seem to be the most bound in time. The kind of anachronism I'm talking about doesn't deny the existence of time but nonetheless holds up the promise that one is not merely bound to time, that there is a flexibility that art affords that allows one to see time differently or see through time in a way that's not normally possible.

MB Many authors in this book propose to think about time differently than as a linear, unified stream. Instead they insist on the co-existence of many temporalities. Does this have to do with the fact that we live in a globalized world and an

1 Fabian, *Time and the Other*.

awareness that even if all the art made in the present moment is contemporary, different artworks bring with them different histories, different temporalities? Do you think that the fact that we try to think about time in more complex ways has to do with the increasing complexity that is linked to a more global way of looking at art?

AN I think that 'comparative temporality', too, has its phases. Johannes Fabian wrote a book called *Time and the Other,*[1] which is about this device of anthropological thinking, to propose that other cultures are not simply other in their habits but in their conception of time. So that relationship has a history that has to do with colonialism and in that sense, sure, the history of globalization since Columbus. That history certainly complicated matters. It definitely brought people into contact and forced a kind of recalibration of times, and that history has a history. We are now at a juncture where the fact that we all have cell phones means that we all know exactly what time it is because we're connected to a time standard that everyone has agreed on. We know exactly what time it is all the way around the world at all times. So, globalization raises the problem but also flattens the problem, demanding that you know where you find yourself in the history of it. You see, I believe in history.

MB Would you say that chronology as an art historical method has largely expired?

AN We are transitioning; we no longer believe very much in historical periods but we're not exactly in a whole other paradigm of thinking either. So, we're in a transhistorical phase, you might say.

MB So we're in this transitional phase in which we still talk about periodization but at the same time we are careful about it.

AN We envision what it might be to think in different ways through time and maybe art is coming into view, in the last two decades especially, as a kind of guide to a different way of thinking.

MB And if art is our guide, what are the journeys that art can provide? What are the outcomes of such endeavours, art historically but also curatorially, what do they look like? Does it mainly result in comparing old and new? Is it trying to find affinities between specific times? What can it yield?

AN I go to see art hoping to find answers to these questions. But maybe rather than comparing the old and the new, it actually will allow for the possibility that the old is not old. And maybe the new is not new, though that's a more familiar thought. At bottom, I suppose when I engage in this kind of thinking and I feel that I'm not simply repeating the routines of my training, I feel a sense of liberation. Not just an anarchic liberation, 'I can do whatever I want' kind of liberation, but really productive liberation in the sense that I find when this happens that I can think outside of the confines of what I've been given and what I've experienced and what signposts I've been given. It becomes possible to imagine the world otherwise.

MB Do you believe that imagining the world otherwise can go beyond seeing the work of art otherwise: going beyond a comparison between works of art or a zooming in into one particular work of art, and this may result in the kind of thesis

2 Nagel, *Medieval Modern.*

building that would allow you to say— let's use your most recent book as an example—that the medieval and the modern/contemporary have a special affinity?[2] Are we allowed to make these statements that are again statements about periods that transcend individual works of art?

AN If we're going to talk about *Medieval Modern*, I'd like to make it clear that mostly that book is a very cautious effort to understand an historical phenomenon: the fact that so many artists in the twentieth century expressed an interest in medieval art, wrote about their interest in medieval art, and engaged with medieval art in their works. At the same time, the book was certainly interested in that impulse inside of art to be oblique to its time or leave its time. And on occasion, no question, I have taken inspiration from the artists in my own work. Since that book I have left off doing the comparisons, teaching the historical lesson. I'm no longer interested in doing lectures where I put two things together that maybe to the audience seem like they're very disparate and showing how they speak to one another or how they once spoke to one another. Instead, in my more recent practice I've just tried to enact the principle. I lecture on the older art in a way that treats it as something that is active and able to have an impact now, without explaining how it relates to contemporary practice. Contemporary practice is our effort to see it and work with it. So, for a curator who is interested in this sort of thing, I think more can be done than to put works of art together from different periods, the transhistorical gesture. I think that trend is sort of on the decline by now, but the deeper impulse to see art in this way is not going away anytime soon. I haven't yet gotten *Artforum* to agree to have articles that address medieval art or Renaissance art without any peg that connects them to contemporary art or modern art. But, editorially, I see no reason why such publications shouldn't do that.

MB Because medieval art, to stay with the example, is equally equipped to provide answers to questions that we struggle with today as is contemporary art?

AN Yes, or maybe earlier examples will rewrite the questions or upset the questions, give a whole different kind of view.

MB Could you give an example of such a question or could you give an example of how an older artwork might integrate in the discourse of contemporary art in such a seamless way that the comparison to contemporary art is no longer needed as a stepping stone to the art from previous times?

AN I think the contemporary is always with us. I can give an example from my personal life. I found myself in the city of Grasse, in Southern France, with a curator named Xavier Douroux, who sadly died last year. He was a cofounder of Le Consortium in Dijon, which over the decades has become a major centre for contemporary art. In Grasse we visited the cathedral, where there are some paintings by Rubens. I pointed out that the paintings weren't made for Grasse but landed there more than a century after they were made. They were originally in the church of Santa Croce in Gerusalemme, a church in Rome that is itself a highly anachronistic space, particularly the chapel that contained these paintings, which is considered a kind of archaeological core of the church and was understood to be a piece of Jerusalem in Rome, hence the name of the church, Santa Croce in Gerusalemme. These paintings were made for that space, which also held a number of relics of the Passion of Jesus. Although they looked like they might belong to a Passion cycle, actually the paintings were commissioned in order to stage and highlight this relic or that relic—*The Crowning of Thorns* the relic of the thorn, *The Raising of the Cross* the pieces of the wood of the cross held there. The paintings are not a narrative cycle, they're connected by their references to these now displaced relics that were collected together in a particular space in Rome. It was a point about recontextualization, about different temporal logics that can connect paintings to one another and to their environment, and also about how environments themselves can be destabilized and made significant, made resonant with other environments. But I didn't really need to spell it out, it was totally clear to him that these were temporal and spatial models to think with as a curator. And he didn't even respond, he didn't say, 'Oh, I see, so it's like site-specificity, but in a different sort of way', or 'Oh, I see, there's an anachronistic element to these paintings', or 'There's a non-narrative logic here', or any number of things that he might have said. He just listened, and I could see his mind turning. And he was maybe going to use those lessons, maybe not, or maybe they would come into his practice in an indirect way, undetectable even to himself.

MB I was also wondering if there is a way of overdoing it? If we stay in the comparative mode, there is a term for it: pseudomorphism, things that just look alike, but are actually not alike. Are there good and bad questions? Are there good and bad anachronisms?

AN I would say there's good and bad in these various ways, just as there's good and bad in artworks themselves. Why do we consider certain artworks less interesting than others? Well, often because they are one-note, or are only working on one level, or are too much of their time in a way that is just not very interesting. We find them limited in one way or another. And I suppose we can speak of the work of curators and historians in similar ways. A given comparison is too formal and is taking everything on the level of similarity of appearance. Are there more interesting ways of talking about how two artworks might relate to one another than composition, or distribution of colours, or mere appearance? Of course. I don't think that questioning certain types of logics of time liberates us from a rigour of thinking. Why would it?

MB To go back to the point you made a little earlier about the fact that the present is so present that we no longer need the comparison. Isn't there a danger in that as well, that we focus too much on the present that we cannot think beyond it? Some might label this as presentism, a less imaginative form of engagement, because it stays conveniently within the familiar.

AN I wouldn't say it's dangerous, since such efforts are almost always boring and short-lived. I think that whenever one is trying to make an effort to make it relevant or make it speak to contemporary concerns, you're almost always really limiting the conversation because, as you just said, what is the present anyway? Isn't it to hypostatize the present to want to make something from the past speak to 'the present'? If you're really so concerned with currency, with the contemporary, you're just going to fall behind. Even by the professed desire to stay contemporary, you will have failed. So why not just abandon that model and that impulse and accept that being oblique to the time, whatever the time is, is the best way of being contemporary.

MB But in an effort of being self-aware, one needs to know which questions belong to the present and belong to things that happen now, and which questions can be situated in the past, right?

AN I don't know—if you come up with a new question, doesn't it belong to a new present? Why presuppose what belongs to the present, why not make it, construct it?

MB I guess this goes back to the good and bad questions. Is one, when confronting a historic artwork, allowed to ask any question at all?

AN In an effort to address a work of art, whether it is old or new, one has to contend with the work. Some works of art call upon one's resources in particular ways and demand that you engage with them and in engaging with them, you engage with their various configurations of time and through that engagement you bring them into a new temporal configuration. It's a challenge, it's difficult to do. If it's done badly it's totally clear to everyone and no one's interested. If it's done well, it seems to be a kind of extension of the work.

Literature

Fabian, Johannes. *Time and the Other: How Anthropology Makes Its Object*. New York, 2014.
Nagel, Alexander. *Medieval Modern: Art Out of Time*. London, 2012.

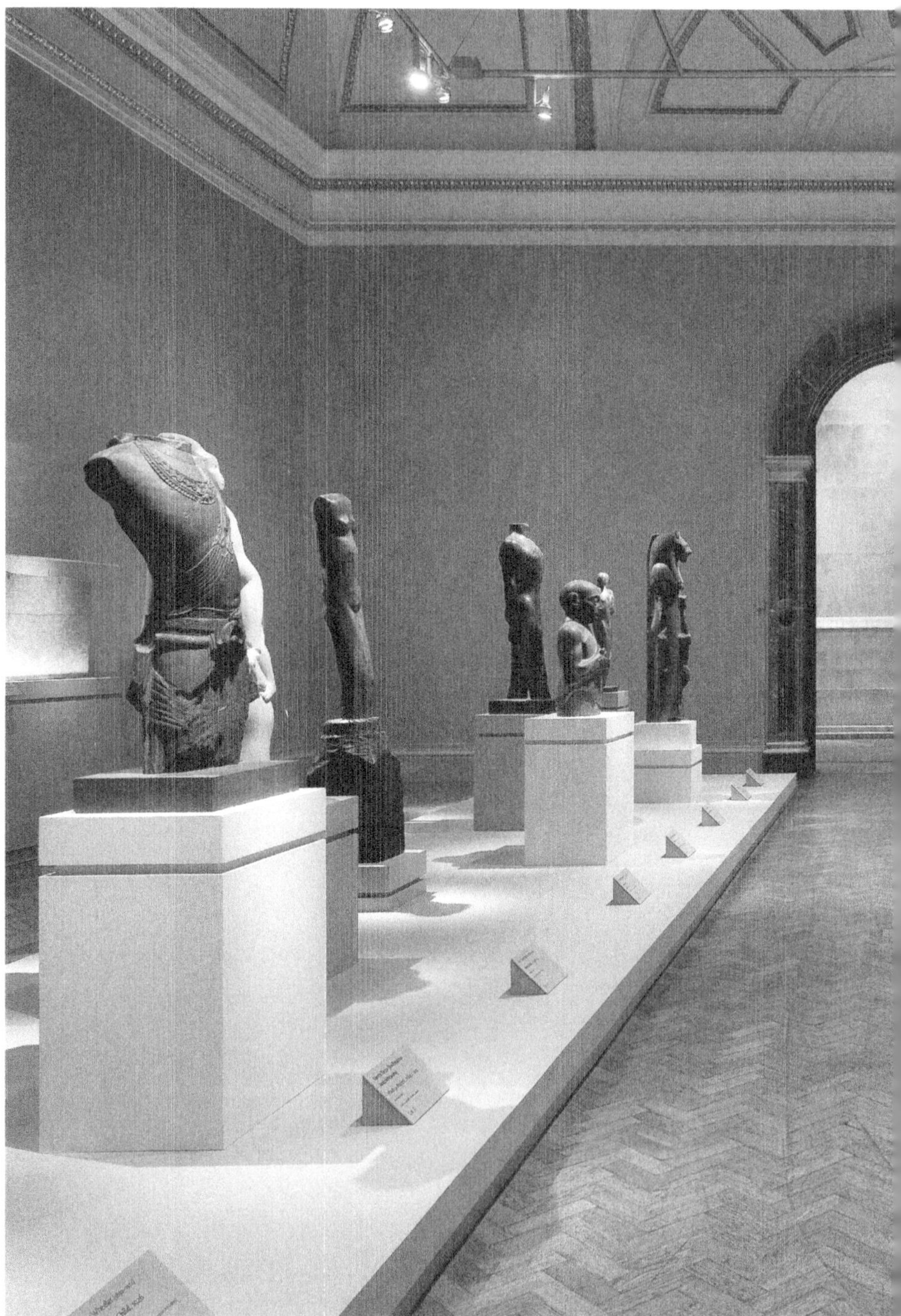

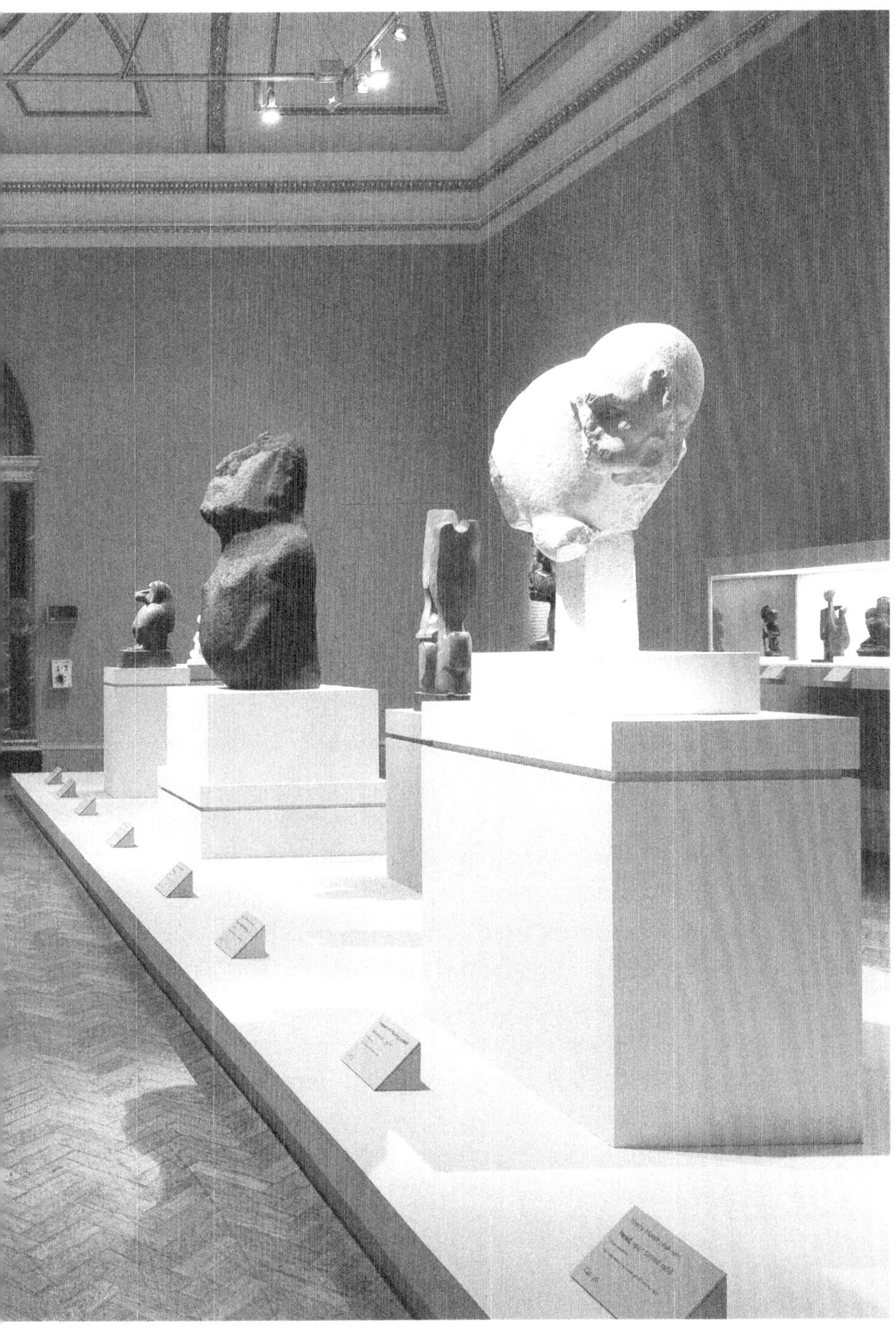

'Modern British Sculpture', installation view, Royal Academy of Arts, London, 2011. Courtesy Royal Academy of Arts/M. Leith. Photo: M. Leith.

In & Out of Time

Penelope Curtis

1 From Lore Van Hees, April 2016. For example: 'Is it attractive, or confusing?' 'Can this create misinterpretations, or just extra meanings?' 'Is there a right way or a wrong way to 'abuse' objects from the past?'

This essay began life with a set of questions which we were presented with in preparation for a conference organized by the Frans Hals Museum | De Hallen Haarlem and M-Museum in 2016. The first question—'Is it liberating to present works across time, or a challenge?'—in many ways foreshadowed the remainder, which could essentially be answered in the same way: it is not a case of 'either or', but of 'and and'.[1]

It can be liberating to present works across time, but it can also be a challenge. The question presumes that the norm is to present artworks within time (if we can use 'within' as the opposite of 'across') but in fact, in everyday life, we see works from across time all the time. In our own houses, to take the most obvious example, we often have furniture from other people's houses, from antique or junk shops, from our grandparents', parents' and our own periods. And our 'own' periods may well end up spanning thirty or fifty years. Most buildings, and most spaces, the streets and squares around us, are quintessentially across time. Most museums have old and new wings.

So why is the transhistorical approach still presumed to be unusual, even innovative, when in fact in many situations, non-artistic, but also artistic, notably with private collections, it is the norm? Is it confusing for the audience? Perhaps only in as far as they are used to nineteenth-century museum typologies, for if they had gone into any private collection of art, things would have been largely mixed up. Private collectors habitually put a medieval sculpture beside a modern painting, and a religious artefact from Indonesia next to a pot from California.

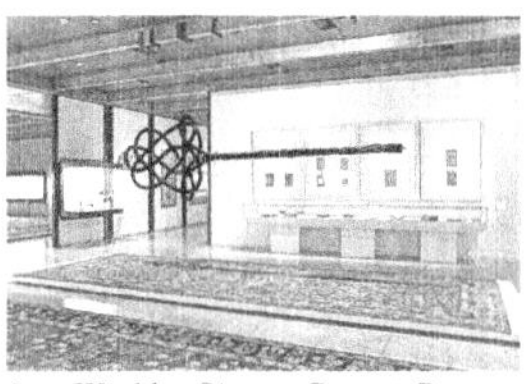

2 Wiebke Siem, *Carpet Beater*, installation view, 'Summer Guests', Gulbenkian Museum, Lisbon, 2016. Courtesy Museu Calouste Gulbenkian. Photo: Carlos Azevedo.

But of course, to mix things up can indeed lead to misreading, and is above all a potential de-specializing or de-professionalizing, removing a piece from its normal curatorial context simply because, to the outsider (or the contemporary curator acting as such), it looks like something else. Or vice versa, adding something contemporary to an historical context because the object, superficially at least, looks like or resonates with the historical object. Misreadings can on occasion be wilful, but are usually well-meaning. And misreadings are rarely one way, so that if a contemporary sculpture is hung over an historic carpet, for example, both lose something of their individual specificity, while communicating on another level altogether.[2] An artwork by a contemporary German artist has really nothing to do with a seventeenth-century Oriental carpet, and it is arguable that neither object contributes to further knowledge about the other, and yet, the juxtaposition may re-awake us to the fact that the carpet was a carpet, and that the carpet-beater, even if outsize, used to have a purpose. Indeed, both objects have fallen into disuse, but only one is a paraphrase of its own source. Their temporary partnership activates each.

And ignorance can have good results. Historic objects with scholarly baggage may be no less misunderstood in their usual context, and of course the 'not knowing' can lead to other kinds of knowing, or fresh knowing. Understanding that bronze mortars of the Renaissance might be cast from the same mould as a bell, and that weapons were melted down to make peace-time objects, provides the background against which to appreciate the work of Fiona Banner, to cite one example. I believe the translation of an object into a foreign context can be more than worthwhile, and lead to deeper understandings of real continuities, both in form and in function. Understanding one can lead to an understanding of the other.

The relationship between old and new can be perceived in a wider range of ways: an understanding of material, of arrangement, of motif, of composition, of social relations, of cultural usage. For example, we understand more about life casting today if we know about its origins in funereal and forensic sculpture. (Before photography, casting was a vital documentary tool, which helped educate scientists and medical students, as well as catching the final likeness of a deceased individual.) We comprehend more fully the impact of coloured sculpture, or of defaced paintings, if we make the link to the Reformation. (The war on the icon meant that Protestant countries became habituated to colour-less sculpture, but colour always used to, and still can, provide a modelled or carved form with uncanny vivacity.) Perhaps this is the more likely if all the objects are moved into a new space, and it is not a question of putting something new into the old museum, or something old into the new museum. If each is put into a neutral exhibition space, there is more chance for dialogue, and less dependence on old hierarchies.

My examples here came from exhibitions made at the Henry Moore Institute in Leeds, looking for instance at the material and cultural meanings of bronze-casting over time;

of casting from the body; of the representation of sculpture within painting, and the use of the Laocoön sculpture by generations of sculptors.[3] In a sense, with these exhibitions, history took a back seat. The exhibitions were not transhistorical in any transgressive sense. The similarity of form and meaning was foregrounded over and above historical progression or change. Transhistorical may be understood to mean spanning a long period of time, or it can mean the juxtaposition of different time periods.[4] It can mean the extension of historical context into a longer timeline to the extent that, rather than being transhistorical, an argument becomes a-historical.

So: does manoeuvring art objects into uncharted contexts produce new insights into the specific qualities of art objects? I am not sure if new meanings are really possible, or can ever be radically or completely new. And new contexts are most likely probable contexts, rather than completely alien ones. Old meanings will continue to exist, but we bring them into play in new ways, juxtaposing common meanings in relation to uncommon pairings or groupings. The meanings were probably already there, but standard museology may well obscure or even eradicate them. New contexts can liberate transversal meanings, if done well.

I am quite interested in looking at historic transhistoricism. For example, in the 'Modern British Sculpture' exhibition at London's Royal Academy (2011), we showed the transhistorical (and transgeographical) bent of British sculptors of the twentieth century, especially of the 1920s.[5] It is utterly wrong, obviously, to think of the transhistorical as something new, even if there is a tendency among museum curators nowadays to jump to this conclusion. People are always transhistorical, and artists and collectors especially. But in this show we

3 Leeds, Henry Moore Institute: 'Second Skin (A fleur de peau)', 2002; 'Bronze: The Power of Life and Death', 2005; 'Towards a New Laocoon', 2007; 'Sculpture in Painting', 2009.

4 I noticed at Tate Britain that the term 'transhistorical' was often used by critics to describe exhibitions with a long chronology (such as 'Art under Attack: Histories of British Iconoclasm', 2013 and 'Artist and Empire', 2015–2016). In many ways this was essentially a criticism of thematic shows and betrays the conventional preference for exhibitions of single artists or recognized groupings.

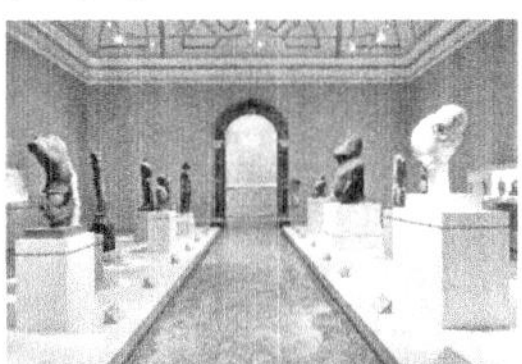

5 'Modern British Sculpture', installation view, Royal Academy of Arts, London, 2011. Courtesy Royal Academy of Arts/M. Leith. Photo: M. Leith.

6 Examples of exhibitions that I curated would range from 'Private View', at the Bowes Museum, Barnard Castle, 1996, which proposed that the original collectors had continued their collecting into the late-twentieth century, and 'La Grande Horizontale', a curated project for TEFAF, Maastricht, 2017 on the reclining figure motif.

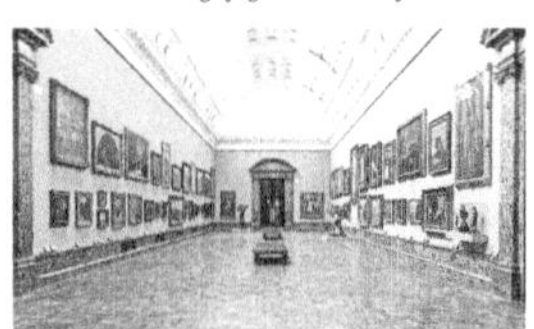

7 'Walk Through British Art', installation view, 1840s gallery, Tate Britain, London, 2013. Courtesy Tate, London, 2018. Tate Photography.

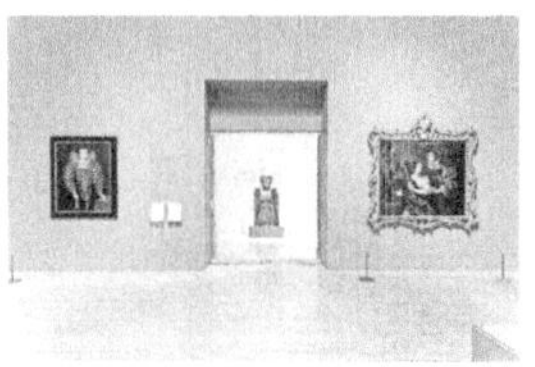

8 Marcus Gheeraerts II, *Portrait of Mary Rogers, Lady Harington*, 1592; Ronald Moody, *Johanaan*, 1936; Sir Peter Lely, *Susanna and the Elders*, c. 1650/55, installation view, 'Migrations', Tate Britain, London, 2012. Courtesy Tate, London, 2018; The estate of Ronald Moody. Tate Photography, photo: Jo Fernandes.

9 Tate Britain: 'Migrations: Journeys into British Art', 2012; 'Looking at the View', 2013; 'Ruin Lust', 2013; 'Fighting History: 250 Years of British History Painting', 2015.

made the point that early-twentieth-century sculptors depended on the very ancient carvings they saw in the British Museum, and that this kind of resource was so essential to modern sculptors that it could (and should) be shown in the same exhibition, and in the same space.

I am not sure I have a personal example of abusing objects from the past, and perhaps I wouldn't be the right person to identify misuse, but an obvious one is the way in which the Third Reich used classical sculpture to assert a hierarchy of race through art. Most national museums in some ways abuse objects from the past, be this in physical terms—the removal of works from their original contexts, poor care, over-cleaning, spoliation—to the wilful appropriation of certain objects for political ends. To paraphrase the original question: is there a right way to abuse objects? Surely this transforms abuse into use?

Other non-linear models—be they thematic, philosophical, fictional—all to a greater or lesser degree will likely use the transhistorical.[6] At Tate Britain, where I was director from 2010 to 2015, and where we rehung the whole collection over 2012–2013, we deliberately offered a classically linear historical chronology[7] as a foil off which to work trans- or a-historically. This also reinforced the *mode d'emploi* of the building, which ran in long enfilades up and down its outer perimeter. We put the collection to use in the chronological *and* the transhistorical sense, with shows such as 'Migrations',[8] 'Looking at the View', 'Ruin Lust' or 'Fighting History'.[9] I would argue that in fact the chronological was the more radical, if chronology was applied rigorously. The transhistorical can indeed be so unanchored in time that it becomes a mix of times, a pluralistic non-time. While 'Migrations' told the story of how non-British artists made it into the national collection (over a time of 350 years, but in date order), and 'Ruin Lust' explored the attraction of a given motif over time, 'Looking at the View' and 'Fighting History' took genres and explored their similarities across time. On the other hand, a properly chronological use of the collection, which seeks to address all the kinds of works within it, and a cross-section of the artists represented, goes further in addressing issues of prejudice and neglect. By working hard on our chronological displays, to include for example not just Turner but those contemporaries who were overshadowed by Turner, and some of those many artists in the collection who had never been shown in the gallery, we probably had a greater impact than in apparently more far-reaching transhistorical shows. For, it seems to me, transhistorical approaches probably largely underscore and re-assert meanings that often are already inscribed in common perceptions, about—to take the aforementioned exhibitions as examples—migration, or ruins, or landscape, or history painting, whereas to see work A (1812) next to work B (1812), when A has never been shown next to B, may be more surprising. Our chronological 'Walk through British Art' aimed to be natural and easy, needing little explication, and yet to do something subtly different. It used the length and walking patterns of the building to assert the movement through time, with thresholds marked with dates, so that one literally stepped through time. The mapping narrative was simply the dateline, and thus needed very much less explication.

What a transhistorical show can do is to open one area of art to another, and one audience to another, and it tends to assert continuities rather than dissonance. In a permanent collection display you can perhaps have a more far-reaching effect on the canon by putting genre painters next to history painters, regional painters next to metropolitan painters,

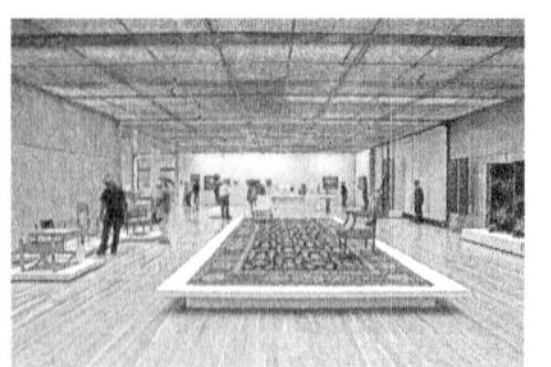

10 Louis XIV fauteuil and Art Deco dressing table, exhibition view, 'Lines of Time', Gulbenkian Museum, Lisbon, 2016. Courtesy Museu Calouste Gulbenkian. Photo: Carlos Azevedo.

women next to men, 'secondary' next to 'primary'. If you do this in date order, it has its own underlying rightness or claim to being. The chronological became a tool or discipline which forced curators to reconsider possibilities. It was absolutely not about narrative, but it was all about the reality of history, in all its dissonance.

I realize increasingly how many kinds of timelines we are always working with, even if we tend to privilege the date of creation. A 2016 project at the Gulbenkian Museum, 'Lines of Time', involved looking with equal attention at the date of purchase. This thinking is especially valid as the works were bought by the same collector, in this case the Armenian-British collector Calouste Gulbenkian (1868–1955), all at the same time. It helps develop the question of taste, and the period eye, which lead to the creation of similar collections at similar times. It also allowed us to think of a collection of early modern objects in twentieth-century terms, given that the opportunities for its assembly mostly occurred between the two World Wars.

Gulbenkian's collection of objects was originally arranged by him in a manner that took account only of functional aesthetics; geography and history were entirely irrelevant. But in the museum that bears his name, and which opened in 1969, the collection has been strictly segregated; 'Lines of Time' was thus an unusual chance to show French eighteenth-century silverware in the context of its sale from the Hermitage by the Soviet authorities after the October Revolution, or an Art Deco table alongside a Louis XIV fauteuil because both were bought in the same year and were used in the same house.[10] This might even not so much be a transhistorical display, but a properly historical one. Gulbenkian was a displaced Armenian oil broker whose love of French eighteenth-century decorative arts spoke of his wish for assimilation, just as his proximity to the Soviet authorities reflects their mutual interest in the emerging oil industry.

I think that it is the work of museums and exhibition-makers to have a strong curatorial construction, but I do not think the transhistorical is a construction as such. It is nothing out of the ordinary, even if it is enjoying a vogue at the present time. In fact, it has been the norm, over centuries, especially with private collections. And museums too are hardly strictly historical, as they have generally privileged geography over history. If the British Museum (for example) were strictly historically organized, it would look very different, effectively becoming transnational. Most museums or galleries of painting are still divided first by national school, and then by period.

The strange thing about history is that a real historical timeline can seem, and is, quite arbitrary. If we wish to say something about artistic production, we may well wish to step outside history. Curatorial constructions, propositions, and arguments may need to ignore the call of history, or at the very least, to look at a longer history as they seek to identify more fundamental meanings. I think this is probably where my own curatorial interests lie: in allowing the 'trans' to be less about disjunction and more about continuity; less about cutting through history, and more about cumulative history. Or, put more simply, less about history in the end, and more about art.

We have got to the strange point when contemporary art is used to bring spectators today into the historic museum. Far from being the shock of the new, this is the new normal, because it is felt that the forms of contemporary art are more known, and more accessible, than those of the past. Placing

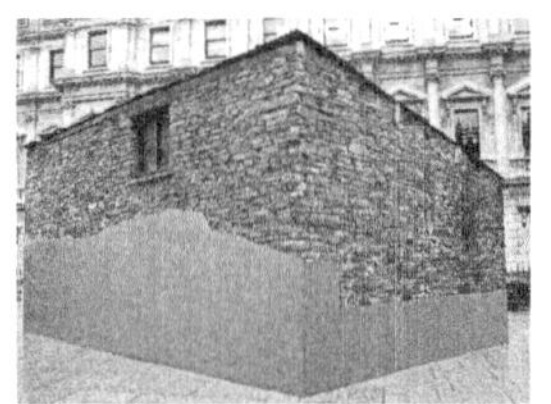

11 Reconstruction of Kurt Schwitters' *Merz Barn* (Ambleside, Cumbria) in the courtyard of the Royal Academy of Arts, London, for the exhibition 'Modern British Sculpture', 2011.

contemporary artworks alongside historical ones can, on occasion, make each more eloquent. At the Gulbenkian we presented a temporary exhibition entitled 'Summer Guests' in 2016, and worked hard to ensure that the guests (the 14 contemporary artworks) were not unwanted, and that they went home before they outstayed their welcome.

But what is more important, I believe, is to combine the possibilities for un-joined-up presentation, which anyone might find in a traditional museum, with the joined-up connections made by a curator within a specific project. Another way of putting this is to allow collection displays to co-exist alongside exhibitions, which make particular arguments. It can be rewarding to have fixed narratives, but it is equally necessary, I think, to allow for others. But though a visit to the storage room can be a liberating escape from an authorial view, it is never sufficient. We need plurality.

Perhaps more important than the transhistorical exhibition, which as we all know can be facile, is the transhistorical programme, which builds up over time into an awareness of continuities in making, looking, and understanding. To make available, to the same potential audience, a programme that uses varying chronological methodologies, rather than always the same one. This is to argue for the co-existence of different kinds of 'contemporary', and for exhibitions that are not always monographic.

Strictly speaking every collection display and every exhibition is transhistorical, bringing together in one place works made in other places and at other times. Perhaps that is why I like the image of Kurt Schwitters' *Merz Barn* in front of the Royal Academy,[11] an institution of the English establishment to which Schwitters was never elected, and where he never showed. The image shows a reconstruction of the simple Lake District hut where Schwitters made his last works, before dying in exile. Two very different realities, two very different places and two very different times for art are brought together here. Co-existing, in one time and place, for an invented but contiguous moment.

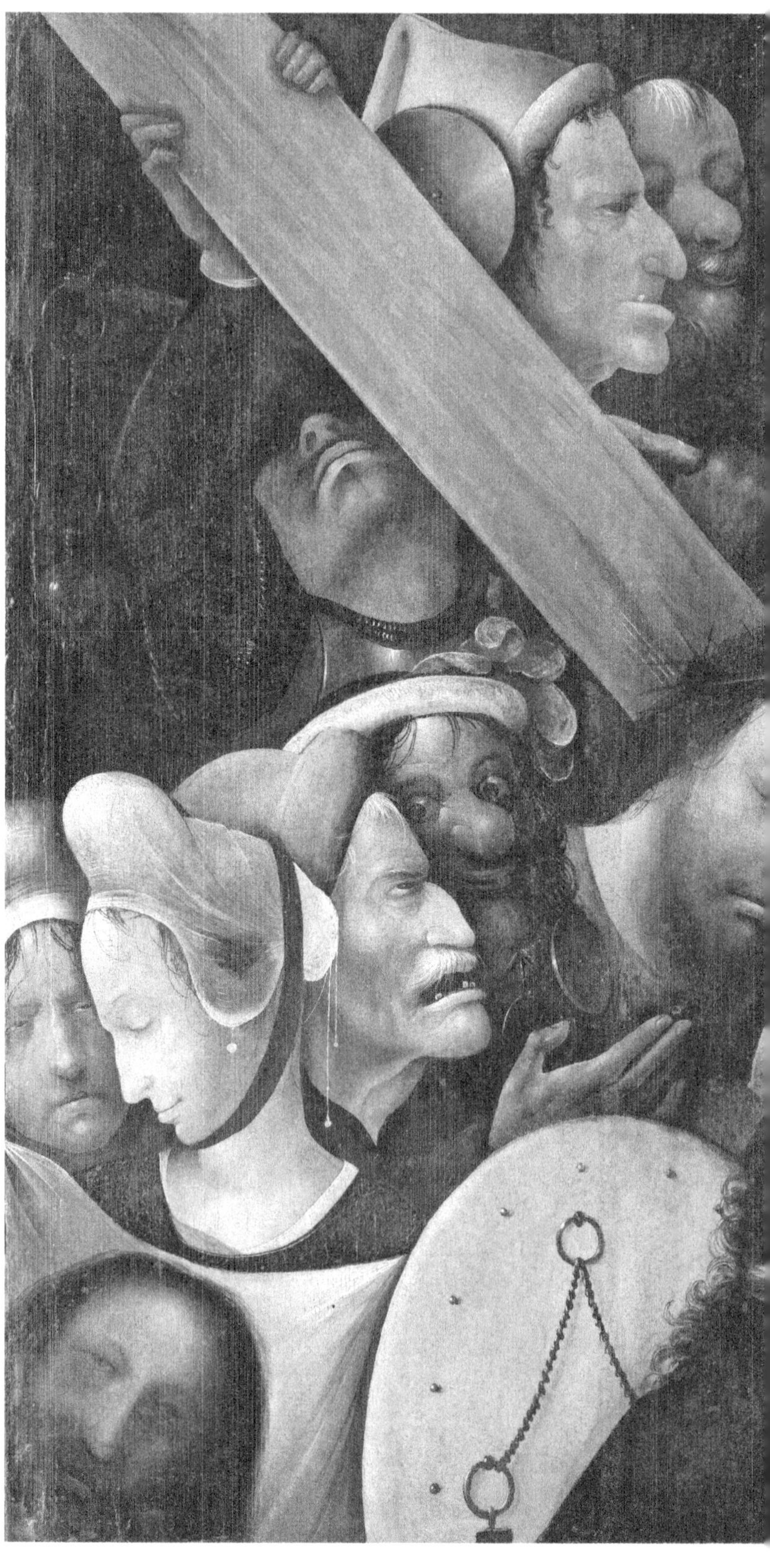

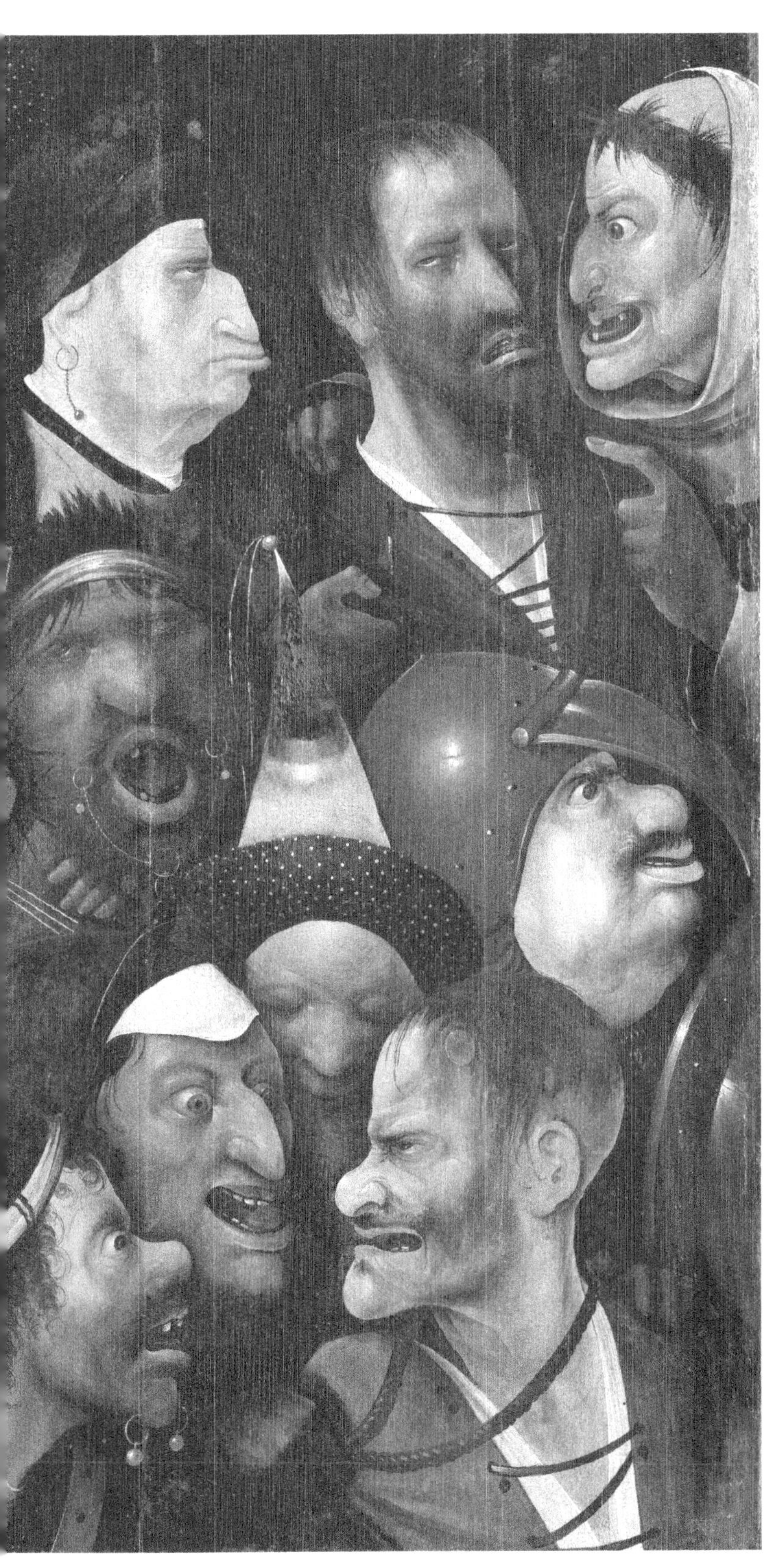

Jheronimus Bosch, *Christ Carrying the Cross*, 1510/35, oil on panel, 76.7 × 83.5 cm, Museum of Fine Arts, Ghent. Courtesy <www.lukasweb.be>—Art in Flanders vzw. Photo: Dominique Provost.

The Paradox of the Value of Art

Constructing Meaning and the Boundaries of History

Peter Carpreau

Hieronymus Bosch's universe is closed to us and, in all probability, we will never be able to re-enter his world of phantasmagorical images rooted in a particular reading of the Christian faith. Some of his works, such as his celebrated *Haywain Triptych* (c. 1516), appear to have a moralizing message, while others have a more mystical feel, including his peerless *Visions of the Afterlife* (c. 1505–1515) and the character heads in *Christ Carrying the Cross* (1510–1535). Many different interpretations have been suggested over the centuries, with meanings sought on the basis of the most divergent ideologies. A variety of characteristics were attributed to Bosch, ranging from madness, through heresy or membership of some licentious sect, to adherence to the 'Modern Devotion'[1] movement. The received wisdom nowadays is that Bosch painted for the bourgeoisie, causing him to critique anything that threatened this segment of the population, such as ecclesiastical corruption or the high nobility. An interpretation of this kind is hardly surprising in the post-war era of European democracies, in which the bourgeoisie has dominated the societal discourse. Whatever the case, even if we no longer

1 A religious and spiritual movement that was started in the fourteenth century by scholars like Thomas a Kempis and Geert Groote who wanted to renew individual and collective spirituality and make it more accessible for a larger part of the population.

know what Bosch's works actually mean, he remains an immensely popular artist, capable of mobilizing hundreds of thousands of visitors, as we saw during the 2016 exhibitions in 's Hertogenbosch and Madrid.[2]

In his study of representations and their significance, Johan Vanbergen describes this phenomenon as a paradox: 'The paradox of artistic value lies in the fact that certain works are acknowledged as valuable, even though their meaning, as a message to us, has evidently diminished in importance.'[3] It is paradoxical, in other words, that a work of art whose meaning no longer has any relation to our own time and has been partially or fully eroded can nonetheless be relevant to us. This paradox touches on the essence of transhistoricity. A transhistorical presentation is one in which at least two artworks from two different historical periods enter a meaningful relationship with one another, with 'meaningful' taken to mean that the two artworks exert an influence over each other's meaning. The first question that arises here is at what point do two works cease to belong to the same segment of time? A working hypothesis in this regard might reflect the idea that 'history starts when people stop remembering', that is when all the first-hand witnesses have died after, say, 50–75 years, meaning that we can speak of a transhistorical presentation if the creation dates of the artworks differ at least 50–75 years.[4] We then have to acknowledge that an incongruence arises between artworks from different temporal segments in terms of their visual language and meaning. Visual language changes over time—sometimes very rapidly—and the historical context as a whole likewise evolves; the standard interpretative models seek and fix meaning in the historical genesis of the work. If works from different periods are compared, using these standard models, then the result is a comparison between totally different worlds, which means

2 The exhibition 'Jheronimus Bosch: Visions of Genius' took place in Het Noordbrabants Museum from 13 February–8 May 2016. The Prado exhibition 'Bosch: The 5th Centenary Exhibition' was on view from 31 May 31–25 September 2016.

3 Vanbergen, *Voorstelling en betekenis*, p. 162. According to Vanbergen, the communicative situation in which the artworks are once again able to convey their meaning must be recovered through art-historical study. It is therefore the task of the art historian to translate the original meaning of an artwork from an obsolete historical visual language to a current language, in such a way that a dialogue is possible with the contemporary artistic context. It is an elegant theory, but the example of Hieronymus Bosch demonstrates that art history is not always up to the task. What's more: it fixes the meaning of an artwork, with the result that transhistorical presentations are no longer possible.

4 I am grateful to Adam Levine for drawing my attention to this approach.

there can be no question of reciprocal influence between artworks. The fundamental question of transhistoricity is, therefore, that of the meaning of an artwork separate from its historical context; precisely the question thus that connects to the enormous popularity of Bosch and the paradox of the artistic value. There are three possible points of departure from which to approach the meaning of an artwork: the artwork itself, the artist and the beholder.

1. The Artwork

The artwork is an inert object: once created, it can no longer change, other than through the natural decay of its materials and through restoration. In this sense, an artwork is a witness to a particular time in history. If we wish to take the artwork itself as the starting point for the determination of meaning, there are various methods, each of which bases itself on the works' historical context. The iconological method, for instance, seeks to interpret a work as a manifestation of the prevailing *Weltanschauung* at the moment of its creation. Cultural-historical and socio-economic approaches, and even the modern versions of stylistic interpretation, also derive ultimately from the historical context. However, seeking the meaning in the period of the work's creation renders it impossible for what a work signifies to be influenced by another work: the meaning is fixed and immovable. At best, this gives rise to a one-way street, with a more recent work being inspired by an earlier one. But there can be no question here of dialogue or, consequently, of a transhistorical approach. In the context of the artwork, consideration ought to be given, however, to the idea of iconoclasm—arguably the only way in which an artwork can change after its creation. It is a phenomenon that has received a good deal of attention recently.[5] On the one hand, there are acts of iconoclasm geared towards the destruction of images. While this is evidence of the power and impact of images, it is not the subject of this text. But there are also, equally well, examples of artworks that have been deliberately altered by other artists. Rubens, for instance, is known to have 'improved' drawings by another master, and we also have Robert Rauschenberg's well-known *Erased de Kooning Drawing* of 1953[6] and the reworking of Goya's *Los desastres de la guerra* prints by the Chapman Brothers in the series *Insult to Injury*.[7] Although these cases initiate a substantive dialogue with the earlier artwork, interventions of this kind represent an artistic practice whereby a new work is created and the old one destroyed, which means they cannot be construed as transhistorical presentations.

5 See Freedberg, *The Power of Images* as the trigger for the renewed interest in iconoclasm.

6 Robert Rauschenberg, *Erased de Kooning Drawing*, 1953, traces of drawing media on paper with label and gilded frame, 64.14 × 55.25 × 1.27 cm, collection SFMOMA, San Francisco. Courtesy Robert Rauschenberg Foundation.

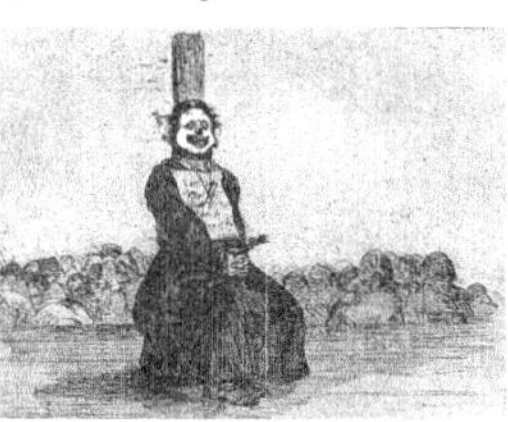

2. The Artist

A second possibility for interpreting the meaning of a work is via the artist, who is at the centre of the current Western perception of the arts. The artist is the one who lends the meaning and even the value to an individual artwork. In so prominent a manner, indeed, that the phenomenon of art as such is structured in terms of 'oeuvres'. Meaning is sought in the biographical data, personality, and individuality of the artist. Expressions such as 'The Age of Brueghel' or initiatives like the 'Rembrandt Research Project' are plentiful. And all because the 'father of art history,' Giorgio Vasari (1511–1574), penned his celebrated *Vite de' più eccellenti architetti, pittori, et scultori italiani, da Cimabue insino a' tempi nostri* in the form of biographies. It was not a new structure: earlier *vitae*

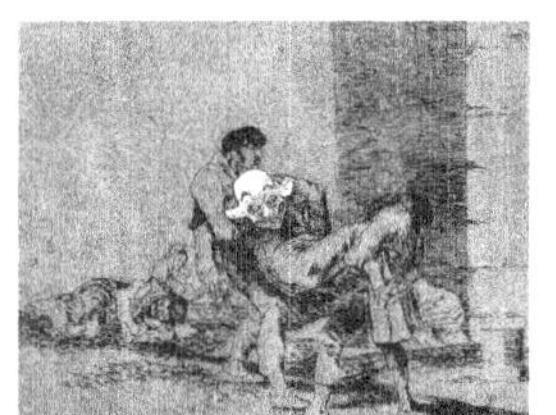

7 Dinos Chapman & Jake Chapman, *Insult to Injury*, 2003, series of etchings, 37 × 47 cm.

had already been written, the most famous of which is the *Legenda aurea* by the Italian Dominican Jacopo da Varazze, also known as Jacobus de Voragine (1228–1298), archbishop of Genoa. Art history is rooted, in other words, in the hagiography. The application of a format that expressed the relationship between humanity and sanctity also led to a shift in meaning, with sanctity now likewise bestowed upon artists. This culminated in the myth of the artistic genius, which reached its peak in the nineteenth and above all the twentieth century.

In his essay, 'The Death of the Author', Roland Barthes dispensed with this notion of the artistic creator. He essentially argued that the meaning of a text does not depend on the person who wrote it[8] but on the reader, since the author is obliged to leave the last word to another[9]. In so doing, Barthes effectively demolished the entire Vasarian order of art, which was based firmly on the hegemony of artists over the meaning of an artwork. He wrote: 'To give a text an Author is to impose a limit on that text, to furnish it with a final signified, to close the writing.'[10] Which brings us to the same conclusion as when we attempted to identify the meaning of the artwork from the work itself: that if meaning is unchangeable because it has been defined on the basis of history, a transhistorical presentation is not possible.[11]

8 In 'The Death of the Author' Barthes draws a distinction, however, between the visual arts and literature. He stated in a 1973 interview, for instance, that the visual arts were seeking to destroy the aesthetic, but that this was impossible in the case of writing, since the destruction of language can never occur via a text. All the same, his analysis of the author in relation to his or her text is perfectly applicable to the position of artists in relation to their artworks.

9 Pieters, 'Wie schrijft moet zwijgen', p. 11.

10 Barthes, 'The Death of the Author', p. 147.

11 'The Author, when believed in, is always conceived of as the past of his own book.' Ibid., p. 145.

3. The Beholder

The final point of departure is the beholder. The idea that the beholder shapes the meaning of an artwork likewise has a long tradition. Alois Riegl acknowledges the importance of the beholder in his book on Dutch group portraits, in which he took his cue from Hegel's ideas on aesthetics.[12] Riegl

12 Riegl, *Das holländische Gruppenporträt.*

sought to explain the phenomenon of these portraits from the point of view of Dutch society, but equally from the 'Seher-erfarung'—the psychological impact a work can have on the beholder. This interest in interpreting an artwork through psychology led to the construction in the twentieth century of an entire tradition, with illustrious names like Ernst Gombrich and his celebrated 'beholder's share', the work of David Freedberg, in which psychology and physical perception are central, and the notion of 'indeterminacy' from reception theory.[13] The basic idea is that viewers create and complete some or all of the meaning of an image through their own experiences.

13 Kemp, 'The Work of Art and Its Beholder'.

This point of departure *does* create the possibility for a transhistorical presentation. If we assume that meaning is realized in the mind of the beholder, this provides a platform on which two artworks can encounter one another, independently of their individual historical context, since the signification is generated by a single historical context, namely that of the beholder. This overcomes the incongruence of the transhistorical presentation and facilitates a reciprocal influence on the respective meanings.

We must take care, however, not to fall into the trap of postmodern relativism: If we leave the meaning of artworks entirely to the personal interpretation of each individual, do we not risk hopelessly splintering that meaning? Several possibilities have been suggested for escaping this impasse. We can continue to opt, firstly, for a hybrid model in which meaning is sought not only through the beholder, but still through the artist and the artwork as well. However, in view of the arguments rehearsed above, this possibility does not appear sustainable for a transhistorical presentation. Another option is to look for objective elements that apply to all beholders. One possibility in this case is provided by the neuroaesthetics of researchers such as Eric R. Kandel and Semir Zeki.[14] While this approach contributes very substantially to our understanding of the perception of artworks, a purely mechanical-biological explanation cannot embrace every aspect of the complex mechanism of meaning-giving. A more fruitful possibility is one based on the visual literacy model, in which the meaning of an artwork is generated in the mind of the beholder, who draws to this end on his or her own knowledge, experiences, and personal image library.[15] This suggests a highly personal interpretation of the artwork, but when all is said and done, the knowledge and image library in question are not all that 'individual': they are constructed instead by a person's societal setting and culture. Education, shared knowledge, mass media, archetypal images and standardized visual topoi all contribute. Consequently, regardless of the historical period in which a particular image originated, beholders will form a meaning based on the prevailing visual culture of their own everyday world. In other words, a transhistorical presentation is possible because beholders assign a meaning to different artworks from within the same historical framework, their own, with this framework laying the interpersonal foundations.

This is a solution to the paradox of artistic value. Artworks do indeed lose their original signification, but each new generation creates its own, fresh meaning using the elements of its own time. Every artwork is a blank canvas, which each beholder paints once more, lending it a renewed personal value and meaning. In this way, the meaning of an artwork emerges independently of its own historical context, which is the necessary precondition for transhistoricity.

14 Kandel, *Reductionism in Art and Brain Science* and Kawabata and Zeki 'Toward a Brain-based Theory of Beauty'.

15 I refer here to the 'Envil model', which Lode Vermeersch, Ernst Wagner, Franz Billmayer, Piet Hagenaars, Peter Carpreau and others further refined through various workshops at M-Museum Leuven. See regarding: Wagner and Schönau, *Common European Framework of Reference for Visual Literacy*.

Literature

Barthes, Roland. 'The Death of the Author.' In *Image Music Text*, pp. 142–148. New York, 1977.

Freedberg, David. *The Power of Images: Studies in the History and Theory of Response*. Chicago and London, 1989.

Kawabata, Hideaki, and Semir Zeki. 'Toward a Brain-based Theory of Beauty.' *PLoS One* 6 (July 2011), doi.org/10.1371/journal.pone.0021852.

Kandel, Eric R. *Reductionism in Art and Brain Science: Bridging the Two Cultures*. New York, 2016.

Kemp, Wolfgang. 'The Work of Art and Its Beholder: The Methodology of the Aesthetic of Reception.' In *The Subjects of Art History: Historical Objects in Contemporary Perspectives*. Edited by Mark Arthur Cheetam et al., pp. 180–196. Cambridge, 1998.

Pieters, Jürgen. 'Wie schrijft moet zwijgen: Over de wedergeboorte van de auteur.' In Roland Barthes, *Het Werkelijkheidseffect*, pp. 7–30. Brussels, 2004.

Riegl, Alois. *Das holländische Gruppenporträt*. Vienna, 1931.

Vanbergen, Johan. *Voorstelling en betekenis: Theorie van de kunsthistorische interpretatie*. Leuven, 1986.

Wagner, Ernst, and Diederik Schönau. *Common European Framework of Reference for Visual Literacy*. Münster and New York, 2016.

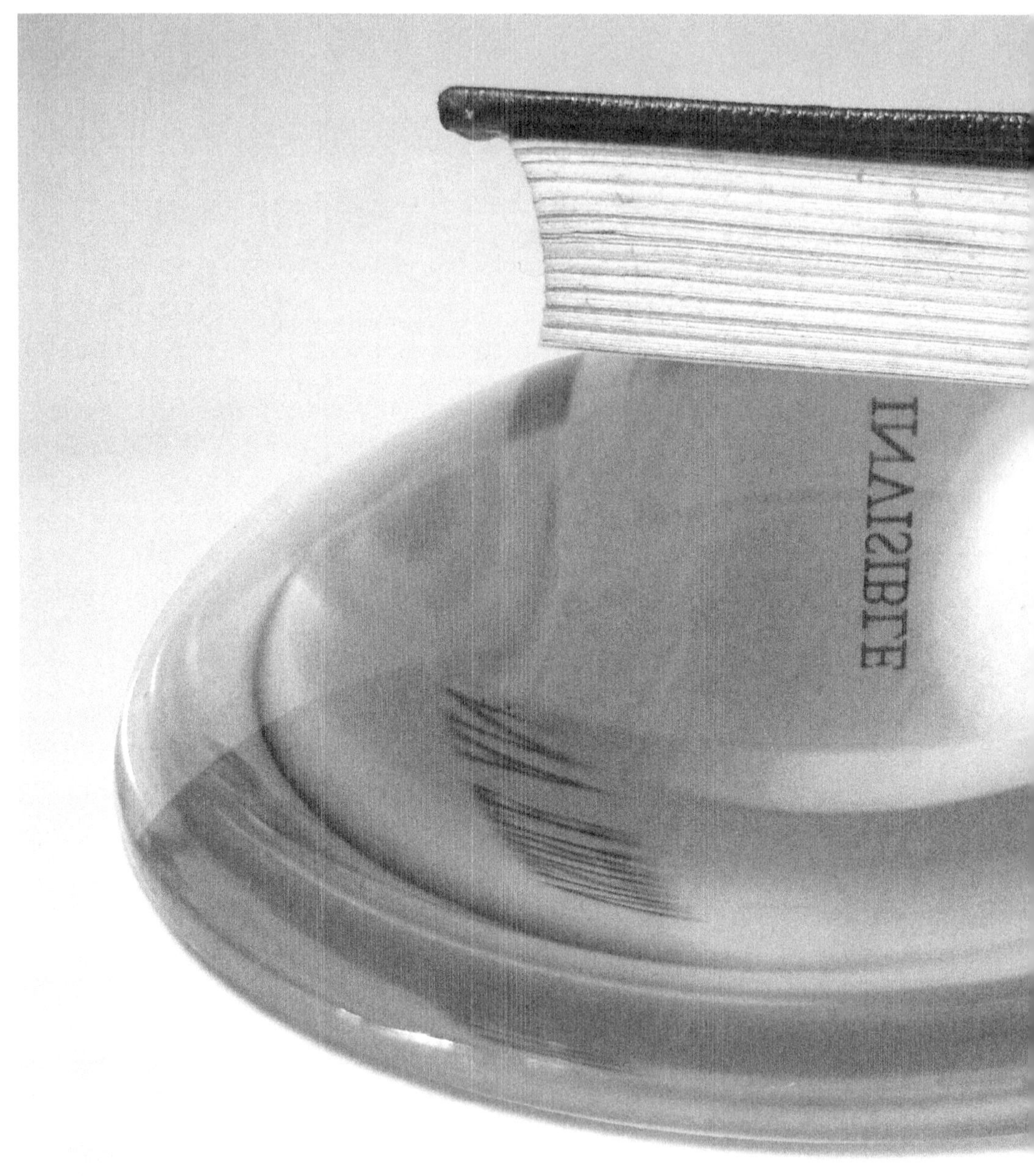
INVISIBLE

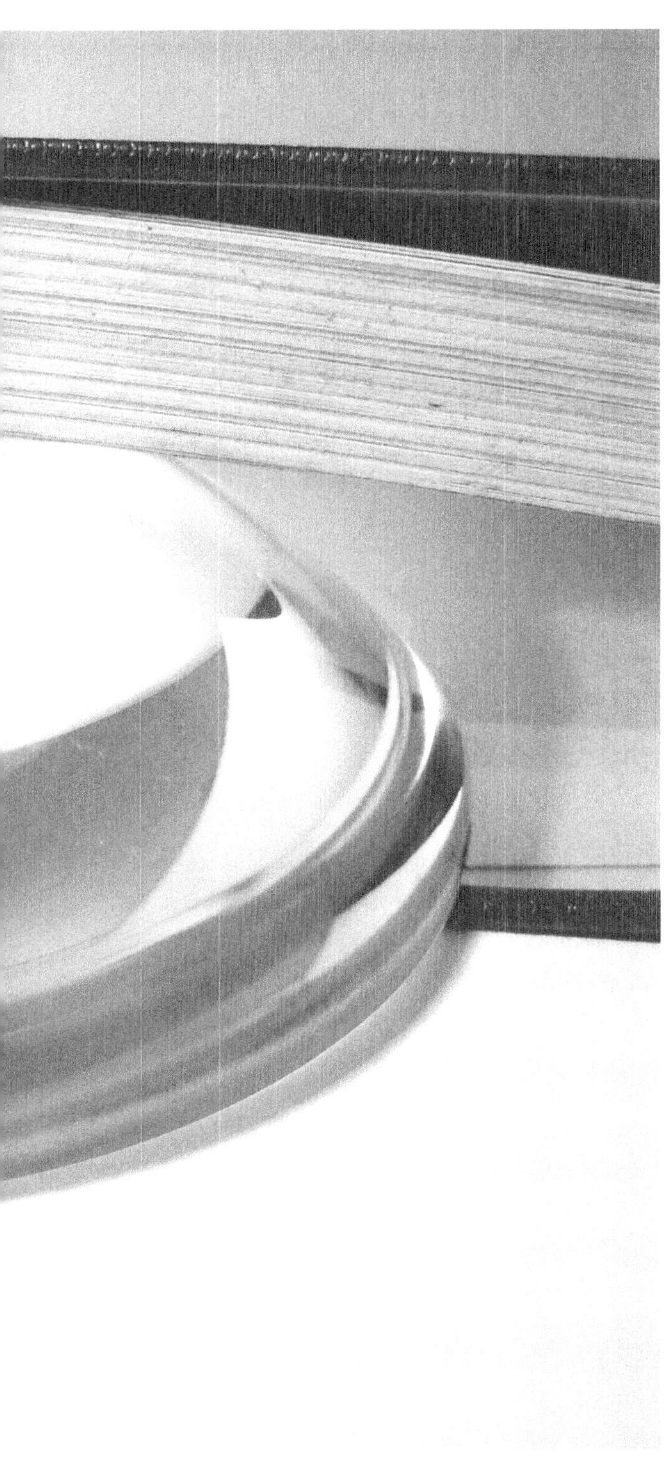

Pavel Büchler, *The Problem of God*, 2007, book, magnifying lens, approx. 3 × 28 × 21 cm. Courtesy Pavel Büchler.

An Emerging Ethics of the Transhistorical Exhibition

Beuys, Büchler, Books

Christa-Maria Lerm Hayes

It was in Venice in 2015, when reflecting on the transhistorical exhibition seemed to become inevitable. The artist Danh Vo then curated 'Slip of the Tongue', installing the Pinault Collection at Punta della Dogana. The exhibition also included his own works: (parts of) crucifixes juxtaposed with items associated with contemporary consumer culture. Vo employed drops of blood as a formal leitmotif—and confronted (albeit in the staircase) his audience with *Immersion (Piss Christ)*, 1987, an icon of artistic and gay rights that, together with Robert Mapplethorpe's works, had sparked the US Culture Wars.[1] Vo's exhibition was as sumptuous and elegantly curated as any manifestation of the presence, indeed normalcy, of (the artist's) homosexuality in art could be: a courageous and activist statement without any raised banners—and thus possibly all the more effective.[2]

Across town from 'Slip of the Tongue', at Palazzo Fortuny, 'Proportio' was another tour de force of artworks—and also furniture—from different centuries, featuring in an array of spaces objects as diverse as a Josef Albers painting, carpets, old oriental measuring instruments, or Le Corbusier's

1 Rugg, 'Rhetoric and Reality'.

2 Claire Bishop comes to a different conclusion in her *Artforum* review <www.artforum.com/inprint/issue=201507&id=54492> (accessed January 2018). To respond to her thoughts in detail is not possible here, but—in relation to the politics of the transhistorical—her assessment that historical items with biographical references have the capacity to become an empty signifier should be taken seriously. In the following, I certainly see this as one of the reasons to propose a 'middle voice'. What she seems to take less seriously than I would is the fact that the artworks themselves are not the only bearers of (their) meaning. They do not function as isolated, talismanic objects, as Gabriel Rockhill would say. Rockhill, *Radical History & The Politics of Art*.

Villa Savoye model. The exhibition was co-curated by interior architect and gallerist Axel Vervoordt. The 'transhistorical' exhibition is not just a recent trend that harks back in exhibition history to the cabinets of curiosity of royalty that were after all the seedbeds of museums. It takes the design choices of many private art collectors (emulating royalty as always) into the public realm and into the white cube space that, since Brian O'Doherty's *Inside the White Cube* essays from the late-1970s, has spelled out its association with real estate and the art market all too clearly. Jean-Hubert Martin, at the Haarlem conference preceding publication of this volume, explained that his 'Magiciens de la terre' exhibition had taken into the museum the kinds of juxtapositions that he had seen in many homes of collectors.

There is thus not one politics of 'the' transhistorical. In the following, I will, after some introductory notes featuring Aby Warburg and Harald Szeemann, try to explain what this approach's liberating elements can be. My main examples will be Joseph Beuys' and Pavel Büchler's work, and I will end with remarks on books in exhibitions: arguably tokens of transhistorical thought. I will keep in mind that a 'middle voice', a position between 'perpetrator' and 'victim' is ultimately inevitable when we speak of the transhistorical exhibition—as is the case probably of all art and all exhibitions.[3] That we understand the white cube as a space that is not neutral, lets us assume also that the non-white cube (as in 'Proportio') is far from agenda-free. This high-end, curated interior design does not only let new money look old, but is also part of a cultural shift away from modernism,[4] which insisted on the separation of art forms and wished to purge history, literature, religion, time, the viewer, politics et al. from its supposedly neutral, self-referential spaces.

3 Boletsi, 'From the Subject of the Crisis to the Subject in Crisis'. I consider this *Documenta Reader* a transhistorical document also, as it features several 'Documents of Empire/ Documents of Decoloniality', alongside Flaubert.

4 Esche, 'The Demodernizing Possibility'.

To reject history, or to have the hubris to complete it, to insist that one does not depend on anything or anyone, but that art means perpetual newness: all this has functioned, of course, as an essential attitude to facilitate modern consumer society. The Bauhaus (somewhat in vain) wished its products to reach wide distribution and its 'Masters' houses in Dessau, 1925, provided no space for old things. Yet, there is a difference between their avant-garde spaces—which (in Kandinsky's house) included a 'spiritual', icon-like gold leaf-covered wall beside the tiled stove—and the Nazis, who were soon to close that institution and kill some of its staff and students. Their scorched earth, tabula rasa policy went hand in hand with an obsession with all things homely and (selectively) historical. If modernity is now seen as inherently chauvinist and colonialist, the transhistorical exhibition, in including pre-modern and extra-modern ('non-Western') material, may be part of an attempt to overcome it, but a focus on history and the attempt to link oneself to its elements is also clearly the tried-and-tested strategy of every despot to establish his own credentials to lead in chauvinistic or colonial ways.

It follows that the most powerfully critical artworks can adopt both synchronous and diachronic strategies: Fred Wilson's 'Mining the Museum', 1992–1993, takes its poignancy from juxtaposing (under the heading of 'metalwork 1793–1880') elaborate silverwork and slave shackles from the *same* time. This synchronicity establishes the two items as causally linked. The project only becomes a 'transhistorical' one, when it is taken as a contemporary artwork, which utilizes historical material (nearly in the way that Vo does). Hans Haacke's tracing of the ownership of a Seurat painting is also transhistorical (in narrating a history and referencing an 'old' artwork) and not (in its single authorship, date, material and form—featuring a mere reproduction of the Seurat). What Haacke shows us, however, is that such investigation—also called art history (or maybe art sociology)—is always transhistorical. Aby Warburg's *Mnemosyne Atlas*, 1920s, is a beautiful example of a transhistorical exhibition.[5] It encompasses also the difficulties encountered here: the art and non-art materials he thematically grouped—as photographs on black panels and exhibited in his research institute's library—are ascribed value if the focus is on their iconographic tradition: to be part of a historical, canonizing narrative most often pays off. If we look further, however, and see how Warburg pursued a comparative psychology (via gestures 'frozen' in the images: *pathos formulae*), then an emancipatory, humanist project emerges: knowledge of historical expression for Warburg became an indispensable means for analysing the place of a given society on the continuum between rationality and an irrationality that would be dangerous for potential scapegoats (such as artists and 'others'). Warburg developed—and needed—such knowledge as a Jew in the Weimar Republic.[6] A transhistorical view is a necessary basis for (art-historical) research, for positions that wish to substantiate their liberating impetus through historical knowledge and example. All thematic exhibitions (and artists' research projects) are thus transhistorical, looking at the past from the present and presenting 'peer practices'. That this does not mean relinquishing a public, or presenting dry, academic curating is evident from the institution that pioneered a broadly thematic display of its collection: Tate Modern (since 2000). I wish to devote my attention to examples in this field where I see that liberating elements take precedence.

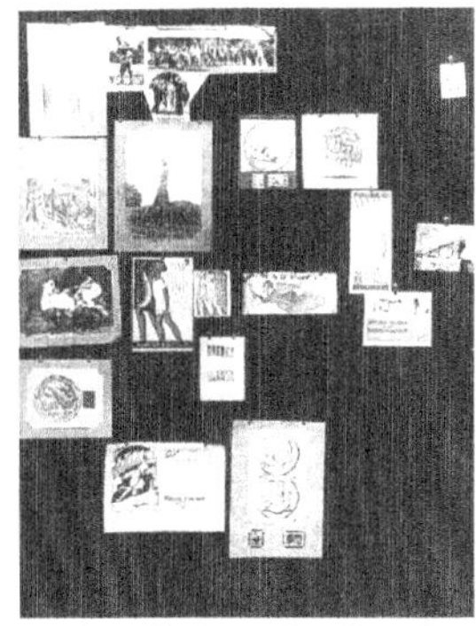

5 Aby Warburg, Panel 77 of *Mnemosyne Atlas*, 1929, historical picture of the original. Courtesy of Warburg Institute, London.

6 Lerm, 'Das Jüdische Erbe in Aby Warburg's Leben und Werk'.

The thematic exhibition is in exhibition history connected with the curatorial practice of Harald Szeemann (documenta 5, 1972). He at times worked in long, diachronic lines, such as his 1983 exhibition 'The Inclination Towards the Gesamtkunstwerk' (total work of art), reaching from Wagner to the present, or his exhibition on Monte Verità, a colony of artists and life reformers: he wished to give form to artistic 'attitudes'. One artist had pre-eminence in Szeemann's universe: Joseph Beuys (1921–1986). Beuys' works, such as those for documenta 5 and 6, can be thought to have lived very much in the present, as they consisted of Beuys entering into long discussions with audience members about political matters, ecology, migration, history, et cetera, captured by 1977 as activities of the Free International University for Creativity and Interdisciplinary Research. Beuys' performances and discussions were accompanied by sculptural manifestations and drawings—and these privilege 'old' materials: items showing traces of use and decay. The transhistorical nature of Beuys' exhibitions thus involved speaking (in academically-related ways) about the diachronic: history and change, and the objects themselves were and are subject to change: a restorer's nightmare. They even sometimes smelled. In Venice, where he exhibited in the German (Nazi-built) pavilion in 1976, he had a hole drilled into the lagoon, to bring historical material to the surface—and he combined this vertical axis with tram tracks on the ground, which literally and figuratively make the horizontal connection in space: from his home on the German/Dutch border across Europe —with the inference that this is how the Jewish citizens of Europe had to travel to their deaths. When martial law reigned in Poland, 1981–1982, he gave work to the Muzeum Sztuki in Łodz (geographically close to Auschwitz) that featured such connections also—specifically those to Ireland, where he had travelled in 1974. I have argued elsewhere that Beuys used James Joyce's literature to link Ireland, especially its megalithic passage tombs and the basalt columns (quickly cooled lava) of the Antrim coast, to the recent World War II and genocide.[7] Such a time-frame from the geological and Neolithic past to the present may today sound more familiar, as we have begun to think in categories of the Anthropocene. In Beuys' time, such a position, which may have the side-effect of lessening the exceptionality of the Shoah, was hotly debated (the so-called 'Historikerstreit'). Transhistorical lines in Beuys' work also reach into the future: his early ecological credentials manifested in becoming a co-founder of the Green movement (and one-time election candidate), but also in the large *7000 Oaks* project, documenta 7, 1982, completed after his death, documenta 8, 1987. 7000 deciduous trees were planted, mainly in the city of Kassel, heavily bombed during the war (due to its arms industry). Each tree Beuys accompanied with a basalt column, taken one by one from the triangular heap on which he had placed them in the main city square—the site that had served citizens to gather the charred remains of their loved ones after the bomb nights. Thus, the anthropomorphic, formerly fluid piece of lava both 'nourishes' and shields each growing tree, measuring (like plants on the mounds of rubble) the distance from day zero. The initial ratio of a tree's height and thickness to its companion changed soon, and it still does.

7 Lerm Hayes, *Post-War Germany and 'Objective Chance'*.

In this kind of oeuvre, historical materials take on a different value: they are chosen rather than made. They are present, partly because it would be damaging to the world for the artist to choose (and thus manufacture) new things. The world should not be littered with newly produced art, but old objects (alongside living things and contact with people) are prioritized as resilient markers of sustainability and critique of consumer society: someone cares. Beuys kept a store of objects, waiting for them 'to call' him, and he also knew that memory (and thus history) does not simply exist, but is produced by consistent effort of re-selecting objects, re-telling (and in the process making) (hi)stories.[8] Certain histories have to be held awake, in order not to repeat themselves, while knowing (or so we can surmise was Beuys' view) that in the largest historical frameworks, human beings will keep committing incomprehensible crimes. This perspective clarifies that the transhistorical is not—or should not be seen as—a straight connection, a teleological worldview: it can be an ecological one, a cyclical perspective. The respect that Beuys had of what he found and re-used or re-cycled was nurtured by his reading of Joyce's *Finnegans Wake*, a 'cyclical book' that speaks of 'recirculation' in its first sentence (which completes the last one of the book): 'riverrun, past Eve and Adam's, from swerve of shore to bend of bay, brings us by a commodius vicus of recirculation back to Howth Castle and Environs.'[9]

In contemporary art, Tacita Dean, born 1965, appears to echo and carry on such respect for the past—e.g. in her poetically activist film *Block Beuys*, 2008, which joined forces with many Beuys scholars, who were at that time (ultimately unsuccessfully) attempting to convince the Hessisches Landesmuseum, Darmstadt, not to turn the spaces with Beuys' work into a white cube.[10] Dean's work focuses on the lovingly mended jute fabric that covered the walls of Beuys' five-room installation in the museum. Beuys had chosen to retain the existing fabric and had incorporated its dimensions, colour and insulating qualities into his installation, produced over many years (1967–1986) as a truly transhistorical curatorial project. Dean works in the medium of 16mm film, now considered obsolete by many (and owing to its scarcity it becomes a more auratic and highly-prized commodity, as well). The film, in its multiple bridging of time, becomes another site of transhistorical attention, an artwork that turns

8 Beuys, having first served as the exemplary Modernist in relation to his public strategies, is now understood as someone who sought to overcome modernity. See: *Joseph Beuys: Greetings from the Eurasian*, esp. Nav Haq's introduction.

9 Joyce, *Finnegans Wake*, p. 3, lines 1–3. The pagination and line numbering are the same for all editions.

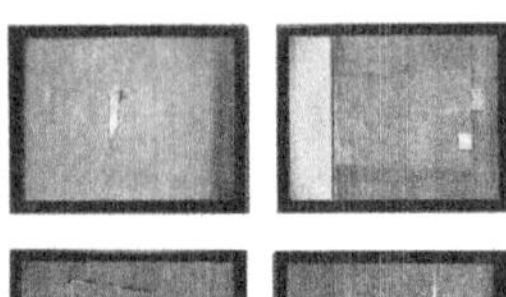
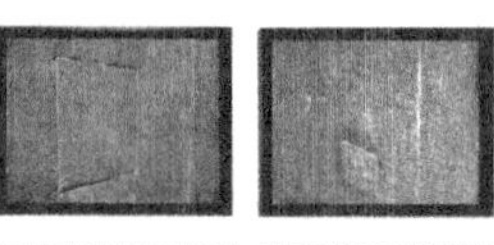
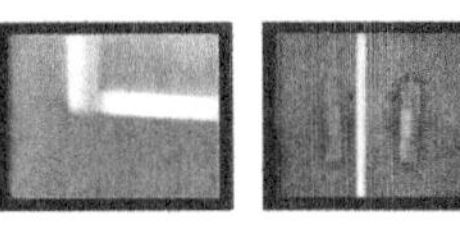
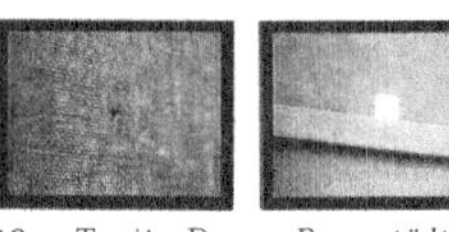
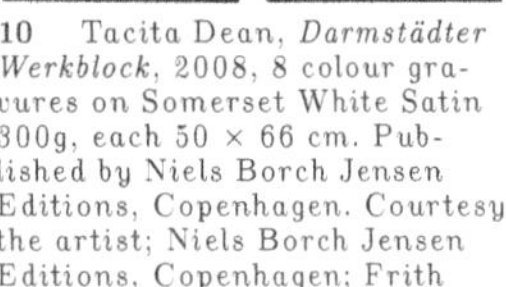

10 Tacita Dean, *Darmstädter Werkblock*, 2008, 8 colour gravures on Somerset White Satin 300g, each 50 × 66 cm. Published by Niels Borch Jensen Editions, Copenhagen. Courtesy the artist; Niels Borch Jensen Editions, Copenhagen; Frith Street Gallery, London, and Marian Goodman Gallery, New York/Paris.

into an act of resilience and an atypical, activist display of object-based, analogue respect in the digital era. It insists on the physical traces and materiality of both room and celluloid as witnesses to the long-term commitment of artist, collectors and the institution that had brought about this work in the first place.

Pavel Büchler, like Dean, has observed that art academies, in their quest for the amnesiac bigger and better, tend to acquire recent technology and de-accession anything old. They do this, despite the fact that retaining analogue machinery for the creation, restauration, and display of both older and current—i.e. transhistorically operating—work could be an asset to such institutions that is likely to be viable financially, especially when the associated skills could be taught and kept alive (the 'employability' of students enhanced and the business model of the institution as lenders of such technology diversified). Such a long-term way of thinking, however, appears neither to be sexy enough for the managers of such institutions, for whom innovation is a mantra inherited from modern and contemporary art (although it is incompatible with it),[11] nor for many students, whose incessant digital image production holds them in a permanent, 'cloud'-based present,[12] where the idea of printing one out, holding it, seems outlandish.

We are reaching a point where more and more people find such contemporary, progress-oriented institutional practices lacking, knowing that they are not sustainable. Now, not only museums discover the transhistorical that has always been within their realm of possibilities, but other public institutions too are adopting theoretical positions that show the value of a historically connected, i.e. transhistorical way of thinking and living: Jane Jacob's dictum 'New ideas must use old buildings' is the motto of the UK Heritage Lottery Fund.[13]

11 See: Büchler, *Somebody's Got to Do It*, pp. 126, 157.

12 See ibid., p. 216 on the unchanging times of/in Western art.

13 Heritage Lottery Fund website: <www.hlf.org.uk/new-ideas-need-old-buildings> accessed January 2018.

While more art academies, universities, and even museums look like bank HQs, bankers are seeking the services of Axel Vervoordt. Classrooms become devoid of books, when lessons are just screen-based, while Silicon Valley professionals are sending their children to schools banning screens. When noting such 'transhistorical' lifestyle choices and educational developments, it would be important to be guided by early practitioners of transhistorical thinking.

Pavel Büchler, trained as a typographer and producing samizdat publications in his native Prague before being incarcerated and, later, moving to England, encountered the West and its art world as a place where, already in the 1970s, there was 'too much'.[14] He developed an art practice that shares Beuys' penchant for selecting objects with traces, especially writing materials (pencils with which he assembles Kafkaesque 'castles') and books that become sculptural objects (e.g. *The Problem of God*, where a lens placed between two pages reveals the word 'invisible', see pp. 118–119). Büchler's work's motto is 'making nothing happen'.[15] It is a commitment not to create material extravaganzas, but find things (often 'obsolete' technological objects such as megaphones, slide projectors, et cetera) that, in the way Büchler installs them, reveal deeper meanings and enable analysis—epiphanies, as James Joyce might have said.[16] With that special way of evolving the found object, this 'transhistorical' art practice goes hand in hand with an advanced institutional wisdom born from Büchler's experiences under a dictatorship and practiced in leadership roles at universities in Glasgow and Manchester.

Deliberately lowering the level of spectacle is inherent in this longitudinal, performative work, using any and all of the affordances of art and its institutions. Indeed, Charles Esche's category of experimental institutionalism[17] can be viewed as

14 Büchler, *Somebody's Got to Do It*, pp. 210, 78. Also: 'tr[y] to give these leftovers-of-meaning one last chance before they drift into ambiguity. It is as if every attempt to hold onto the affective ties to tradition and heritage were also a small rebellion against their persistence … for the time being.' Ibid. p. 78. 'There are some books … [that] made a gesture of resistance and struggle to which I pay respect. Badly printed … these books are monuments to a political attitude. They were published to challenge the neglect of the continuity of culture, which was brought about by a popular submission to the belief that culture is a historical convention. They were published out of necessity, out of a sense of urgency: not to "break a silence" but to speak clearly in the prattle of so many obedient voices, to act, to participate, to continue….' p. 85.

15 Büchler, *Somebody's Got to Do It*, p. 198.

16 See Büchler's work on Joyce: Lerm Hayes, 'Bloom Stool'.

17 Esche, '"We were learning by doing"'. Büchler would call those engaged in experimental institutionalism '"tactical practitioners" [, who] prefer to work in the interstices and gaps left unclaimed by politics and art'. Büchler, *Somebody's Got to Do It*, p. 163.

inspired by Büchler, whom he centrally featured in his first curated exhibition.[18] Using what is there in terms of historical material, both object-based and intellectual, is an attitude that was a necessity behind the Iron Curtain: Friedrich Schiller taught the importance of aesthetic education in the aftermath of the French Revolution, transferrable to other violently oppressive situations. Cut off from current debates, dissidents had to think for themselves and value what could be learned from reading Marx against the grain, or the Bible for early Christian experiences in illegality.[19] Valuing certain liberating cultural traditions—the ones Gilles Deleuze and Félix Guattari would call minor[20]—enabled debates that connected through time and space: dialogues with other readers and with authors, who were often too canonical to be censored and could be adapted to use both in the future and elsewhere, i.e. in the West. Books opened and still open other worlds and sharpen the necessary sensitivity for analysis of one's own position in history. The one thing that is a constant in history is change. (Joyce's *Finnegans Wake* as a cyclical 'world history' was mentioned). Even if one was told that one lived in the regime to end all and to which there were no alternatives—as every totalitarian state tells its subjects—it gives hope to know that these claims were already made by any number of no longer reigning dictators. History can free the mind.

With Warburg, one could use culture—e.g. the rise of the transhistorical exhibition—as an indicator of the place of current societies on the continuum between rationality and irrationality, or the level of orthodoxies in our time. I prefer to note that artists such as Beuys and Büchler and curators such as Esche enhance through their work the complexity of both object-based and institutional practice with which they construct social situations (aka artworks and exhibitions). That

18 It was: 'Excavating the Present, Kettle's Yard', Cambridge, 1991. This also applies to me in one of my first curated exhibitions: 'Pavel Büchler: Old, Rare and Unusual Roses.' 'Return' Gallery, Goethe Institut Dublin, 7 December 2006–15 January 2007.

19 I developed arguments related to this point in recent conference papers: 'Conceptualisms and Liberation Theology Behind the Iron Curtain', *Conceptualism: Intersectional Readings, International Framings: Black Artists and Modernism in Europe after 1968*, Van Abbemuseum, Eindhoven, 9 December 2017; and: 'Formering the West Today Through Attention to Activist Practices Behind the Iron Curtain', *Art & Activism*, University of Leiden, 14/15 December 2017.

20 Deleuze and Guattari, *Kafka*.

art institutions are now, e.g. through transhistorical exhibitions, more open to generating and exhibiting diverse, lateral knowledges of the past, cannot but mean that these practices are needed—undoubtedly in order to generate visions and manage the problems of both present and future.

Historical objects with which we are connected affectively, such as real paper-and-print books, have, in my view and as Büchler's work also suggests, a definite role in this constellation. Behind the Iron Curtain, books were a prized, and shared, intellectual status symbol. They have in the twenty-first century become a new commons, something of little monetary value that is passed on through impromptu 'community libraries', sheltering in the last few public phone booths. Many artists and curators are creating opportunities to read as a form of art and exhibitions,[21] and the 2015 Venice Biennale staged a central, communal reading of Marx' *Das Kapital*. The status-quo-changing, modernity-overcoming reading[22] of potentially liberating (minor) literature is a central experience of the slowly,[23] respectfully transhistorical. As a community-building measure and alternative to inadequate/tendentious (art) education, it helped to bring about the peaceful revolution of 1989. Who knows what might be possible today, when we transhistorically make 'nothing happen'?

21 See e.g.: Heman Chong and Renée Staal, 'The Library of Unread Books', CASCO, Utrecht, 2017–2018. Or my own curated: 'Convergence: Literary Art Exhibitions'. Golden Thread Gallery, Belfast, Limerick CCA, 2011.

22 Büchler, *Somebody's Got to Do It*, pp. 91, 137.

23 Ibid., p. 208.

Literature

Bishop, Claire. 'History Depletes Itself: Claire Bishop on Danh Vo at the Danish Pavilion and Punta della Dogana.' *Artforum* 54, no. 1, September 2015, pp. 324–329.

Boletsi, Maria. 'From the Subject of the Crisis to the Subject in Crisis: Middle Voice on Greek Walls.' *The documenta 14 Reader.* Edited by Quinn Latimer and Adam Szymczyk, pp. 431–468. Munich, London and New York, 2017.

Büchler, Pavel. *Somebody's Got to Do It: Selected Writings by Pavel Büchler Since 1987*. Edited by Nick Thurston. London, 2017.

Esche, Charles. '"We were learning by doing," an interview with Charles Esche by Lucy Kolb and Gabriel Flückinger.' *(New) Institution(alism)*. On-curating Vol. 21 (January 2014), ‹www.on-curating.org/issue-21-reader/we-were-learning-by-doing.html#.WlzGAiMZNE4› (accessed January 2018).

———. 'The Demodernizing Possibility.' In *How Institutions Think. Between Contemporary Art and Curatorial Discourse*. Edited by Paul O'Neill, pp. 212–221. Cambridge and London, 2017.

Deleuze, Gilles, and Félix Guattari. *Kafka: Toward a Minor Literature*. Minneapolis [etc.], 1975.

Joseph Beuys: Greetings from the Eurasian. Exh. cat. M HKA. Antwerp and London, 2017.

Joyce, James. *Finnegans Wake*. London, 1939.

Lerm Hayes, Christa-Maria. 'Das Jüdische Erbe in Aby Warburg's Leben und Werk.' *Menora 5: Yearbook for German-Jewish History 1994*. Edited by Julius H. Schoeps for the Salomon Ludwig Steinheim Institute of German-Jewish History at the University of Duisburg, pp. 141–169. Munich and Zurich, 1994.

———. *Post-War Germany and 'Objective Chance': W.G. Sebald, Joseph Beuys and Tacita Dean/Nachkriegsdeutschland und 'Objektiver Zufall': W.G. Sebald, Joseph Beuys und Tacita Dean*. Göttingen, 2008.

———. 'Bloomova Stolice/Bloom Stool.' In *Pavel Büchler: Marná práce/Labour in Vain*. Edited by DOX Centre for Contemporary Art, pp.104-107. Prague, 2010.

Rockhill, Gabriel. *Radical History & The Politics of Art*. New York, 2014.

Rugg, Whitney. 'Rhetoric and Reality: O'Doherty Between the Art World and Arts Endowment.' In *Brian O'Doherty/Patrick Ireland: Word, Image and Institutional Critique*. Edited by Christa-Maria Lerm Hayes, pp. 81–96. Amsterdam, 2017.

Part 3

Curatorial Strategies

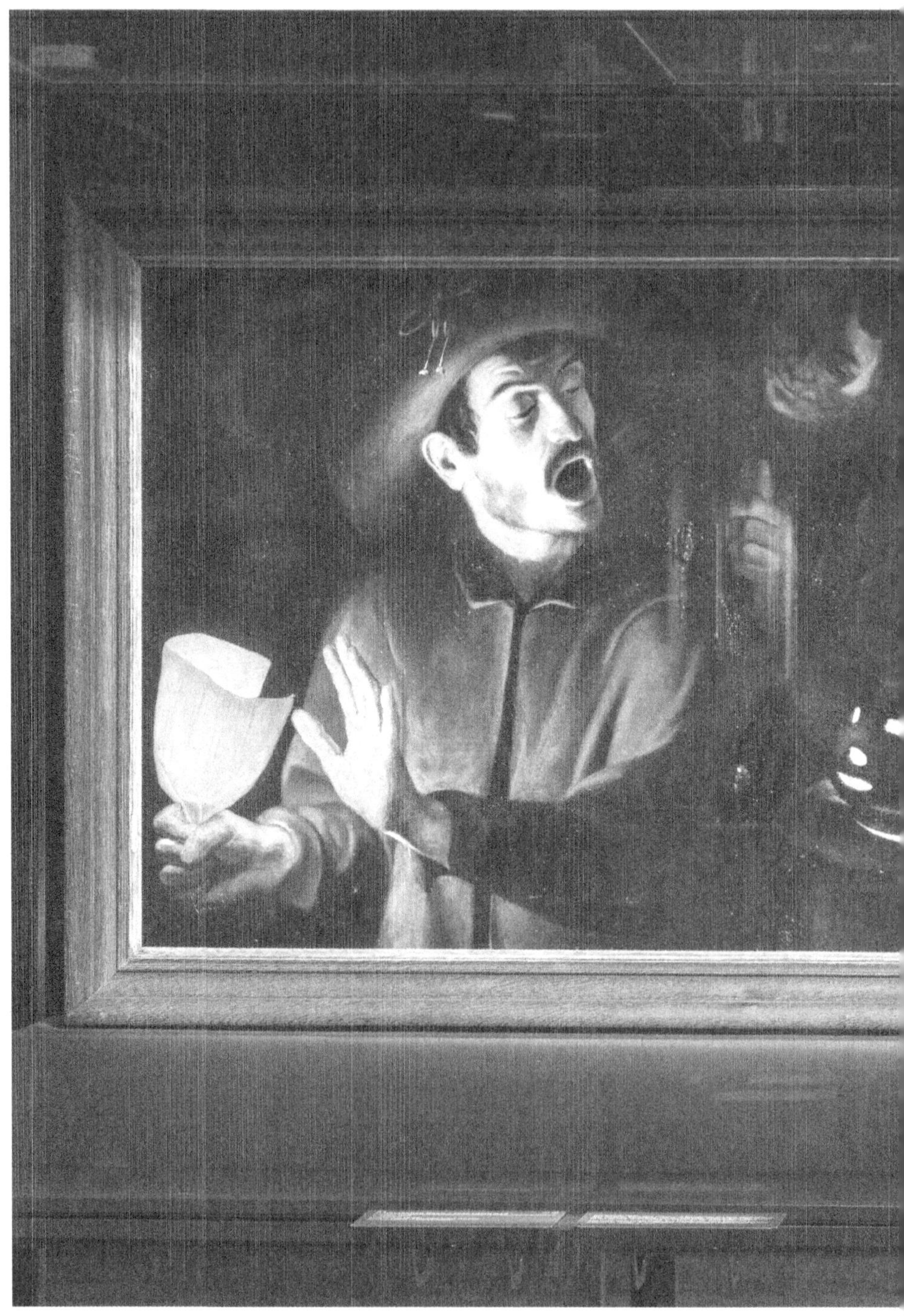

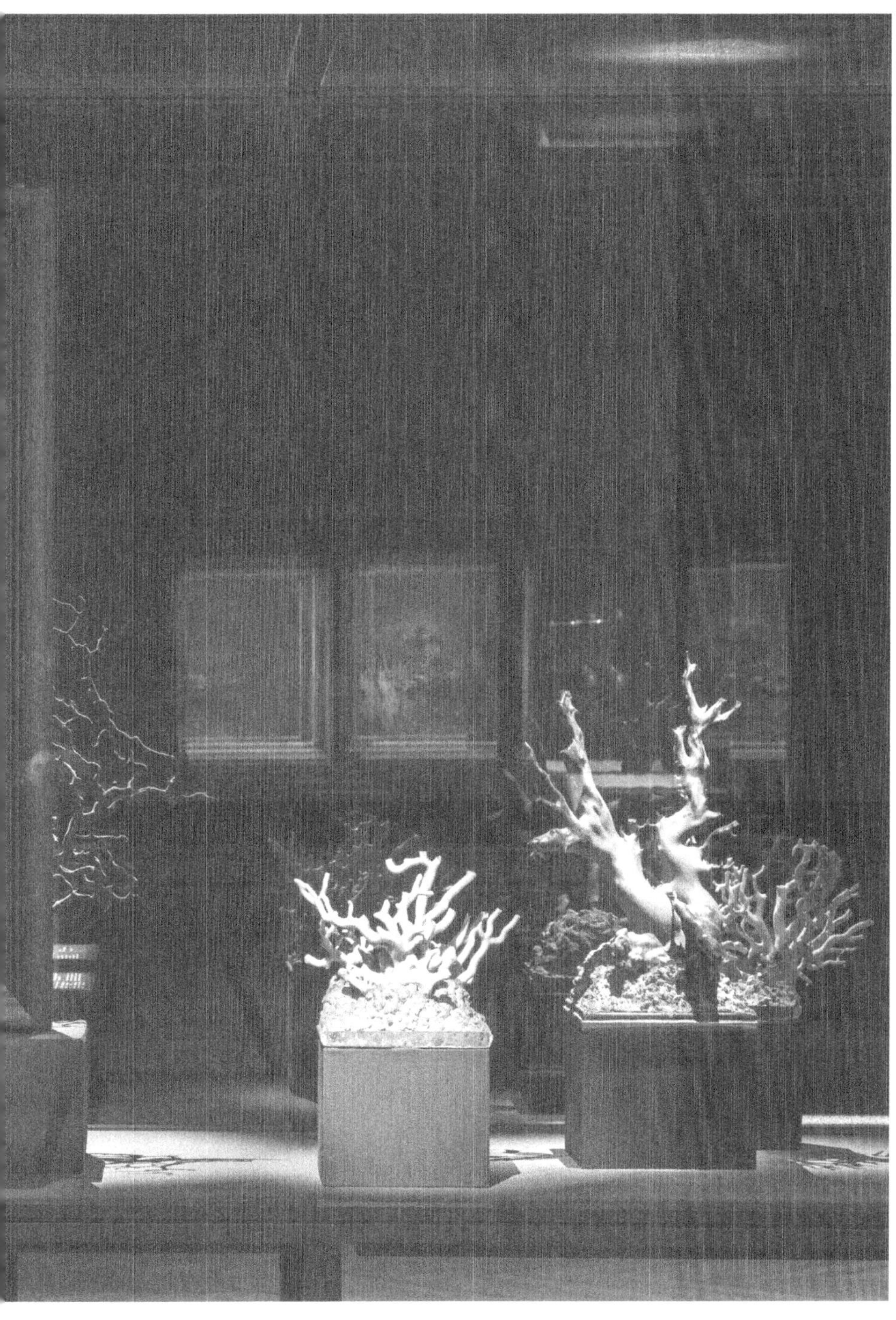

'During the Night: Edmund de Waal meets Albrecht Dürer', curated by Edmund de Waal, installation view, Kunsthistorisches Museum, Vienna, 2016. Courtesy Kunsthistorisches Museum.

The Book in Which We Learn to Read

Contemporary Artists and their Place within Historical Museums

Jasper Sharp

... And this, gentlemen of the press, curators, critics, experts and others, is the claim we painters make in regard to the old masters. They are ours, not yours. We have their blood in our veins. We are their heirs, executors, assignees, trustees. We are pious sons, but henceforth it is we who are the interpreters of their wishes, with full power to set them aside, and substitute our own, whenever and wherever it seems fit for us to do so. They would have wished it so.[1]
—Walter Sickert (1860–1942)

1 Walter Sickert, quoted in exhibition catalogue *The Artist's Eye*.

The painter Walter Sickert was a partisan and a provocateur, but his strong-worded assertion quoted above is not entirely without basis in fact. The presence and engagement of living artists within the halls and galleries of historical collections has long been taken for granted, since it was primarily for their benefit that many such museums were conceived. When the Muséum central des Arts (today known as the Louvre) opened its doors on 10 August 1793, it did so under the directorship of its first governors, the painters Hubert Robert, Fragonard and Vincent, the sculptor Pajou, and the architect de Wailly. Admission was free, but the museum was open to the general public for just three days of the ten day week of the new revolutionary calendar. Priority was given on the remaining days to artists, many hundreds of whom took the opportunity to study paintings formerly hidden from view in the private collections of the French royal family and aristocrats who had since fled abroad.

A decade before the Louvre began drawing its first crowds, the imperial Habsburg picture collection in Vienna had been installed at the Upper Belvedere, the former garden palace of Prince Eugene of Savoy, at the instigation of Empress Maria Theresa. For the first years of its presentation, only academic pupils (and the occasional travelling aristocrat) were granted access to the collection, which was documented in one of the first public catalogues to be compiled according to scholarly criteria.[2] Over the course of the next century, one great museum after another was founded with the same purpose: to educate, encourage, and inspire the contemporary artist. The Rijksmuseum, Amsterdam (1815), the Prado, Madrid (1819), The National Gallery, London (1824), and the Altes Museum, Berlin (1830) each set about collecting and presenting objects which living artists could study. All over Europe, students of art and practising artists were invited to listen in on the conversations that had taken place across the centuries, and to become part of the conversation themselves.

During the years since the founding of such museums, living artists have continued to make use of them. If nothing else, they provided answers as to how artists of the past had solved certain problems. Sir Herbert Read's 1954 lecture 'The Museum and The Artist' listed a number of specific cases in which museums and their collections had shaped the development of contemporary art: the influence of Japanese prints on Whistler and Gauguin, of Persian miniatures on Matisse, of non-western sculpture on Picasso, 'all fruitful influences

2 In 1891, the picture collection was relocated (along with the other imperial collections) to the recently completed Kunsthistorisches Museum on Vienna's Ringstrasse.

3 Read, 'The Museum and The Artist'.

4 Paul Cézanne, quoted in Read, 'The Museum and The Artist', p. 289.

5 Sir Joshua Reynolds, quoted in Hall, 'A Sublime Roller Coaster Ride Through Art History'.

6 Rosenblum, 'Remembrance of Art Past', p. 8.

which came from museums'.[3] But such influences were very often tempered by resistance. Paul Cézanne famously referred to the Louvre as 'the book in which we learn to read', but it is the subsequent, less often cited part of his statement that is perhaps more revealing. 'We must not be content to memorise the beautiful formulas of our illustrious predecessors. Let us get out and study beautiful nature. Let us try to discover her spirit. Let us express ourselves according to our own temperaments.'[4]

His contemporary Camille Pissarro went further, describing the Louvre as a graveyard of art and insisting that it should be burnt to the ground. The Italian Futurists, had he lived long enough to know them, would have gladly helped him find the fuel. Whether or not he was serious, this was just one example of many repeated attempts on the part of artists to annihilate tradition and dismantle what they perceived to be the cult of the past. In words attributed to the eighteenth-century painter Sir Joshua Reynolds, the Old Masters were both 'models to imitate… and rivals with whom to contend'.[5] In a National Gallery catalogue essay titled 'Remembrance of Art Past', Robert Rosenblum attempted to rationalize such arguments, calling it a 'precarious balance between respecting and destroying tradition is at the very roots of our heritage'.[6]

Some of the greatest artists of the twentieth century were content to mock historical museums while simultaneously absorbing and appropriating from them with ironic detachment and a certain promiscuous abandon. But as Rosenblum points out, the revolutions of modern art faced backwards every bit as much as forwards.

> Picasso, once heralding everything new in the twentieth century, has slowly been transformed into the guardian

> of the past, as we discover that his terrorist attacks on tradition turn out to be a way of rejuvenating, not destroying, our heritage, even preserving for us the conventional subject hierarchies of ambitious figure paintings, ideal nudes, portraiture, landscape and still-life.[7]

7 Ibid., p. 13.

Tucked into the middle of that last sentence is a word which has come to define the complex relationship between living artists and the history of art: tradition. That which is passed down from one generation to the next, and, should it be judged to remain relevant, to successive generations beyond. It is a common instinct within human nature to develop a certain antipathy towards that which one has been taught to admire. Many artists through the ages have proclaimed themselves to be against tradition, by which they mean the art of the past. As has been often pointed out, the difference is between those who have studied the past and need to unburden themselves from it in order to find new means of expression, and those who have refused or failed to learn from it and are therefore likely simply to repeat it or to register forms of hollow protest. In certain cases it is more a question of semantics: artists have spoken out against tradition when in fact what they mean to attack is academicism, and its lifeless, inevitable predictability.

The educational-academic role prescribed to historical museums by their founders, and the nature of the relationship between those museums and living artists, have become increasingly ambiguous over time as the institutions and their collections become ever more gradually removed from the present day. The points in time at which their collections suddenly stop—1848 in the case of the Louvre, for example, or 1900 in the case of The National Gallery, London—drift further away from us with each new year that passes. As a result, museums that no longer collect the work of artists practising today, or indeed of several generations before them, are having to rethink the way in which they engage with living artists.

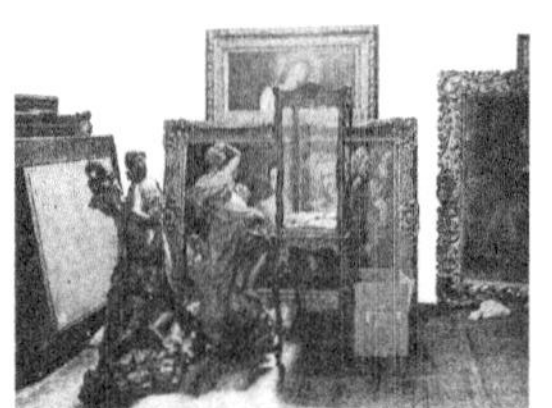

8 'Raid the Icebox I with Andy Warhol', installation view, Museum of Art, Rhode Island School, Providence (RI), 1970. Courtesy of the Museum of Art, Rhode Island School of Design.

More than thirty years ago, The National Gallery in London initiated a series of exhibitions titled 'The Artist's Eye', in which prominent artists such as David Hockney, Lucian Freud, Bridget Riley and Francis Bacon were invited to disrupt temporarily the usual historical display of the Gallery's paintings by making a selection of works and then hanging them in his or her own way. A small, personal 'collection', if you like, assembled from one much larger. At the time of her exhibition, Riley was asked how an artist's view of a collection differs from that of a scholar or member of the public visiting the museum. 'An artist', she replied

> sees the collection in much the same way as any visitor: he likes or dislikes certain paintings, and he benefits, like everybody, from some historical knowledge to help him bridge the gap to the art of the past. But an artist cannot help but be drawn, consciously or unconsciously, by interests particular to his work. He will be looking for points of contact through which his own problems may become a little clearer to him and, although no artistic intentions are ever the same, he may find comfort and encouragement in realising that certain fundamentals of making a painting remain fairly constant.

The format took its cue from an earlier curatorial experiment, Andy Warhol's 'Raid the Icebox'.[8] Initiated by Dominique de Menil, the project presented an eclectic selection of objects hand-picked by Warhol from the storage vaults of the Museum of Art, Rhode Island School of Design, at museums in three different cities in the United States during 1969–1970.[9] The selection of objects that Warhol made, and the methods that he chose to present them, were provocative and unconventional, assaulting the principles of connoisseurship and established institutional rules about the display and value of certain objects over others. Writing in the small catalogue that accompanied the exhibition, Dominique de Menil provided an insight into her thinking.

> Like a bewitched castle in the fairy tales of old, the world of art lies asleep. To break the spell unusual gifts or thorough preparation is needed. Occasional good will is not enough. Sunday visitors roam museum galleries lost and bored... If critics and scholars can open many doors, only seers and prophets open the royal gates... For what is beautiful to the artist, becomes beautiful. What is poetical to the poet, becomes poetical. So let's visit museums with poets and artists.[10]

This approach has been taken up in recent years by the Kunsthistorisches Museum in Vienna, with a series of exhibitions for which guest curators have been invited to select objects from the museum's collections. The first exhibition in 2012 was curated by the American artist Ed Ruscha. Ruscha made repeated visits to the museum, acquainting himself with its collections, visiting its storage spaces, meeting with its curators and conservators, in order to assemble his own 'private collection' of works from among the many hundreds of thousands of objects assembled over centuries by the museum's imperial founders.[11] His exhibition's title, borrowed from Mark Twain, was wonderfully appropriate: 'The Ancients Stole All Our Great Ideas.'[12] The series continued in 2016 with a deeply personal selection made by the British writer and artist Edmund de Waal. The troubled history of

9 'Raid the Icebox I with Andy Warhol' travelled from the Institute for the Arts, Rice University, Houston, Texas (29 October 1969–4 January 1970) to The Isaac Delgado Museum, New Orleans (LA) (17 January–15 February 1970) to the Museum of Art, Rhode Island School of Design, Providence (RI) (23 April–30 June 1970).

10 Dominique de Menil, 'Foreword', in *Raid the Icebox 1*, p. 5.

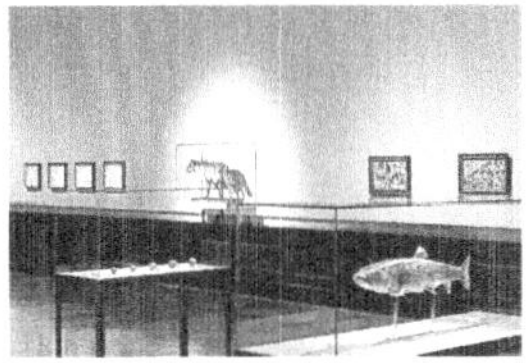

11 'The Ancients Stole All Our Great Ideas', curated by Ed Ruscha, installation view, Kunsthistorisches Museum, Vienna, 2012. Courtesy Kunsthistorisches Museum.

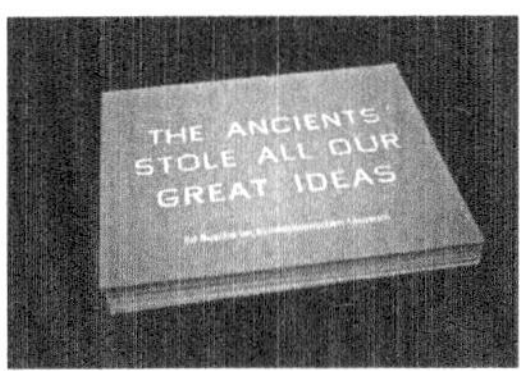

12 Ed Ruscha, *The Ancients Stole All Our Great Ideas*, exhibition catalogue, Kunsthistorisches Museum, Vienna, 2012. Courtesy Kunsthistorisches Museum.

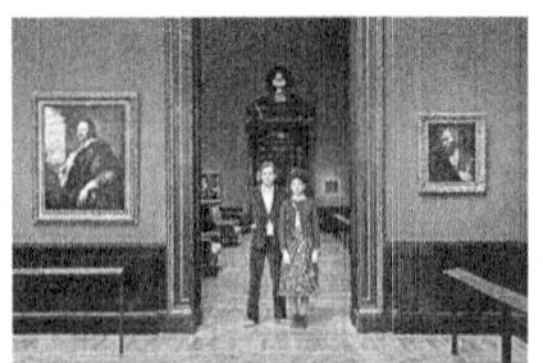

13 Wes Anderson and Juman Malouf at the Kunsthistorisches Museum, Vienna. Courtesy Kunsthistorisches Museum.

14 In recent years The National Gallery has taken further steps to integrate contemporary artists into the activities of the museum. Its board of trustees, for example, always includes at least one artist whose point of view is considered crucial in determining important questions of policy or direction. Since 1990, the museum has also operated a two year artist-in-residence programme, during which time Associate Artists including Paula Rego, Peter Blake, Ron Mueck and, most recently, Michael Landy have been given the opportunity to work within the museum. A similar programme has operated at the Isabella Stewart Gardner Museum in Boston since 1992.

De Waal's family in Vienna, their persecution under the National Socialists, and the role that the Kunsthistorisches Museum played in this, contributed to a charged and emotional atmosphere. The third exhibition in the series is in development at the time of writing, and will open in September 2018. The guest curators on this occasion are the American film director Wes Anderson and his partner Juman Malouf.[13] Their exhibition promises to be the most expansive so far, with objects drawn from all fourteen of the museum's collections and an unexpected concept of display.

Where such projects succeed is in their dismantling of conventional methods of historical display, and the questioning of the value of certain objects over others. In giving these guest curators carte blanche to select art works in different media, from different cultures and from different periods, one reveals unfamiliar aspects of familiar objects by altering their position and context. Tidy and familiar curatorial structures are dispensed with in favour of a more personal reinterpretation of the past, a form of historical argument that engages the museums' works as evidence and in doing so contributes to our reading and understanding of them.[14] The process also serves to illuminate the selecting curator's own work, and the thinking and decisions that inform it. The thread that unites the works is the eye of the person or persons who chose them. The challenge and pleasure for the visitor is to try to match our eye to theirs, to understand the reasoning behind certain decisions.

This is just one of many contrasting approaches adopted by historical museums in their engagement with contemporary art and its makers. In examining their methods for such engagement, it is also interesting to examine their motives. Among the most frequently cited reasons for presenting projects with contemporary artists is the desire to increase the number of visitors, in large part through the capture of younger, more contemporary-minded audiences, without overly antagonizing the more conservative elements of their museums' regular constituency. But beyond swollen attendance figures and the column inches of press attention that tend to accompany them, there are more essential, more fundamental reasons for historical museums to engage with living artists, reasons that take us back to their beginnings and to the spirit of Enlightenment that provided their ideological foundation. One of the primary objectives of such museums is to show their visitors where they stand in time and place, within the broader evolution of mankind. The great art of the past is great precisely because it manages to communicate with us today in a manner independent of its time, that collapses time. 'There has always been good painting and bad painting', wrote Hsieh Ho in the sixth century in 'Six Principles of Chinese Painting', 'but in art, the terms ancient and modern do not have citizenship'.[15]

To hold a conversation with the past, to seek a natural continuity even when it might at first appear both improbable and unpredictable, demands both simplicity and sophistication. It will provoke endless debate and the risk of failure, but it can also bring great reward. 'The existing monuments form an ideal order among themselves', wrote T.S. Eliot,

> which is modified by the introduction of the new work of art among them. The existing order is complete before the new work arrives; for order to persist after the supervention of novelty, the whole existing order must be, if ever so slightly, altered; and so the relations, proportions, values of each work of art toward the whole are readjusted; and this is conformity between the old and the

15 The Six Principles of Chinese Painting were established by Hsieh Ho (also known as Xie He) a writer, art historian, and critic in sixth-century China.

new. Whoever has approved this idea of order … will not find it preposterous that the past should be altered by the present as much as the present is directed by the past.[16]

16 Eliot, 'Tradition and the Individual Talent, p. 37.

Literature

The Artist's Eye: An Exhibition Selected by R.B. Kitaj at the National Gallery, London. Exh. cat. London (The National Gallery), 1980.

Eliot, T.S. 'Tradition and the Individual Talent.' *Perspecta* 19 (1982), pp. 36–42.

Hall, James. 'A Sublime Roller Coaster Ride Through Art History.' *Tate Etc.*, no. 17 (Autumn 2009), ‹www.tate.org.uk/context-comment/articles/sublime-roller-coaster-ride-through-art-history›.

Raid the Icebox 1. with Andy Warhol: An Exhibition. Exh. cat. Providence, RI (Rhode Island School of Design), 1969.

Read, Herbert. 'The Museum and The Artist.' *College Art Journal* 13, no. 4 (Summer 1954), pp. 289–294.

Rosenblum, Robert. 'Remembrance of Art Past.' In *Encounters: New Art From Old*. Edited by Richard Morphet, pp. 8–23. Exh. cat. London (The National Gallery), 2000.

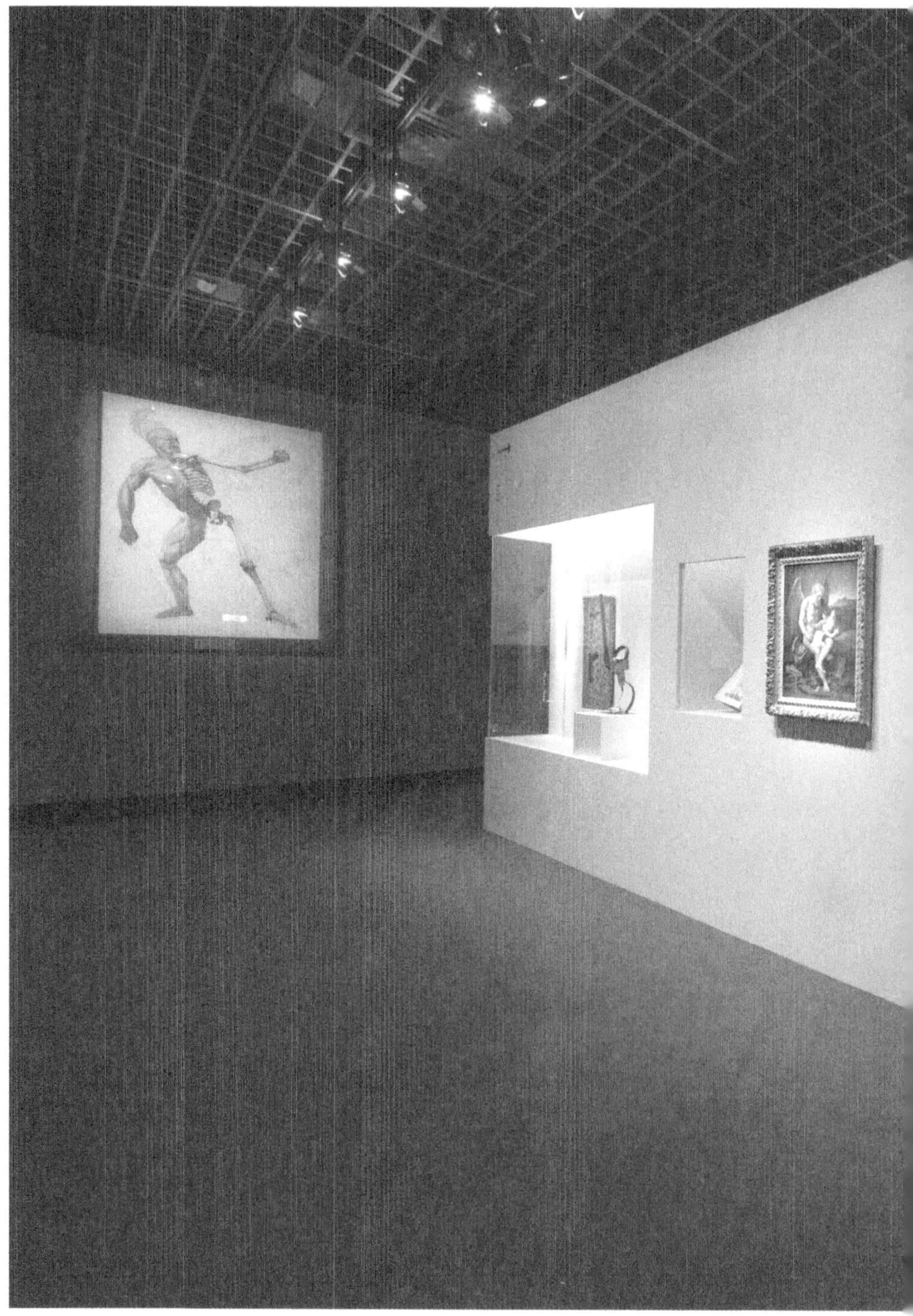

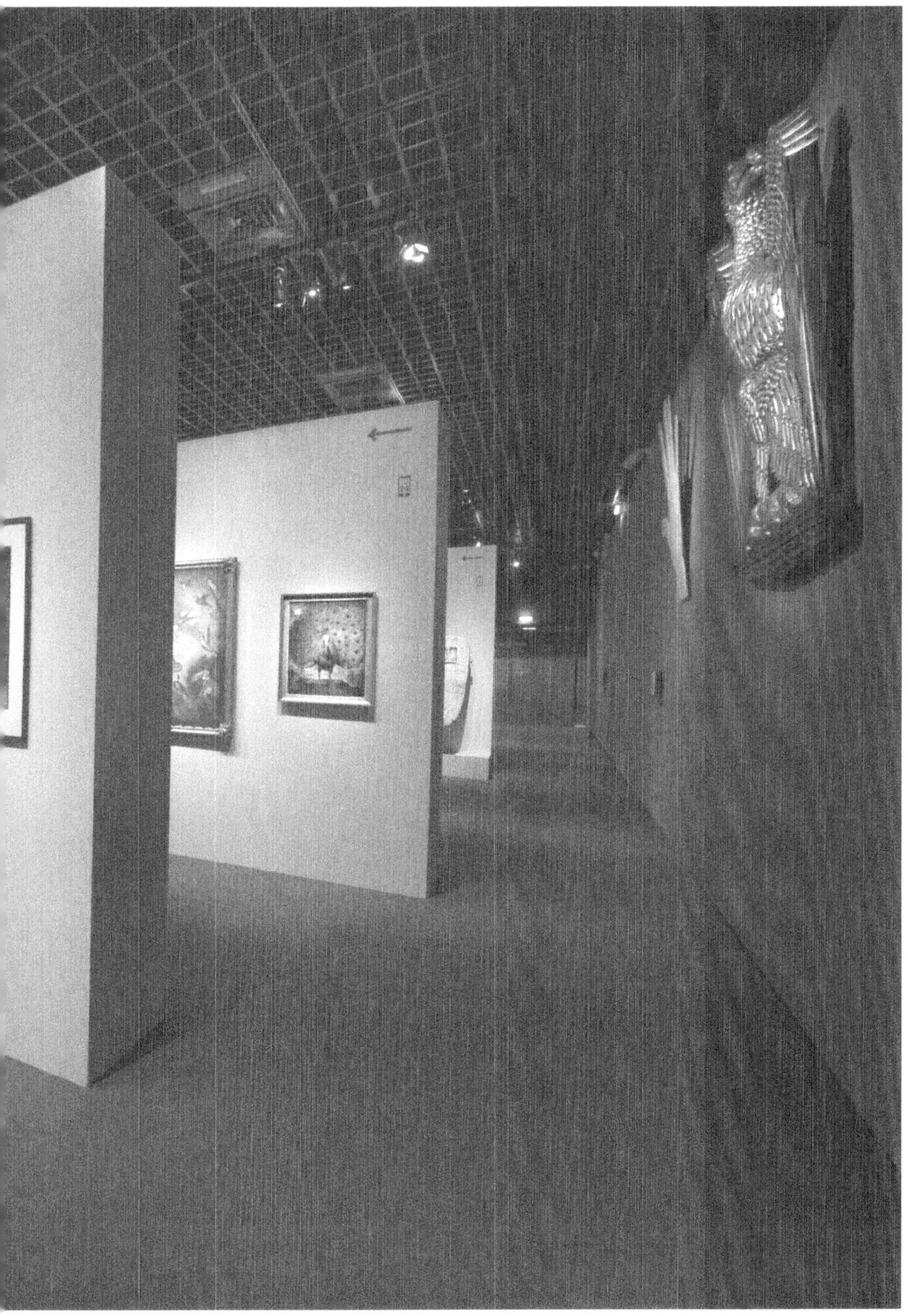

'Carambolages', curated by Jean-Hubert Martin, scenography by Hugues Fontenas Architectes, installation view, Grand Palais, Paris, 2016. Courtesy Rmn-Grand Palais. Photo: Didier Plowy, 2016.

Visual Thinking

'Carambolages' at Grand Palais Paris

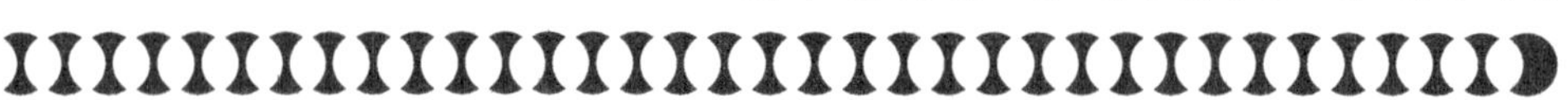

Jean-Hubert Martin

'Carambolages' was an exhibition at the Grand Palais in Paris that took place in the spring of 2016. It included 180 works from antiquity to contemporary art, from many different cultures, chosen for their correspondence with the present. The following directives were essential for the concept of the exhibition:

1. Attachment to things

Recent anthropology[1] has defined objects in their intense relations to humans up to the point that they may be considered personalities with their own biographies and destinies. The goal was to translate this thinking into the exhibition format. As a counterpoint to the abstraction of language, it is linked to an interpretation of the world as an experiential whole that takes the engagement with material objects seriously.

1 See for instance: Kopytoff, 'The Cultural Biography of Things', and Bonnot, *L'attachement aux choses.*

2. To assemble and compare artworks of all origins, to avoid technical and chronological categories and to replace chronological linearity by analogical sequence[2]

Contextualization has long remained the untouchable paradigm of museum organization: all works in a museum were to be surrounded by others of the same period and origin. In truth, however, a museum is a receptacle for objects extracted from their context. The only exceptions to this rule are artworks that are contemporary with the museum movement of the nineteenth and twentieth century. The museum creates its own context: its own architecture, décor, and furniture. Since the museum always already is an artificial context, it is delusive to pretend that we can re-create an original context. Rather than attempting to revive the past, we might consider all museum objects contemporary to the extent that they are encompassed by our own gaze. This is the sense of Duchamp's famous remark that he borrowed from Odilon Redon when he said that the spectator makes the picture.[3]

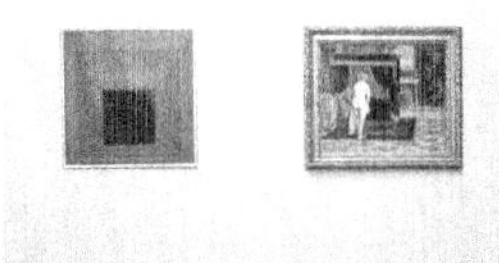

2 Josef Albers, *Porta Negra*, 1996; Eglon Hendrik van der Neer, *Candaules and Gyges*, 1680, installation view, 'Künstlermuseum: eine Neupräsentation der Sammlung des Museum Kunst Palast', Düsseldorf, 2001–2003.

3 Duchamp, Sanouillet and Peterson, *Duchamp du signe*, p. 105.

This shift in agency to the spectator's gaze suggests new possibilities for juxtapositions—new kinds of association can be established relating to the kind of formal comparison that everyone constantly makes. Rational arguments and historical logic have dominated art history to the detriment of the kind of analogical thinking that prevailed during the Renaissance before it gave way to rationalism. From a more universal perspective, the classic period of Western mimetic representation is a unique exception.

3. To select works according to their visual impact and their correspondence with modern and contemporary art. To avoid the usual hierarchies between major and minor, high and low

Artists, like collectors, admit no constraints in the connections that they make with the past. When artists don't collect artworks, they collect images: pinning on the wall of their studios reproductions of pieces that, in their eyes, have a referential value. These works act as a kind of reminder and often have no formal relation with the artist's oeuvre but offer solutions to certain questions the artist contends with. Analogical associations often guide artists in their creative processes. Aesthetic judgement can only be elaborated through comparison—and it is much more exciting to compare heterogeneous than homogenous objects. The juxtaposition of two heterogeneous objects can illuminate their meaning or function by visual means alone. It can also suggest a third idea that was not inherent in either. The stimulating aspect of comparison is the quest for similarity in difference and vice versa.

4. To take the experience of previous transhistorical exhibitions into account

Art history tends to confine itself to textual references, whereas many significant curators prefer to trust their visual experience. Their memories are marked by exhibitions that they have seen, artworks that have strongly impressed them 'in the flesh'. This form of transferral is difficult to talk about because it has been little studied. It rests on oral testimony and photographs that convey the ways in which an exhibition was hung—the study of such photographs in their own right has barely begun. Exhibitions and the display of a museum are ephemeral and leave few traces. It is all too easy to defer to texts when they are available, rather than attempting to understand how visual thought is developed and transferred.

I have attempted several experiments in transhistorical exhibition making that were formative in conceptualizing 'Carambolages': in 2001, I asked two artists, Thomas Huber and Bogomir Ecker, to work with me on a new display of the collection of the Museum Kunst Palast in Düsseldorf. Called 'Künstlermuseum', it was an attempt to answer current social questions with artworks. In 2007, at Palazzo Fortuny in Venice, the exhibition 'Artempo', organized by Tijs Visser, Axel Vervoordt and myself, created a considerable stir. The aim was to show the time dimension in art by confronting contemporary works with ancient ones.[4] 'Theatre of the World' went from MONA, Hobart to La Maison Rouge, Paris in 2013 and gathered works from all origins along creative aspirations that they share. It was dealing as much with anthropology as with art history.[5]

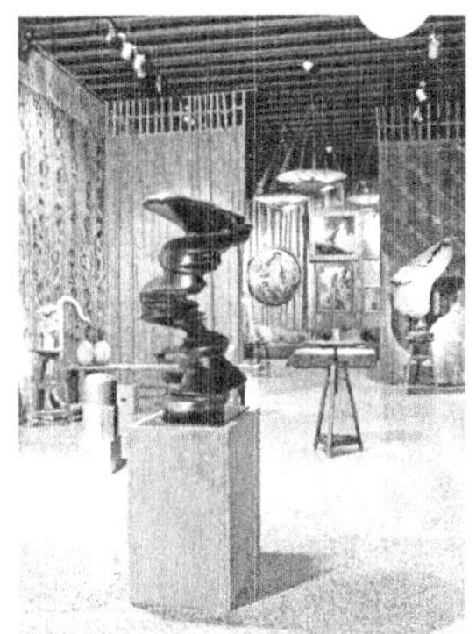

4 Tony Cragg, *Bent of Mind*, 2006, exhibition view, 'Artempo', Palazzo Fortuny, Venice, 2007.

5. Visual thinking and interpretation from sight

The numerous references, be they copies or reproductions, that are found in artist studios indicate that visual thinking exists. It has long been believed that in order to identify a form one must be able to name it, but this is not true. Signs can be anonymously transmitted from one artist to another and one culture to another and in this process often acquire a new meaning. Thus, there exists a visual memory shared within a particular culture that can enable communication by image. These semiotic links are not universal, but often they are not too difficult to decrypt. The misunderstandings that

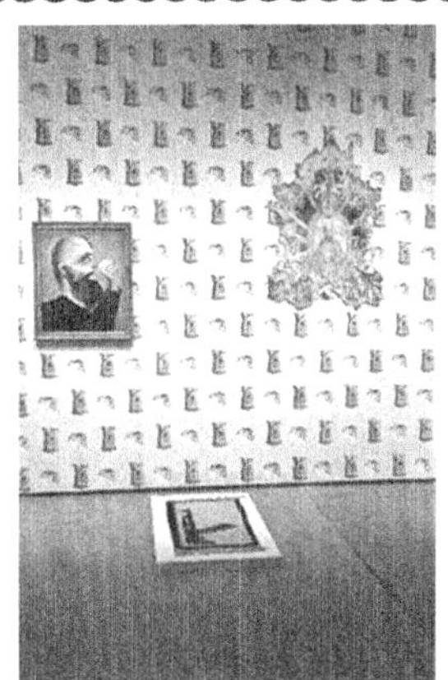

5 Robert Gober, *Hanging Man/Sleeping Man*, 1989; Sidney Nolan, *Colonial Head-Kelly Gang*, 1943–1946; Wim Delvoye, *Untitled (Osama)*, 2002–2003; *Afghan war rug*, c. 1993, installation view, 'Theatre of the World', MONA, Museum of Old and New Art, Hobart, 2012–2013.

inevitably occur are part of the game. This visual memory can instigate all sorts of comparisons that transcend the categories of art history and deserve greater attention and consideration. There is a need to exercise this form of knowledge and confirm visitors in the validity of their own judgements. Works of art are vehicles for dreams; they stimulate the imagination and inspire emotion. One goes to a concert or play not to learn, but to enjoy. Similarly, the experience afforded by an exhibition should be one of pleasure, not discipline. The goal thus was to create an experience that was first and foremost visual; to appeal to the visitor's sensory and emotional capacities, scholarship, and pedagogic language were regarded as secondary.

How can these directives be translated into an exhibition? One could imagine all sorts of methods: an alphabetical order derived from the artworks' titles, a classification by size, a narrative where each work represents a word, thematic groups, et cetera. For previous exhibitions, I had to work mostly from existing collections. The choice of artworks was therefore reduced, which limited the possibilities. The 'Carambolages' project was much more ambitious, as it went beyond a single collection and included loans from all over, though there were the usual practical and financial restrictions.

I created a database of images, which I selected based on their visual effect. The images were grouped into themes. This allowed me to choose among several possibilities to build up sequences. In contrast to the usual exhibitions—which are conceived from a historical, philosophical or anthropological point of view, which is to say from an idea that postulates the interpretation of the works—the method here led to questioning each work in connection with the others. This associative process also produced the way in which the artworks were installed. Each item was predicted by the previous one and announced the next one. The scenography presented a long series of perpendicular walls, which obliged the visitor to follow a serpentine route through them, from left to right and right to left. This visual chain can be compared to a well-known French nursery rhyme 'Trois p'tits chats, chapeau de paille, paillasson…', which is passed on from one generation to the next in school courtyards. It is also connected to the phenomenon known from film that the same indifferent and neutral face of an actor is interpreted differently depending on the image shown prior. This new linearity can also become sinuous and make some detours. When an association of two items generates an interesting comparison, it remains within a back-and-forth dialectic, in a trio; when an additional element is introduced the ideas circulate in multiple directions. This leads from ping-pong to billiard, from which the word 'carambolage' comes.[6]

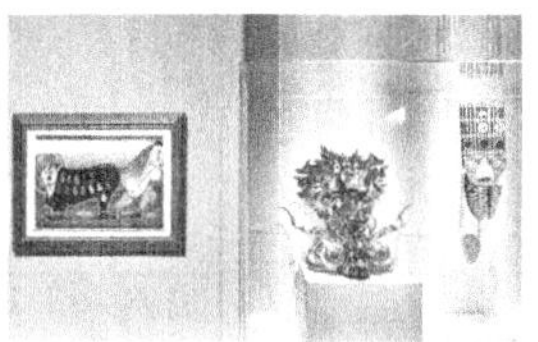

6 Friedrich Schröder-Sonnenstern, *The Diplomatic Couple*, 1955, Centre Pompidou, Musée national d'art moderne, Paris; mask of Nauplo Diablo, Oruro, Cercado Province, Bolivia, 1955, Musée du quai Branly, Paris; Konden mask, Malinke, Guinea, twentieth century, installation view, 'Carambolages', Grand Palais, Paris, 2016. Courtesy Rmn-Grand Palais. Photo: Didier Plowy, 2016.

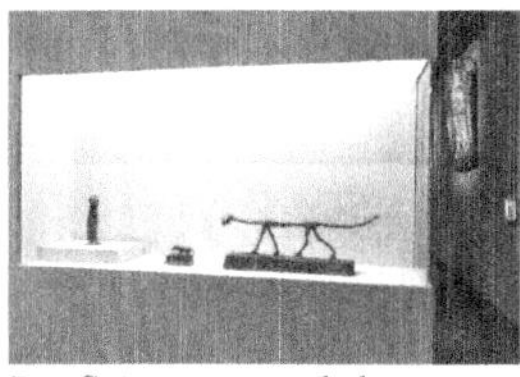

7 Cat mummy and shrew-mouse coffin, Egypt, 664–332 BC, Musée du Louvre, Paris; Alberto Giacometti, *The Cat*, 1951, Fondation Alberto et Annette Giacometti, Paris, installation view, 'Carambolages', Grand Palais, Paris, 2016. Courtesy Rmn-Grand Palais. Photo: Didier Plowy, 2016.

The linking followed simple formal or semantic associations, which don't request scholarly knowledge like, for instance, being familiar with Greco-roman or Christian mythology. Some connections could be playfully guessed, others required close attention to the work in order to grasp the significant detail that led to the next work. With its poetic effects, the presentation called upon the imagination of the visitor. These links could be made by everyone individually, according to their knowledge and memory, as absurd as they may appear to a rational mind.[7] Instead of repressing them, the exhibition 'Carambolages' sought to stimulate and lend credibility to them, akin to what the Surrealists attempted with their dictionaries and their magazine *Documents* (1929–1931) as they propagated the values of nonsense, the absurd, and the irrational.

8 Breton, *L'amour fou*, p. 42.

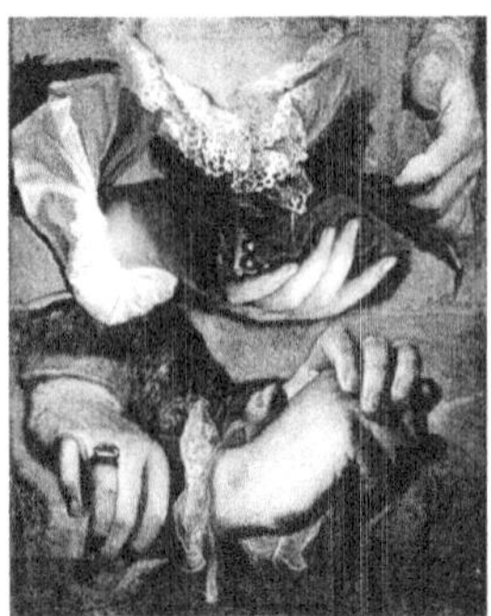

9 Hyacinthe Rigaud, *Étude de mains*, 1715–1723, Musée Fabre, Montpellier.

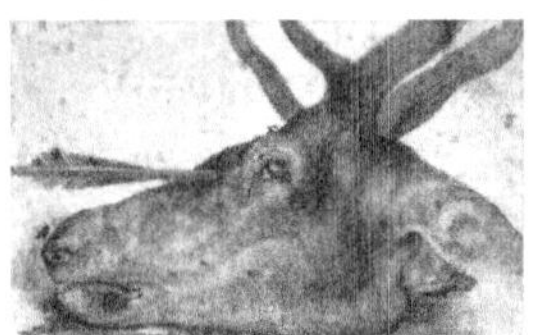

10 Albrecht Dürer, *Tête de cerf percé d'une flèche*, 1504, Bibliothèque nationale de France, Paris.

This equally applies to the neophyte, who is able to discover an array of unusual images, and the connoisseur who can discover objects from fields unfamiliar to him. André Breton coined 'L'attraction du jamais vu',[8] the emotion of the never-seen-before. Surprise is a fundamental incentive of aesthetic pleasure that lies much higher on an emotional level than seeing that which is already known. Nevertheless, it is the urge for the latter that drives the crowds towards the blockbuster exhibitions.

Modern and contemporary art delivered the basis for the criteria to choose the works. The dozen of living artists represented were among those who inspired me most, with whom I had regular discussions and from whom I had learned most. The purpose of the exhibition was not to deliver a pedagogy of quasi-mechanical formal connections between ancient and modern works. Many of the exhibited works are considered secondary or minor. They will very soon get upgraded, because they mean much more to us today than the consecrated masterpieces. In the past, we have seen similar shifts in the canon. For instance: after having long been considered a minor artist, Giuseppe Arcimboldo is now considered a great master. The hand study of Hyacinthe Rigaud[9] is probably better known today than any of his completed portraits. The arrow in the head of Albrecht Dürer's deer[10] is an image of greater pain for us today than the martyrdoms of many saints. There are many more examples: objects that touch us today because of the affective projections that we overlay on them. These interpretations—as far as they might depart from the original context of creation—are valid, because objects travel in time and space. Many works requested for this exhibition have long been relegated to minor galleries or storage, but since taste evolves, they are today appreciated anew. By way of exhibiting them, they have gone from a status of atypical or minor to the status of major work. Could we postulate that some of these works may become the masterpieces of tomorrow? The question seems arrogant because the selection depends completely on the curator and is therefore immediately deemed subjective. Thus it relies on the taste of the times, the Zeitgeist, and the paradigmatic change underway since a classical canon was given up. Feeding into this Zeitgeist are the most refined connoisseurs: the artists with their intuition and affinities. Not that they are prophets, but, more simply, they are human beings who are able to distil the diffused phenomena of the present and translate them into their works.

The exhibition unwound a sequence of analogies and associations, not a real narrative, because it was up to the visitors to build it up according to their own knowledge. It followed *The Way Things Go*: the marvellous film by Fischli and Weiss in which the movement of each object provokes another one in a chain reaction that becomes an allegory of the flux of life. No labels were installed next to the works. Instead, written information was provided on screens next to a group of images of works. For those visitors who wanted more context, the catalogue, the digital book, and the Internet provided this. In the middle of the exhibition, there was a wall with all the images of the exhibited works so that visitors could make up their own sequence of objects and posit an alternative to the curator's one.

Just as the various media before it, the Internet will not kill the museum as long as it will know how to adapt to renewed forms of pleasure and avoid to isolate itself in academic and doctrinal knowledge. The objective of 'Carambolages' was not a nostalgic immersion in history but an insight into the desires, fears, and hopes of humanity as these manifest themselves in material culture. The quote 'The

11 Quoted in Adler, *Six Great Ideas*, p. 17.

ancients stole all our great ideas'[11] from Mark Twain's autobiography fits this type of exhibition so well that I chose it for my next show at the Pushkin Museum Moscow, in 2021.

Literature

Adler, Mortimer Jerome. *Six Great Ideas: Truth, Goodness, Beauty, Justice, Equality, Liberty: Ideas We Judge By, Ideas We Act On*. New York, 1981.

Bonnot, Thierry. *L'attachement aux choses*. Paris, 2014.

Breton, André. *L'amour fou*. Paris, 1937.

Duchamp, Marcel, Michel Sanouillet and Elmer Peterson. *Duchamp du signe: Écrits*. Paris, 1991.

Kopytoff, Igor.'The Cultural Biography of things: Commoditization as Process.' *The Social Life of Things. Commodities in Cultural Perspective*. Edited by Arjun Appadurai, p. 64–91. Cambridge, 1986.

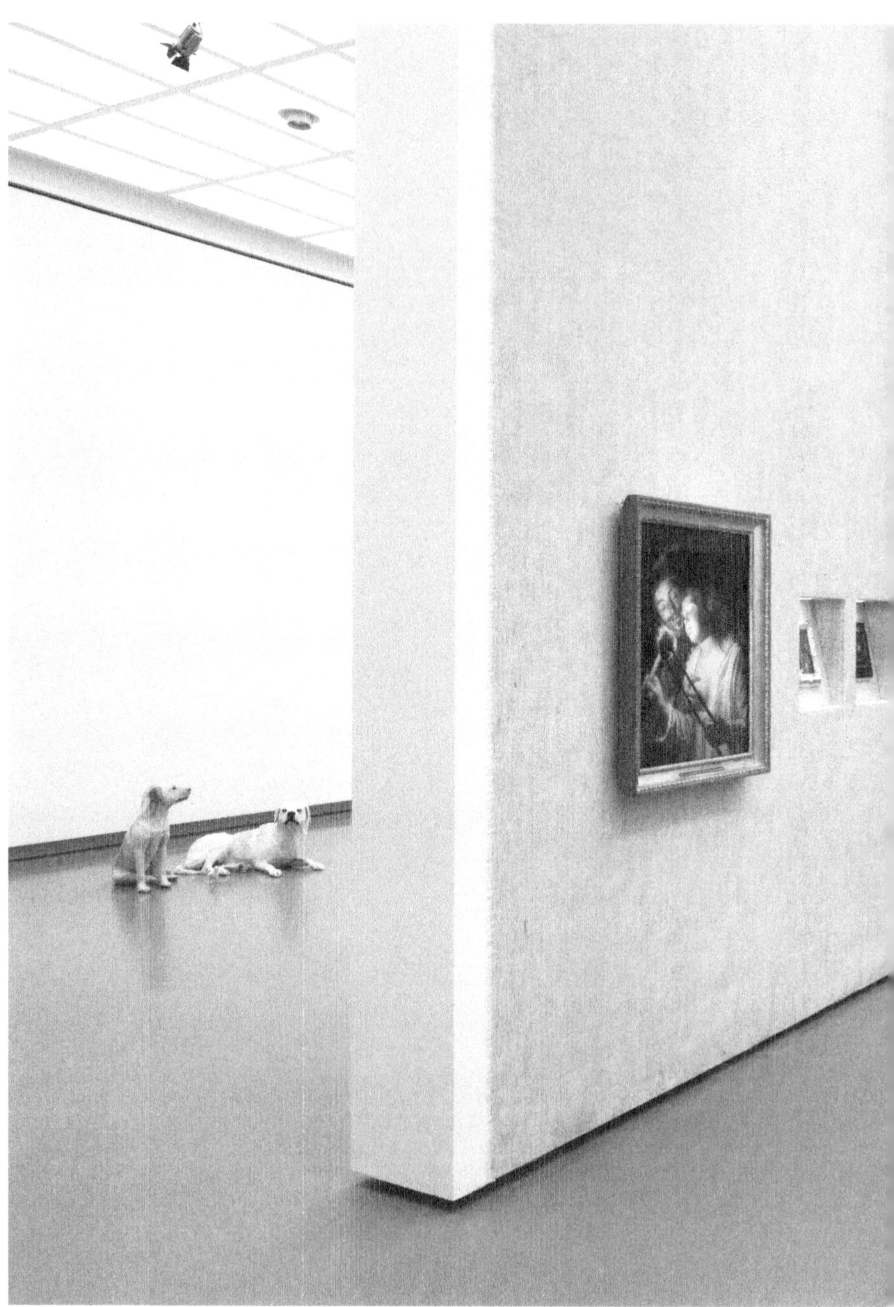

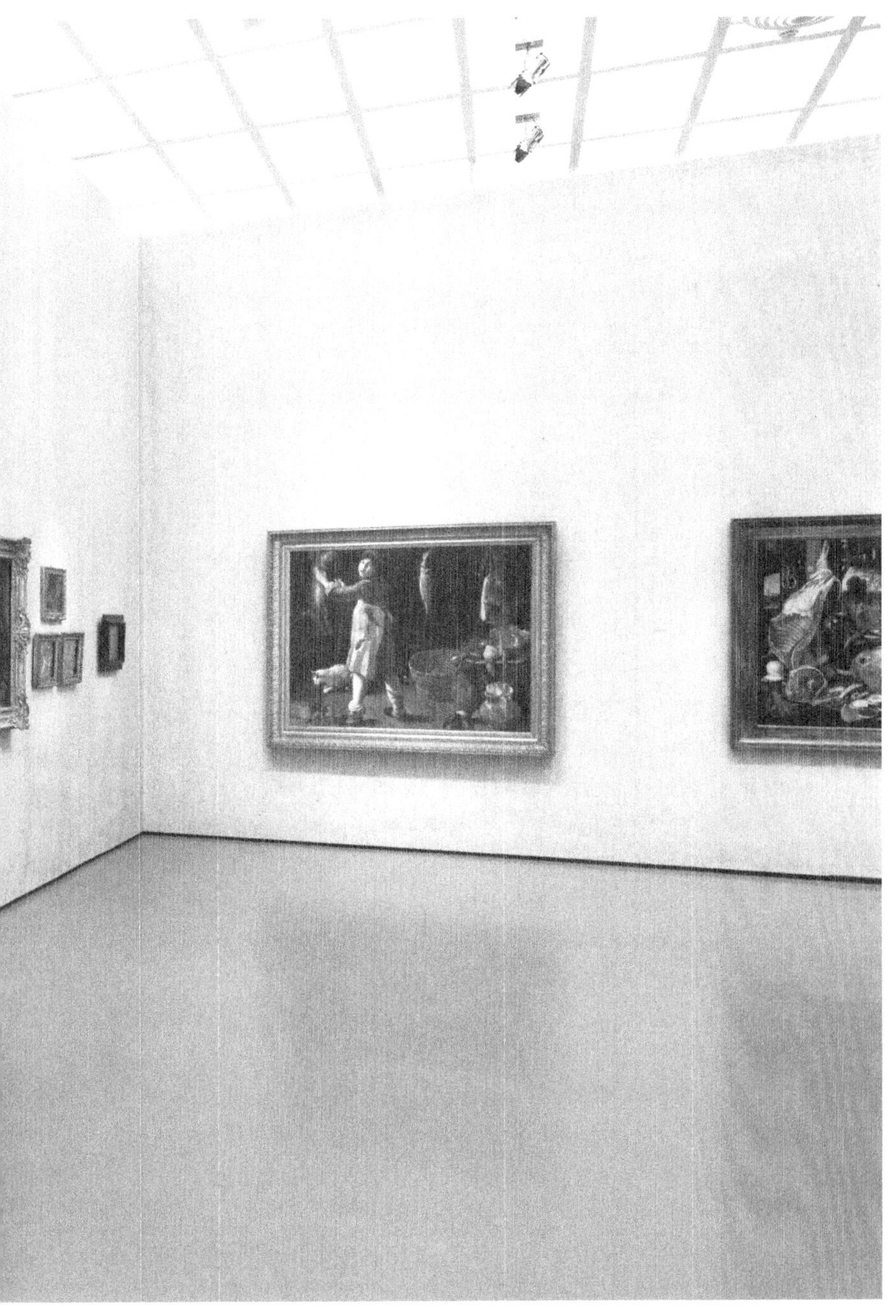

'Riotous Baroque', exhibition view, Kunsthaus Zürich, 2012. On the left: Maurizio Cattelan, *Untitled*, 2007, taxidermied dog, taxidermied chick, expanded polyurethane; first painting left: Gerrit van Honthorst, *The Soldier and the Girl*, c. 1622, oil and canvas, 83 × 66 cm, Herzog Anton Ulrich-Museum, Braunschweig. Courtesy Kunsthaus Zürich.

Film Montage as a Curatorial Method

Bice Curiger

I've always been annoyed at having to do what people in the film industry or in real life call 'telling a story', meaning starting at zero hour, creating a beginning and then arriving at an end.[1]
—Jean-Luc Godard

In place of a *hermeneutics* we need an erotics of art.[2]
—Susan Sontag

1 Quoted in Robé, 'Jean-Luc Godard'. The quotation is from a transcription of lectures that Godard gave in Montreal at the Conservatoire d'Art Cinématographique, April-October 1978.

2 Sontag, 'Against Interpretation', in *Against Interpretation and Other Essays*, p. 14.

More and more exhibitions are beginning to experiment with the juxtaposition and indeed confrontation of historical and contemporary works. This goes hand-in-hand with a clearly critical awareness of the entrenched conventions that underpin the presentation of historical exhibitions and also with the growing interest of younger people in eliminating the divide between audiences focused exclusively on contemporary art versus those focused on the works of old Masters.

A project organized in 2012 at Kunsthaus Zürich serves to illustrate this point. Titled 'Deftig Barock/Riotous Baroque', the exhibition moved on to the Guggenheim Museum Bilbao a year later, where it was titled 'Barocco exuberante'. The show explicitly treated contemporary art and seventeenth-century art as equals, working on the basis of a principle that might be described as montage.

Let me first comment briefly on the institution where the project was planned and carried out. Its name is unusual: Kunsthaus Zürich. This museum with its large collection was thus named to establish an affinity with other democratic institutions in the city, such as the Rathaus (town hall) and the Schulhaus (schoolhouse), and to underscore that its founding was indebted neither to a prince nor to a prominent statesman, seeking, for instance, to consolidate his status. On the contrary, back in the eighteenth century, a group of artists had already begun collecting art in exchange with colleagues in Germany. Kunsthaus Zürich therefore looks back on a memorable history in which a contemporary artistic view of the past inspires the practice of mounting exhibitions. My activities as a curator since 1995 have always drawn on this special tradition.[3]

And it was in this spirit that I organized my first exhibition in 1995 in the museum's second-story gallery of 1300 square meters. It was to be an accentuated confrontation, as indicated in the title: 'Zeichen und Wunder—Niko Pirosmani (1862–1918) und die Gegenwartskunst/Signs and Wonders—Niko Pirosmani (1862–1918)' and Contemporary Art'.[4] Pirosmani, a Georgian artist, created vibrant iconic paintings on black oilcloth, seeking to render archetypical ideals of life in a rural community.[5] The exhibition showcased the Georgian artist in combination with the work of younger practitioners who recur explicitly to a pictorial idiom. Confidence in the persuasiveness of contemporary art was to be the context that would liberate Pirosmani's work from the grip of such condescending labels as 'naïve' and 'primitive', the more

3 It was here, in 1978, that Harald Szeemann first presented his exhibition 'Monte Verità—Berg der Wahrheit. Lokale Anthropologie als Beitrag zur Wiederentdeckung einer neuzeitlichen sakralen Topographie' (Monte Verità—Mountain of Truth. Local Anthropology As a Contribution to Rediscovering a Modern Sacred Topography), in addition to other idea-oriented and monographic projects.

4 Peter Fischli and David Weiss, Robert Gober, Katharina Fritsch, Mike Kelley, Tony Oursler, Jean-Luc Mylayne, Cindy Sherman, and others were represented in the exhibition, which was on view in Zurich in 1995 and at the Centro Galego de Arte Contemporáneo in Santiago de Compostela in 1996.

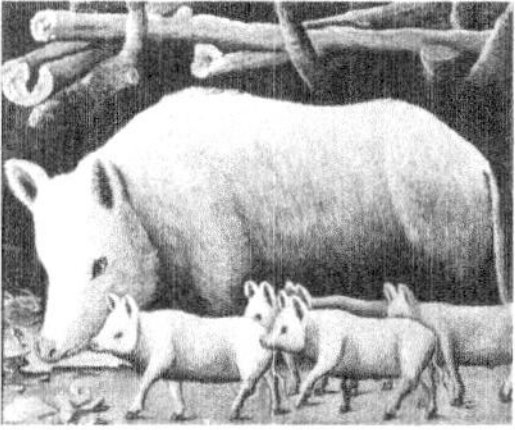

5 Niko Pirosmani, *White Sow with Piglets*, early twentieth century, 80 × 100 cm, oil on cardboard, Art Museum of Georgia, Tbilisi.

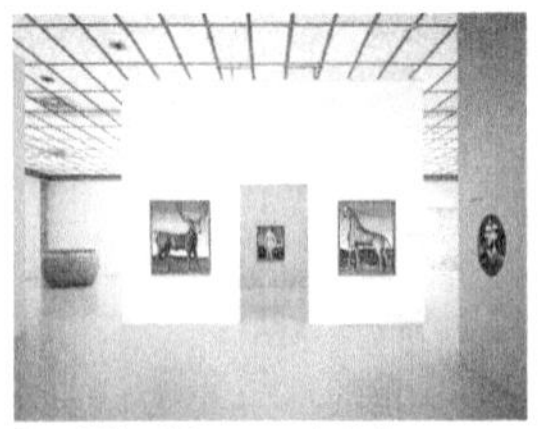

6 Niko Pirosmani, Lily van der Stokker, Fischli Weiss, exhibition view, 'Signs and Wonders', Kunsthaus Zürich, 1995. Courtesy Kunsthaus Zürich.

7 Here, the meaning of the word in German deviates from the Dutch meaning, a phenomenon known in linguistics as 'false friends'.

so, considering the fact that he was largely known as the 'Douanier Rousseau of the East'. I intentionally aimed to generate the sense of an alien body catapulted out of the heavens and into the current art scene. The subtle impact of Pirosmani's large-format works suggested ever new areas of common ground and rapport, for instance, with Jeff Koons *Wall Relief with Bird*, 1991, or the deceptively naïve questions in the big *Question Pot* (1985–1986) by Peter Fischli/David Weiss.[6] On the other hand, his somewhat exaggerated idealization of collective existence stood in fruitful contrast to the more menacing mood of works by such artists as Mike Kelley or Cindy Sherman.

In the aforementioned 'Riotous Baroque' exhibition, organized seventeen years later at Kunsthaus Zürich, the montage principle culminated in the conspicuous juxtaposition of two artistic eras that were not merely decades but hundreds of years apart. The calm, matter-of-fact presentation of such widely divergent, if not diametrically opposed work was an intentionally radical curatorial decision, which revealed an astonishingly rich fabric of relations and affinities. Let a few keywords suffice: existential, erotic, travesty, exaggeration, human all too human, and cartoon.

The theme of the show also involved a juxtaposition—between vibrant vitality and vulnerability. Hence, the subtitle of the exhibition: 'Tributes to Precarious Vitality'. The German etymology of the Baroque word 'deftig' takes us back to seventeenth-century Dutch, where it translated as 'capable, strong, mighty, solid'. Here in this exhibition, the art was *deftig* in being so immediate and intensely alive, and the word might also be applied to the principle of confrontational encounter in the contemporary sense of being drastic and riotous.[7]

The notion of the Baroque was to be stripped of its conventional clichés and stylistic emphasis: none of the ornamental excesses, the sumptuous pump and gold, but rather peasant life in deliberate contrast to kings and courts, the grotesque in contrast to the classical, and, at the other end of the scale, extravagant artificiality and affectation.

The first thing visitors encountered on entering the exhibition were Baroque paintings of peasant life by Dutch Masters, scenes of partying, drinking, brawling, scurrilous protagonists as well as Bartolomeo Passarotti's *Crazy Lovers*,[8] only to be astonished in the next room by Maurizio Cattelan's real stuffed dogs sitting on the floor and protecting a little chick. The unusual intrusion into a museum of imagery bursting with life also inspired the snapshots Juergen Teller took of two friends who seem to have snuck, naked, into the Louvre at night.

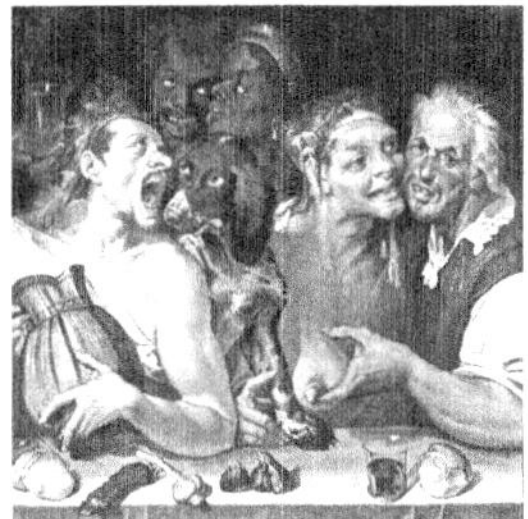

8 Bartolomeo Passarotti, *Crazy Lovers*, c. 1577, oil on canvas, 114 × 118 cm. Private collection.

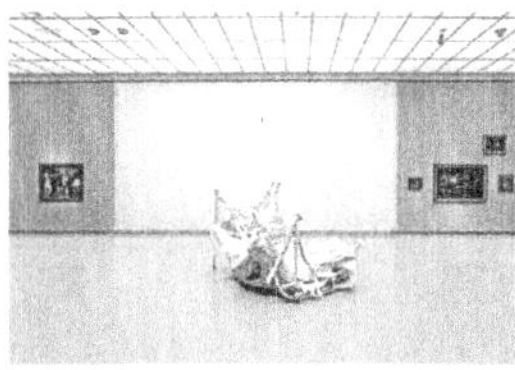

9 'Riotous Baroque', exhibition view, Kunsthaus Zürich, 2012. Foreground: Urs Fischer, *Untitled (Soft Bed)*, 2011. Courtesy Kunsthaus Zürich.

10 Compiled by Bice Curiger, Muriel Perez, Filine Wagner, and Gabrielle Schaad, in: *Riotous Baroque*, pp. 153–164.

The exhibition 'Riotous Baroque' consisted of chapters. To definitively preclude the impression of imposing a common denominator on different eras, the old Masters were mounted on walls that were painted a light yellow and then covered in burlap, while the contemporary art appeared in front of or on white walls.[9] A number of keywords was assigned to each of the chapters; these were fleshed out in a detailed glossary at the back of the catalogue.[10]

Under the entry 'actualization', for instance, readers find the following:

> actualization is a common practice in the theatre. Different temporal planes are synchronized on stage by virtue of the fact that the actors are interpreting their individual roles. ... In the field of fine art exhibitions, by contrast, a diachronous understanding of time obtains as a condition in order to arrive at a useful synthesis. The

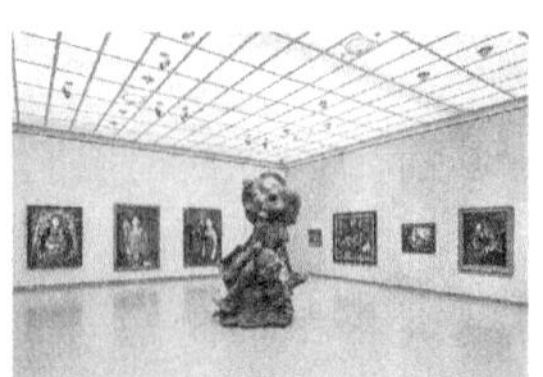
11 'Riotous Baroque', exhibition view, Kunsthaus Zürich, 2012. Foreground: Paul McCarthy, *Snow White and Dopey*, 2011. Courtesy Kunsthaus Zürich.

> dangers of superficial analogies and interpretative short-circuits lurk in both disciplines.

The art market also emerged in the age of Baroque, and in consequence, painters began adapting their choice of motifs to a new clientele and their wishes. It was only logical, therefore, to inquire into a certain pop factor, which was also addressed as follows in the glossary:

> A prior affinity with pop culture would appear to be given in the Baroque by virtue of its inclination towards theatricality (→ theatricality), fun (→ amusement → humour), intensity (→ excess) and also the disregard for boundaries (→ classicism/anti-classicism). Likewise, the vital immediacy of its expression—as is the case in pop—might derive from the view that 'even uneducated people can have aesthetic experiences' (Thomas Hecken) (→ popular topics). As is the case in the pop world, contradictions coalesce and dissolve once more in the Baroque: life and death, high culture and low culture, typical regional features and the cosmopolitan, virtual and real (→ illusion → immersion → Europe → world domination).

The largest gallery presented numerous allegories, vanitas paintings and voluptuous, exotic, sumptuous still lifes. These collided with a sculpture by Paul McCarthy, and Cindy Sherman's satirical and yet somehow moving portraits of aging socialites. McCarthy's large rendition, carved in wood, of *Snow White and Dopey* (2011) alludes not only to Walt Disney but also clearly to Gianlorenzo Bernini's extremely erotic sculpture, *Saint Teresa in Ecstasy* (c. 1650).[11] The artist's audaciously sexualized amalgam links his repeatedly addressed critique of Disney's puritanism with the hypocritical sensuality of propagandistic church art during the counterreformation.

The exhibition deliberately shied away from superficial analogies of form and motif. However, in the chapter flaunting the exaltation of courtly still lifes with their multifarious allegories, and in portraiture, the reins were intentionally handed over to superficial 'bling-bling' in order, once again, to provoke a collision of contrasting worlds and catapult them into a fruitful and surprising dialogue. The conspicuously decadent portrait of the effeminate Marshall Charles Auguste Matignon, painted by Hyacinthe Rigaud in 1708, pictures him against a distant scene of battle.[12] He is attired in gleaming armour with a silk sash draped around his waist and tied in an enormous, extravagant bow. At one particular spot in the exhibition, visitors simultaneously saw this painting along with a hyper realistic work by Marilyn Minter, which zooms into a huge red mouth with silver paint flowing over it. These two extremely contradictory and mutually incendiary works made manifest the 'pathology of glamour',[13] which is often held to characterize the age of Baroque and has undoubtedly infected ours.[14]

In view of an art historical matrix that still relies heavily on style, form, and period, works occasionally found a place in the exhibition not because of their exceptional artistic rank but rather thanks to their visual immediacy. Many gripping and even at times deeply disturbing works were on display, culminating in Christiaen van Couwenbergh's shocking *Rape of the Negro Girl* (1632),[15] in which three white men are seen raping a black slave.[16]

At the risk of being accused of resorting to a voyeuristic gaze on an elevated, cultivated level, as daily brandished by the Boulevard press with hypocritical indignation, the

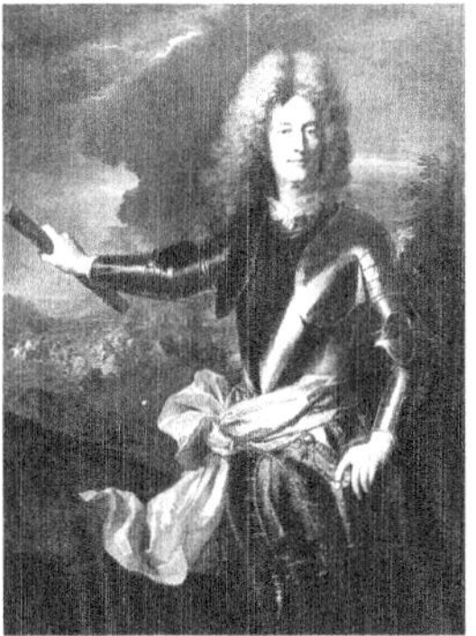

12 Hyacinthe Rigaud, *Marshall Charles Auguste Matignon*, 1704, oil on canvas, 147 × 113 cm, Staatliche Kunsthalle, Karlsruhe.

13 The term was originally introduced by Holland Cotter in an article about Marilyn Minter, in 'Art in Review Marilyn Minter'.

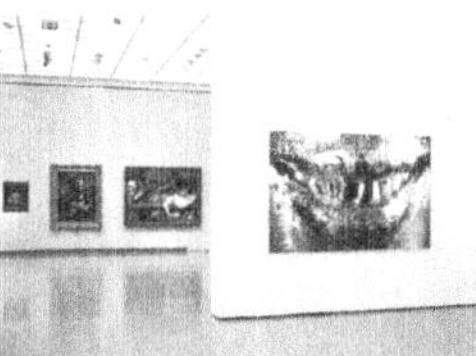

14 'Riotous Baroque', exhibition view, Kunsthaus Zürich, 2012. Foreground: Marilyn Minter, *Cheshire (Wangechi)*, 2011, enamel on metal, 152.4 × 243.8 cm. Courtesy Kunsthaus Zürich.

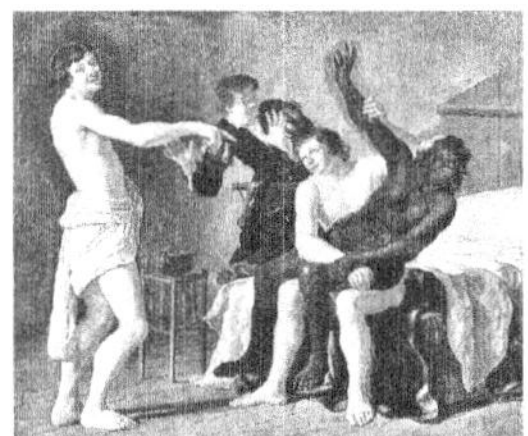

15 Christiaen van Couwenbergh, *Rape of the Negro Girl*, 1632, oil on canvas, 104 × 127 cm. Musée des Beaux-Arts de Strasbourg.

16 We do not know whether the artist took inspiration from a literary source, the sensationalism of newspaper fillers, or the lurid comedies so popular at the time in Amsterdam. The Musée des Beaux-Arts in Strasbourg acquired the painting in 1970.

17 See also additional information on the historical context, for instance under '→ world domination' and the significance of colonialism.

18 'After all, an exhibition should also be seen as an offer to promote the sheer delight of thinking and not necessarily inaugurate a new category or even a new canon. This flexibility in thinking and an openness with regard to the references, ought to be given'. Nike Bätzner, in *Riotous Baroque*, p. 27. Participants in the conversation included Victoria von Flemming, Michael Glasmeier, Tristan Weddigen, and Bice Curiger.

exhibition firmly banks on the mature, adult viewer and the power of reflection in the special context of the museum.[17] Similarly, we may and, indeed, should count on the viewers' sense of humour. In the exhibition, a comic strip by Robert Crumb detailed the predicament of a weak little man, utterly cowed by the overpowering desires of a gigantic woman.

Art is a field that aims at intersubjective experience. As such, the subjectivity of visitors is of general interest as a *commonly shared* subjectivity. This begins early, with the choice of the exhibition title, which refers to ordinary everyday experience and not necessarily to the theories communicated by art historical terminology. In my case this was misunderstood by critics, who promptly classified the exhibition as 'radically subjective'. Wouldn't it then be time for me to be committed to the asylum? After years of inquiry into the subject, one speaks to the public, one explains and presents a publication, all of which is done in order to responsibly communicate the objectification of subjective perception, which was to be the key concern of the exhibition.

One of the Baroque specialists who participated in a conversation printed in the catalogue commented that 'an exhibition should also be seen as an offer to promote the sheer delight of thinking...'.[18] In her 1966 publication *Against Interpretation and Other Essays,* Susan Sonntag took a stand against the traditional claim to a singular semantic hegemony and the dictates of the 'hypertrophy of the intellect', drawing early attention to the philistine refusal to give interpretation a rest. Even though the thrust of her essay may at times pay tribute to dated aspects, her thoughts on the sensibility of the recipient and the sensual experience of the work have lost none of their currency and significance.

The practices of montage and collage acquired crucial and, indeed, near monumental status in the history of the avant-garde in the twentieth century. Art historian Werner Hoffmann characterizes the principle of montage in cubist collages as a form of 'disjointed contrast that occupies at least two distinct zones of reality', a 'kaleidoscopic order' and a 'polyphony of procedure'.[19] Hoffmann (1928–2013) also pioneered the notion of the curator of 'the thinking look', as he called it,[20] and in his 'discursive exhibitions' he targeted a 'visual, tactile essayism, of clearly unpredictable outcome'.[21]

In a reality that has long since been arrogated by acceleration, exposing people to ever more complex visual stimuli, altered capabilities of perception must necessarily be taken into account in organizing exhibitions. However, this cannot be achieved by inundating viewers with all the latest technical gadgetry or mounting increasingly elaborate scenographic productions without fundamentally revisiting the principle of the conventional narrative.

How uncommonly inspiring and essential, then, is the return to the filmic concept of montage, as discussed and analyzed by Jean-Luc Godard and Walter Benjamin! Both referred to the dynamic technique of montage employed in Russian movies of the revolution and in surrealism. According to Eisenstein, the 'mono-perspective' must give way to a fragmentary form of narrative, in other words multiple perspectives. In his famous essay 'Montage mon beau soucis' (1956),[22] Godard criticizes the conventional, illusionist mode of telling stories. Basically his opposition derives from the insight that film and cinema are an accumulation of 'bits'.[23] Pieces glued together (viz. collage) can lead to unique visual outcomes and experiences through mutual contagion.

A tour through an exhibition can certainly be compared to the byways of such considerations. Temporary exhibitions

19 Hoffmann, *Grundlagen der modernen Kunst*, pp. 47ff.

20 Warnke, 'Nachruf auf Werner Hoffmann'.

21 Ziegler, 'Eine Favela, die sich Montmartre nannte'.

22 Godard, 'Montage mon beau soucis', pp. 30, 31.

23 *The Cinema Alone*, esp. pp. 38ff.

and presentations of collections often act as if a heavenly order, following a red thread, has arranged everything on the basis of a rationale so irrefutably linear and true that we visitors can easily follow it. But what about the latent potential of accepting and even emphasizing the fact that single works are always fragments of a larger whole or a slice of time—molecules perpetually bonding and repelling each other in the energetic field of the vibrant museum that we must protect from the all too reasonable interference of uninspired communicators and merchandizing technocrats.

Literature

The Cinema Alone: Essays on the Work of Jean-Luc Godard, 1985–2000. Edited Michael Temple and James S. Williams. Amsterdam, 2000.

Cotter, Holland. 'Art in Review Marilyn Minter.' *The New York Times,* 5 May 2000, ‹www.nytimes.com/2000/05/05/arts/art-in-review-marilyn-minter.html›.

Godard, Jean-Luc. 'Montage mon beau soucis.' *Cahiers du cinema* no. 65 (December 1956), pp. 30, 31.

Hoffmann, Werner. *Grundlagen der modernen Kunst: Eine Einführung in ihre symbolischen Formen.* Stuttgart, 1978.

Riotous Baroque. Exh. cat. Zurich and Cologne (Kunsthaus Zürich), 2012.

Robé, Chris. 'Jean-Luc Godard: A Montage of Attractions.' *Pop Matters,* 22 June 2015, ‹www.popmatters.com/194263-jean-luc-godard-a-montage-of-attractions-2495522044.html›.

Sontag, Susan. *Against Interpretation and Other Essays.* New York, 2001.

Warnke, Martin. 'Nachruf auf Werner Hoffmann.' *Die Zeit,* 21 March 2013, ‹www.zeit.de/2013/13/Nachruf-Werner-Hofmann›.

Ziegler, Ulf Erdmann. 'Eine Favela, die sich Montmartre nannte: Vermutungen über eine zeitgenössische Methode, Kunst auszustellen: Ein Rundgang durch drei Museumsschauen.' *taz,* 6 May 2014.

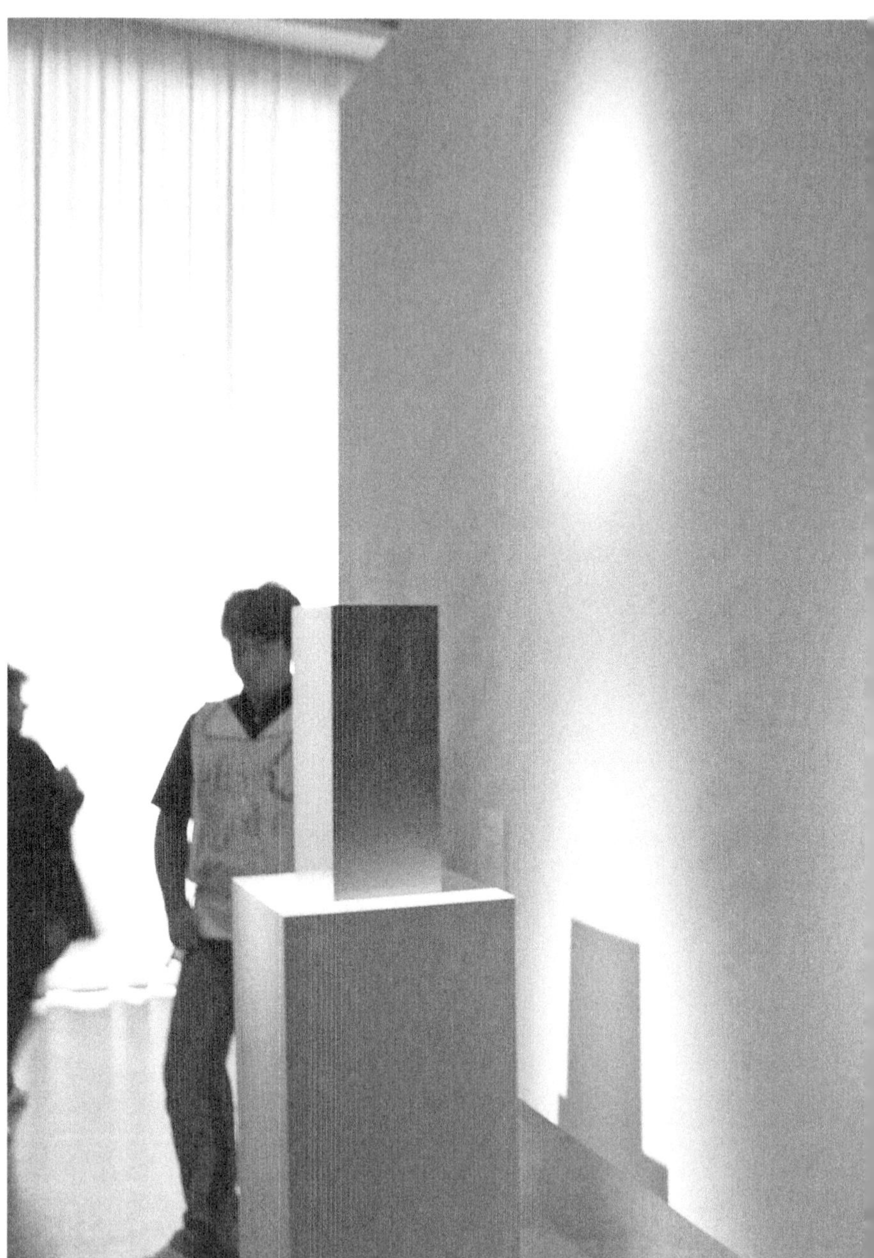

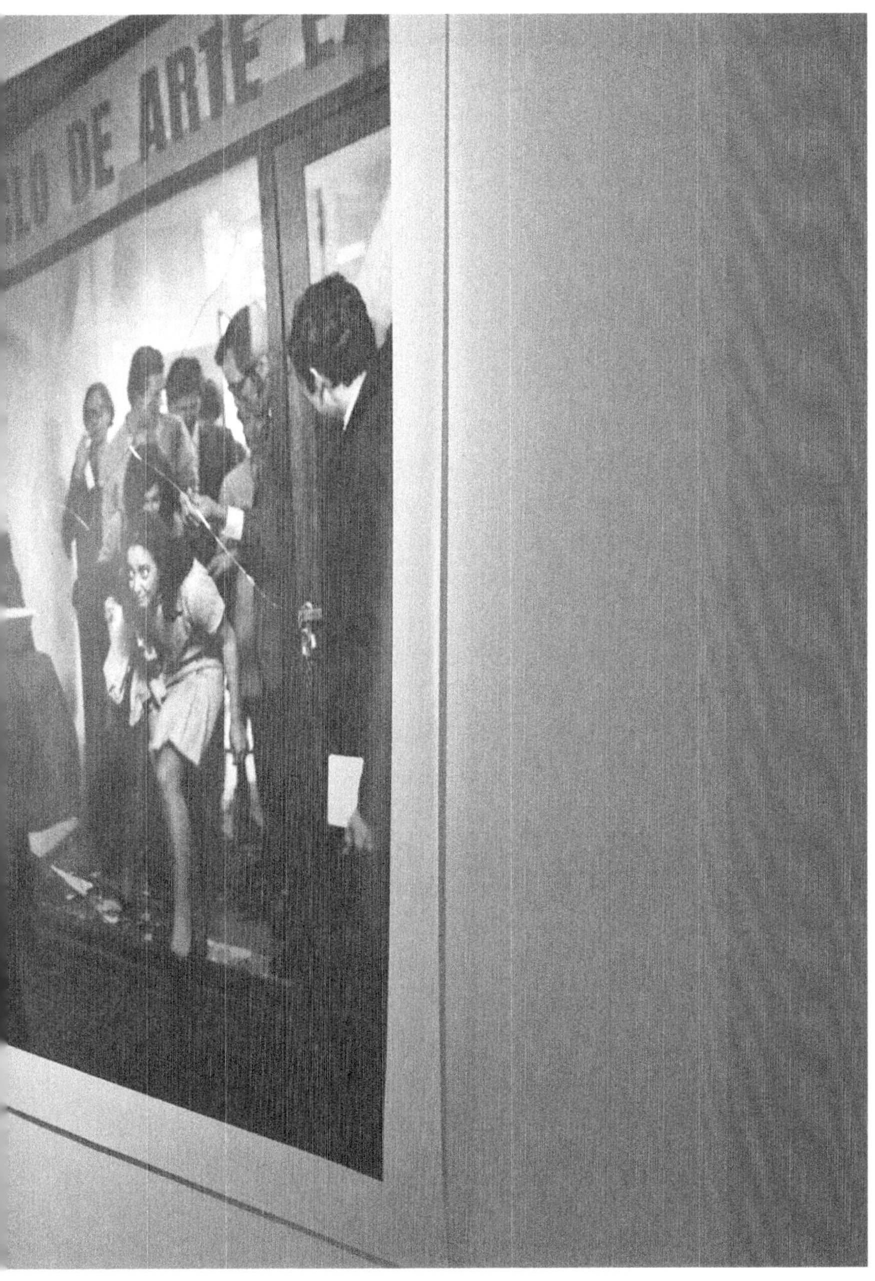

John McCracken, *Song*, 2004, and photograph by Ryszard Kasiewicz of Graciela Carnevale's documentation of her action for the 'Ciclo de Arte Experimental', 1968, installation view, documenta 12, Kassel, 2007. © documenta archive, inv. no. docA_MS_d12-10030287/photo: Ryszard Kasiewicz, courtesy Graciela Carnevale.

‘Migration of Form’ at documenta 12

Ruth Noack

‘inter-, multi-, trans-, de-, anti-, in-, meta and post-’ Can prefixes ever be anything but a sign of trouble? Can they point forward, instead of backward? This seems unlikely. To a large extent, prefixes remain symptoms of a problem of the past. Their presence indicates the ambivalent position we find ourselves in when we want to acknowledge past fallacies but have (or seek) no other means than a quick fix of language to redress them.

How then to address the problems of the past? This is one of the first questions anyone invited to curate a documenta will ask themselves. Not because previous iterations of this show have done such a bad job—the opposite is the case: one cannot but be impressed by the depth of awareness with which one's predecessors have approached the complexities of hegemonic exhibition making. Rather, curators must address the problems of the past, because the symbolic positioning of documenta sets it up as part of a historical genealogy. It is never just the present that is represented at documenta, but a present that reflects upon its past and reaches into its future. In this, documenta differs from biennales and from this, no curator can escape.

'One of the key operations of documenta 12' writes Annie Fletcher,

> was to incorporate art history while reflecting on the historicising nature of the exhibition itself, as if saying that history is important, but it can't be dealt with exclusively through documents. Rather it must be approached by way of a willing and knowing adaptation, distortion and activation of that history. As a result, the exhibition display managed to contribute to the understanding of the more contemporary works while allowing the 'historical' works to operate as documents or models and, at the same time, as contemporary positions in their own right. The fact that feminism was one of the axes along which this dialogue between the historical and the contemporary was established offers some hindsight about where we might go from here.[1]

1 Fletcher 'On Feminism (Through a Series of Exhibitions)'.

The dialogue between the historical and the contemporary was one of several modes of associating works with each other, associations that were loosely defined by what became the catchphrase of documenta 12, the 'migration of form'. There were manifold reasons to call into question normative ordering, but let us not forget one of the most important: The majority of documenta's lay audience would not have known the predecessors to works they were seeing, because they were not used to seeing works of art at all. Introducing historical works into an exhibition of contemporary art was a means to materialize history so as to allow viewers to learn for themselves about what they are seeing—as well as to begin to reflect on the historicizing nature of the exhibition itself.

What held for historical works and a lay audience in 2007, also held for contemporary work and the (Western) professionals: the relevance of what was shown needed to be materialized because its context was unknown even to the professional audience. In documenta X (1997) and documenta 11 (2002), Catherine David and Okwui Enwezor, respectively, had used discourse to supply missing contextual information. By 2007, the scope of what constituted contemporary art had widened yet again, so it was doubtful that any one viewer would be able to study up on such diverse political and aesthetic geographies. Given the production of discourse necessary to allow viewers to engage with the works on the basis of contextual knowledge, it seemed reasonable to assume that the risk of shattering the exhibition was rather high.

As the curators of documenta 12, Roger M. Buergel and I therefore needed another than a purely discursive, knowledge-based model of spectatorship, one that emphasized the possibility, nay *necessity* to engage in the act of viewing and making sense of what is presented *in the face of the impossibility to do so* in any absolute way hence the feminist approach to complex and polyvalent, even inconsistent story-telling.

Take the highly constructed association between a sculpture by John McCracken, *Song* (2004) and a photograph of Graciela Carnevale's famous performance for the 'Ciclo de Arte Experimental' in Rosario (1968). Carnevale had just locked the doors of her gallery in Rosario, effectively trapping her own public inside. A passer-by freed the unfortunate art lovers by throwing a stone through the front window. The photograph of people climbing out into the street has become an icon of an era when artists all over the globe were leaving the institution in order to self-define their practice or to make their art adhere to everyday life. But at documenta 12, it was placed at such an angle that it looks as if Graciela climbs straight into the exhibition place, where she must inevitable stumble upon John McCracken's highly abstract, spiritual-sculptural object. At first glance a visual joke, this installation nevertheless introduced two artists we very much revered into one curatorial trajectory, which privileged production over representation and inspired story-telling over conventions of art historical coherence.

In other words, the organizing principle of the show, the 'migration of form', an expansive and sometimes eccentric layering of correlations that worked thematically as well as aesthetically on different levels of complexity, was also meant as a negotiation with the audience. For in an exhibition, form (and its migration) cannot be solely thought of as an essential attribute of an object, but involves a viewer who is interested in making sense of the presentation. Meaning takes the form of an engagement between the viewer and the work, and this means that meaning can also escape us. Some juxtapositions are more successful than others and there are criteria for such juxtapositions that can and must be defined. One criterion is whether particular combinations infuse the individual work with resonances and make it shine. Another criterion is the audience's relational habits: does the exhibition manage to transform people from passive, appropriating subjects into active collaborators? The phrase we used was 'emancipated spectatorship'.

It is a historical fact that forms have migrated. Yet we all know that there is no neutral, free movement. Within the European context, the irrational fear of migrants is accompanied by an astonishing lack of knowledge about globalization—people still imagine themselves to be in the centre of the world. We therefore found it necessary to provoke ambivalence by introducing the term migration into the discussion of an exhibition with at least some hegemonic force, both

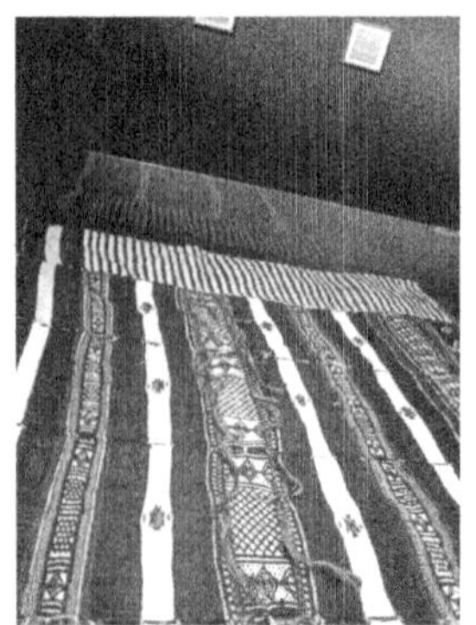

2 Anonymous, Arkila Kerka, woven textile, twentieth century. Photo: Roger M. Buergel, 2007.

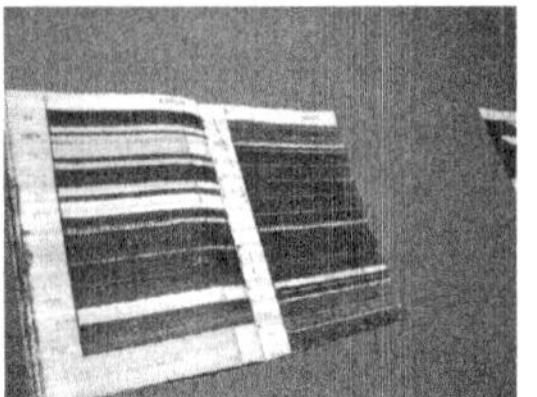

3 Nasreen Mohamedi, *Diary* from the 1970s. Photo: Roger M. Buergel, 2007.

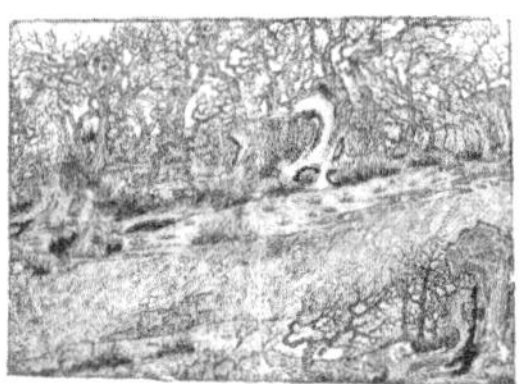

4 Anonymous, *Saray Albums* (Diez A Fol. 71), fourteenth-sixteenth century, miniature on paper, 20.3 × 29.1 cm, Staatsbibliothek zu Berlin—Preussischer Kulturbesitz, Orientabteilung, Berlin.

nationally and internationally. It also seemed imperative to provide the audience with evidence of the long history of globalization, a history in which Europe seems to be almost an afterthought.

At the time, very little art-historical research into transcultural migration of form had been done. As a discipline, art history was and mostly remains nationalist and bound up with hegemony. Nasreen Mohamedi's work, for example, has been placed in the context of an art scene invested in the constitution of independent India. It has also been compared to Western abstraction, but it had not yet been related to Islamic art and philosophy, despite the fact that the drawings, photography, and diaries all point to it. So when we installed a traditional Muslim textile[2] next to Mohamedi's diaries,[3] we were not simply making curatorial use of formal correspondences. Both, the stripes in the diaries and in the Arkila Kerka from Mali, a twentieth-century example of an eleventh-century woven pattern, refer to coded information. We were making a speculative argument on their common foundation in the iconoclast tradition of Islam. More importantly, the formal comparison was a curatorial way of expressing a desire for another history, not yet written, and thus less about filling a gap than about making a gap visible.

The exhibition also showed factual migrations of form. Take the Persian drawing contained in the Berlin *Saray Albums* (fourteenth-fifteenth century).[4] While the landscape depicted here recalls the visual language of Persian art, two elements stand out: colourful shapes looking almost like dragons, and a river rippled by what can be characterized as 'Chinese' waves. While the river is perfectly readable as river, the colourful shapes remain enigmatic in their pictorial function. They are rocks, transported from Chinese art into a new context in the guise of pure forms. Both elements, waves and rocks, are, in today's parlance, copied and pasted from a different art-historical context. While the waves are perfectly integrated in the pictorial universe of the Persian landscape, the rocks demonstrate the fascination the artist must have felt coming upon this singularly strange shape. This drawing is one of many which trace the appropriation of forms during the century in which Greater Iran was ruled by the Ilkhanids, a Mongolian dynasty.

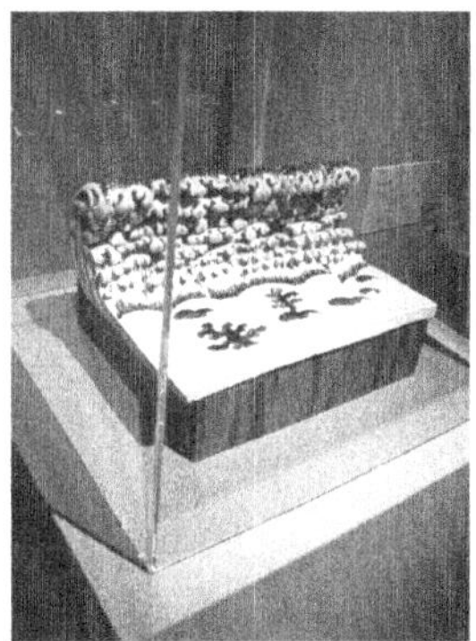

5 Ai Weiwei, *Prototype for the Wave*, 2004, installation view, documenta 12, Kassel, 2007. Photo: Roger M. Buergel, 2007

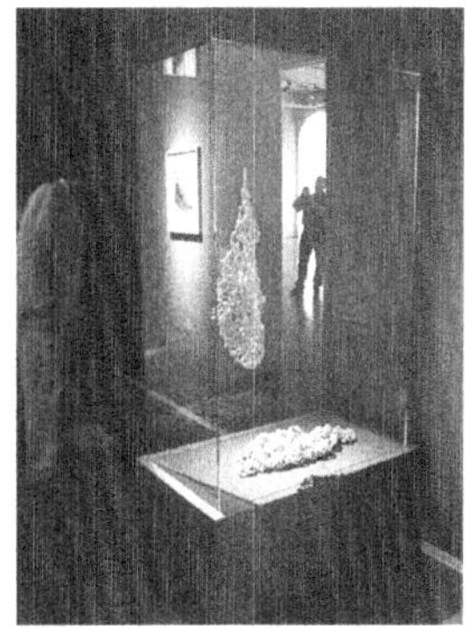

6 Mira Schendel, *Droghuinas*, 1966, installation view, documenta 12, Kassel, 2007. Photo: Roger M. Buergel, 2007.

In the past ten years new transnational research has started to look closer at historical migration of form. I venture that there is hardly a museum depot that does not contain at least one example of work that speaks to the impact on art by the migration of goods along trade routes, the migration of knowledge along educational pathways, or the migration of people along passages of survival. It should be obvious that therefore, art is also implicated in colonialism and other systems of exploitative and unjust exchange of goods, labour, education, services. Because this transnational research is now being undertaken, exhibition making today can start to address these issues in a much less aspirational way than the one we chose with documenta 12.

On the other hand, the lack of research gave us the freedom to use the concept of migration of form in other than factual modes, i.e. in unexpected, associative constellations. Aspects of an artwork that might not have been noticeable within the prevailing framework of interpretation rose to the surface. The Persian drawing, for example, was displayed together with *Prototype for the Wave* (2004) by Ai Weiwei[5]—and two of Mira Schendel's *Droghuinas* (1966).[6] The similitude between the waves in the Persian drawing and the porcelain sculpture is striking. We all know that formal innovation was never really an issue in traditional Chinese art, and this relative conservatism informs Ai Weiwei's piece. However, it would be a mistake to imagine a seamless migration of form across seven centuries, since the contemporary artist is taking up the traditional form in a gesture of interruption: critical of the costs of the 1990s wave of Chinese modernization, a wave that forced itself upon society with the might of a tsunami.

Mira Schendel's *Droguinhas* seem a world apart. Made from rice paper, they change appearance according to how they are handled. They are non-referential. Yet there are subtle connections to the other two works, be it the fragile thingness shared by the two sculptures, be it the way that the surface of the paper objects resonates with the smooth glaze of the porcelain. All three works depict movement or flow, but whereas the Persian drawing and Ai Weiwei's wave have caught the flow in one form, rendering water as a kind of dynamized materiality, Schendel's objects keep flowing, building up and collapsing energized matter.

We cannot touch the *Droguinhas*, yet even at their most inanimate, behind the glass of the display case, there prevails the sense of tactility and flow of energy. Regardless of our historical knowledge, Schendel's biography or lack thereof, this is what we pick up on. The act of comprehension is incomplete and the attempt to rectify the situation by detecting similarities between the individual works is only partially successful. The arrangement will remain a simultaneous projection and negation.

documenta 12 used the concept of migration of form to tell three kinds of—sometimes intertwined—stories: One narrated instances where form has moved across histories, cultures and geographies. The second created synthetic contexts for individual works of art, in which objects were connected in a formal and rhizomatic display, transposing normative Western centrist art history and exhibition practice. The third concept, connecting artistic forms with forms of being, or subjectivity, was not addressed here. However, if one defines transhistoricity as a multidirectional activity of creating a meaningful relationship between art and the world, it does not suffice to rethink display modes. The very least, we would need to think anew what an audience might mean to our own curatorial or institution-building practice.

Literature

Fletcher, Annie. 'On Feminism (Through a Series of Exhibitions).' *Afterall* 17 (Spring 2008), ‹www.afterall.org/journal/issue.17/feminism.through.series.exhibitions› (accessed 15 January 2018).

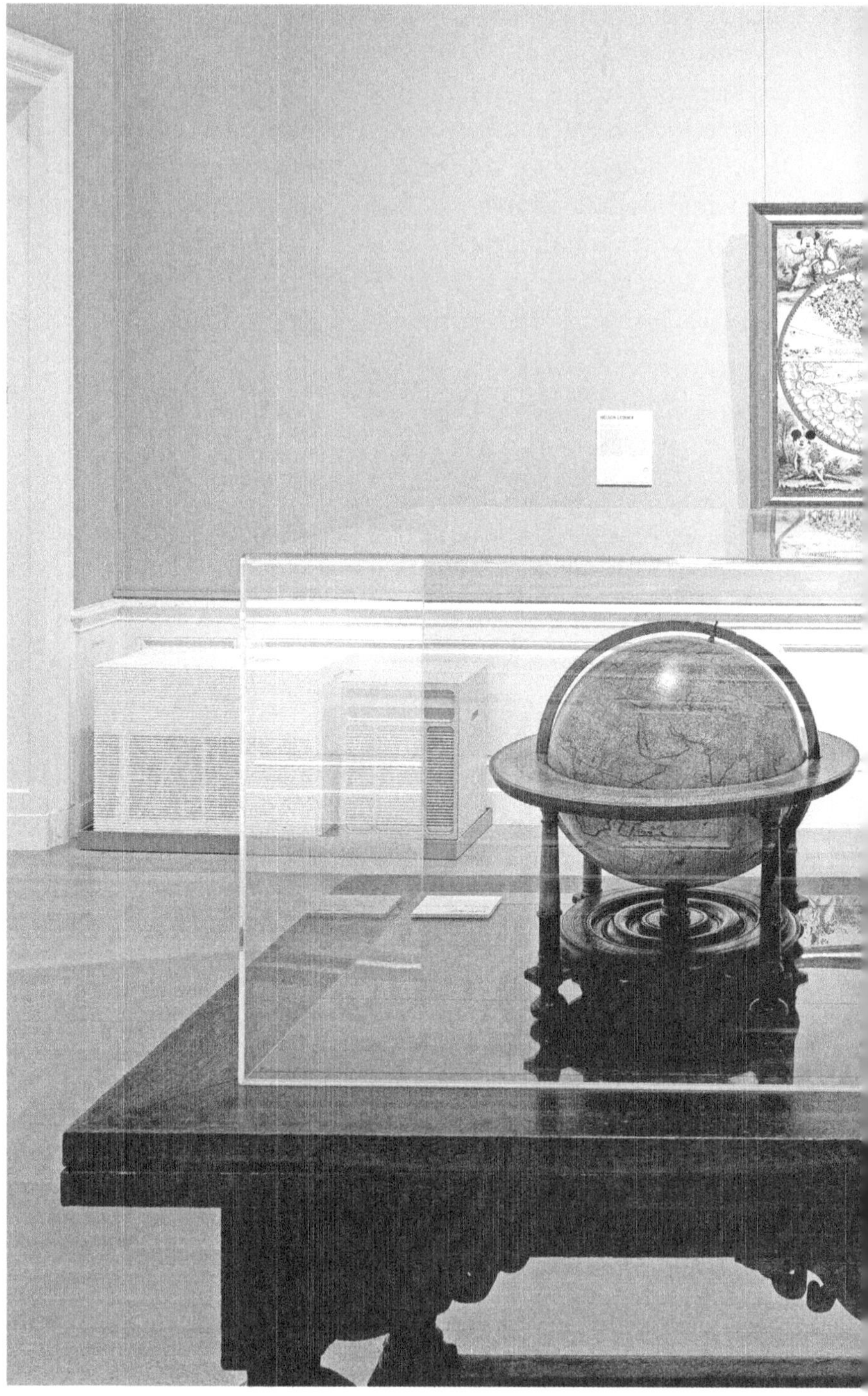

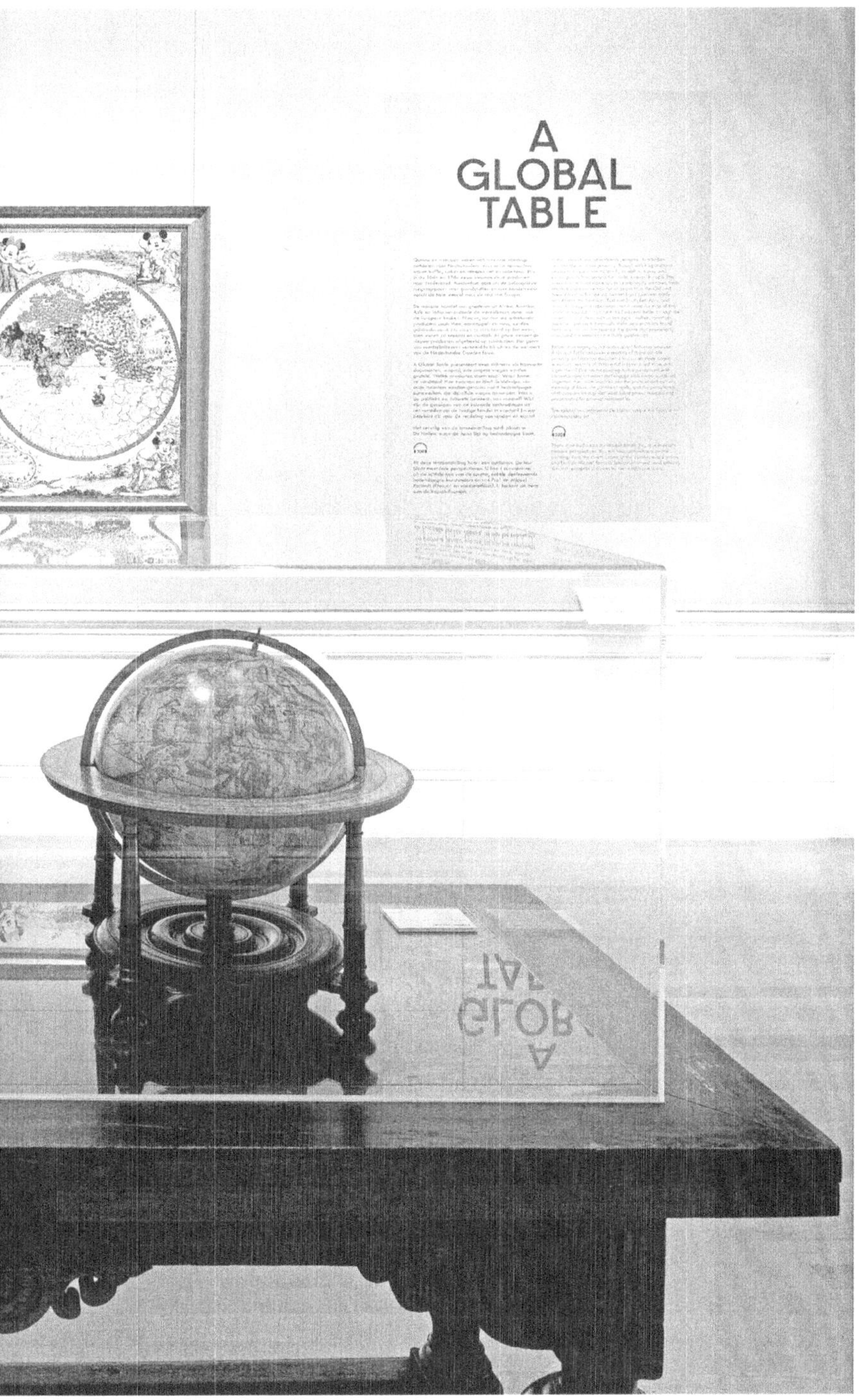

Gerard and Leonard Valck, celestial and terrestrial globe, c. 1750. Noord-Hollands Archief; Nelson Leirner, *Right You Are if You Think You Are*, 2003, photograph, 100 × 130 cm, installation view, 'A Global Table', Frans Hals Museum, Haarlem. Courtesy Frans Hals Museum | De Hallen Haarlem. Photo: Gert Jan van Rooij, 2017.

Setting 'A Global Table'

Seventeenth-Century Still Life, Colonial History, and Contemporary Art

Abigail Winograd

The past is never dead. It isn't even past.[1]
—William Faulkner

In a seldom frequented wing of the Uffizi, Florence, there is something called the Rembrandt Room, a modestly sized gallery housing the museum's collection of Dutch Golden Age painting. In it, seeking refuge from the maddening crowds swarming Botticellis, Caravaggios, and Michelangelos, I happened upon a small still life, *Fruits and Insects,* painted in 1711 by Rachel Ruysch.[2] There, nestled amongst ripe peaches, grapes, plums, slender stalks of wheat, and a gourd, was an ear of yellow corn.[3] Its plump kernels caught my eye and I paused to stare. Having studied pre-Columbian art as a graduate student, I know that corn is a plant native to the Americas—the cereal upon which great Native American civilizations were built—where it was domesticated and refined over the course of thousands of years.[4] When, I asked myself, did corn first arrive in Europe and begin to make its way into still-life paintings? This moment of recognition unsettled my

1 William Faulkner, *Requiem for a Nun* (1959), Act 1, Scene 3.

2 Rachel Ruysch (b. The Hague, 1664—d. Amsterdam, 1750) was one of a handful of female painters who made their living as still-life painters in the seventeenth and eighteenth centuries. Ruysch, Maria van Oosterwijck (b. Nootdorp, Netherlands, 1630—d. Waterland, Netherlands, 1693), and Clara Peeters (b. Antwerp, c. 1594—d. after 1657). Works by Oosterwijck and Peeters were included in the exhibition.

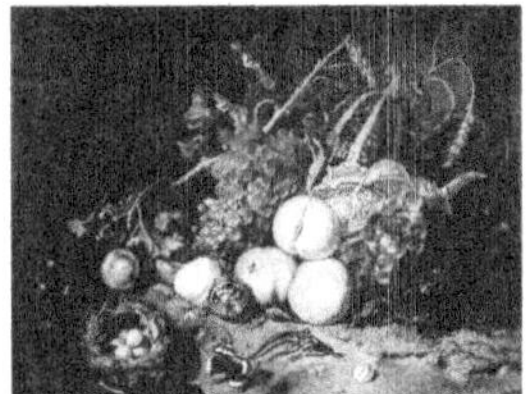

2a Rachel Ruysch, *Still Life with Fruit and Insects*, 1711, oil on panel, 44 × 60 cm, Uffizi Gallery, Florence.

3 It is worth noting that the calabash is also a species of plant native to the Americas that was transported across the globe by European traders. When I first viewed the painting, I was unaware of this fact.

4 Scientists believe that corn was domesticated in Central Mexico about nine thousand years ago. The plant traveled to North and South America via the migration of indigenous communities.

thinking about the genre as a whole. What other stories were embedded in this unassuming canvas?

Ruysch's painting is visual evidence of the expansion of European power in the Americas at the end of the fifteenth century. An interchange not just of peoples and cultures but of flora and fauna as well. The landing of Spanish conquistadors in the New World marked the beginning of the Columbian Exchange: the massive transfer of agricultural products and foodstuffs from the New World to the Old.[5] This exchange of goods was not exclusively a transatlantic affair: new products also came to Europe via overland and overseas trade with Africa, East and South East Asia, and India. As European imperialism transformed the map of the world, establishing a truly global network of trade in the process, so too did it transform the European table through the introduction of items such as tea, sugar, coffee, tomatoes, potatoes, and corn. This transformation was not limited to Europe. Chili peppers (*Capsicum annum*), for example, also native to the Americas, traversed the globe on the ships of Portuguese traders. Their arrival in Asia transformed various cuisines; indeed it is impossible to think of Thai or Indian curries without them.[6] As the masters of international trade, the Dutch in particular saw their economy grow exponentially throughout the sixteenth and seventeenth centuries, based precisely on this exchange of goods.[7] It is no surprise that many of these new products eventually found their way into still-life painting, the genre that exemplarily visualized the 'embarrassment of riches' of the Dutch Golden Age.[8]

Reassessing and redressing colonial history has become commonplace in contemporary museum practice. Yet, this seemed a novel approach to the subject of colonialism, globalization, and trade while simultaneously providing an interesting

5 The term Columbian Exchange was first used by Alfred W. Crosby in his classic environmental history *The Columbian Exchange: Biological and Cultural Consequences of 1492* published by Greenwood Press in 1972. The term is now utilized as shorthand to refer to the set of complex historical and environmental changes initiated by the arrival of Columbus and his crew in the Americas.

6 Evidence of the global exchange of agricultural products is made beautifully visible in the *Hortus Malabaricus*. Compiled over the course of thirty years by Hendrik Adriaan van Rheede tot Drakenstein, who served as the governor of Dutch Malabar between 1669 and 1676, the *Hortus Malabaricus* surveyed the medicinal properties of plants growing on the Malabar Coast. All twelve volumes of the Hortus were published in Amsterdam between 1678 and 1693. The compendium includes plants brought to India from across the globe. The names of which are written in four languages: Latin, Arabic, Malayalam (Malabar), and Sanskrit. The books were displayed in 'A Global Table' courtesy of the Library at the University of Leiden.

7 The Dutch East India Company (VOC) was founded in 1602 and was granted a trade monopoly that stretched over Dutch held territories from the Cape of Good Hope in present day South Africa to the Straits of Magellan in present day Chile. The charter gave the company the right to sign treaties, build forts, maintain armed forces, and to administer the regions brought under their control. This gave the VOC control of Asian trade including spices (pepper, salt, clove, cinnamon, and nutmeg), silk, cotton, rugs, wine, hazelnuts, porcelain, and tea. Its counterpart, the Dutch West India Company (WIC) was founded in 1623 and was granted a trade monopoly over the Caribbean (West Indies), Brazil, and North America, as well as oversight of Dutch participation in the transatlantic slave trade which involved extensive activity on the west coast of Africa. The WIC oversaw the trade in tobacco, sugar, salt, and slaves as well as precious metals, ivory, pearls, and other luxury goods. The paintings in the following galleries feature these items

8 The idiom 'an embarrassment of riches' was used as the title of Simon Schama's now classic cultural history of the Dutch Golden Age in which he explored Dutch identity through the lens of material culture. For the purposes of making 'A Global Table', Schama's effort to understand the impact of the Dutch economic miracle by looking at the quotidian and domestic was also instructive. Schama, *The Embarrasment of Riches*.

opportunity to reframe a genre while encouraging a new way of looking. Would it not be possible to organize an exhibition of still-life painting which, rather than engaging in traditional art historical analysis would read seventeenth-century still lifes as historical texts? Such an exhibition would invite the viewer to ask three simple questions: What is it? Where did it come from? What did it take to get it there? The goal being to use common goods (salt, tobacco, gourds, etc.) as a lens through which to reveal the political and cultural meaning of food, the politics of trade, and the persistence of discrepancies in global wealth and power initiated and perpetuated by colonial relationships. This notion became the basis for 'A Global Table', which opened at the Frans Hals Museum | De Hallen Haarlem on 23 September 2017.

Looking for a theoretical model around which I could mould this exhibition, I turned to anthropology. 'A Global Table' takes its inspiration from Sidney Mintz's *Sweetness and Power: The Place of Sugar in Modern History* (1985), in which Mintz argued that taste and the pursuit of foodstuffs shaped empires. Mintz used the history of sugar as a way to understand global historical, political, and cultural developments from the seventeenth century through the twentieth. In so doing, he described how the politics of food converged with the politics of international trade—with wide-ranging economic, environmental, and social consequences.[9]

Mintz's perspective was transhistorical in that he looked at the effects of a single product across time. If 'A Global Table' was to attempt the same in the visual arts, this would require the juxtaposition of historical painting with contemporary art in order to transform a snapshot of the seventeenth century into a moving picture of global historical, political, and cultural developments to the present. Additionally, an

9 Mintz, *Sweetness and Power.*

exhibition of seventeenth-century still-life painting is entirely univocal as the artists are all Dutch, primarily men, and universally enthusiastic about the colonial enterprise. The addition of contemporary art was essential, not just to ensure the presence of a counter-narrative, but also to allow the audience to grasp the spectrum of consequences instantiated by colonialism. In the past decades, the politics of food have reasserted themselves in the global community's cultural consciousness, and the socio-economics of food production and consumption have become a growing concern of an increasing number of artists. The mechanisms and processes behind the transport and production of basic foodstuffs, such as salt or sugar, was in the seventeenth century, and remains today, an enormously complex enterprise.

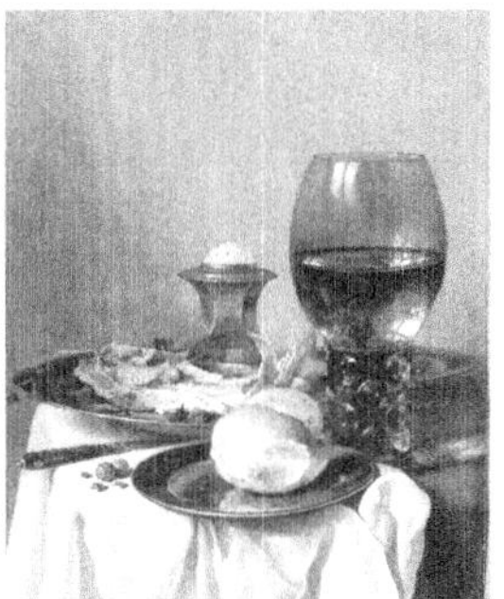

10 Pieter Claesz., *Still Life with a Salt*, c. 1640–c. 1645, oil on panel, 52.8 × 44 cm, Rijksmuseum, Amsterdam.

Look, for example, at Pieter Claesz.'s *Still Life with a Salt* from 1640–1645.[10] Where did that salt come from? The silver salt cellar at its centre contains salt likely shipped from the Caribbean to Amsterdam. The fecundity of the North Sea fisheries was the original source of Dutch wealth. The transport of fish requires its preservation, making salt an essential commodity. The production of salt in the Netherlands was not possible, as it required digging up land, which resulted in terrible flooding. The practice was outlawed following the St. Elizabeth's floods in 1421. In the fifteenth century, Spain was the primary source of salt. However, the break between the northern Netherlands and the Spanish crown in the 1580s required locating a new point of supply. The Spanish were the first Europeans to discover salt flats in the Caribbean in the late 1490s. Bonaire would become the centre of Dutch salt production in the Caribbean and the mining and transport of salt would become a driving force behind Dutch participation in the transatlantic African slave trade.[11] This is, of course, an extremely truncated explanation but it provides a

11 This connection between salt and the transatlantic slave trade was the subject of the work of Patricia Kaersenhout's *Soul of Salt*. The work was included in 'A Global Table' and was displayed in De Hallen.

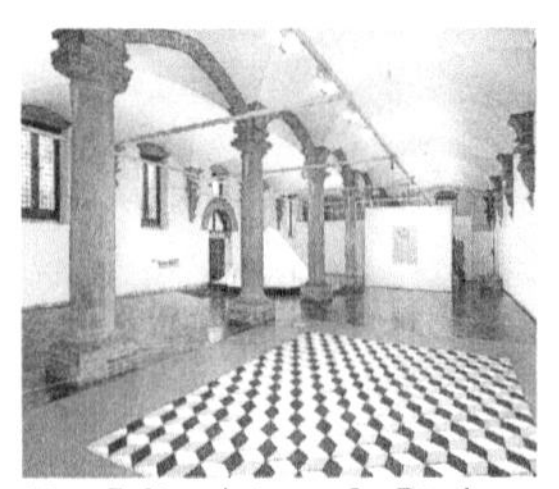

12 Felipe Arturo, *La Disolución de la Geometría*, 2014, brown sugar, powder coffee, powdered milk, 200 × 400 cm; Patricia Kaersenhout, *Soul of Salt*, 2015–ongoing, installation, installation view, 'A Global Table', De Hallen Haarlem. Courtesy Frans Hals Museum | De Hallen Haarlem. Photo: Gert Jan van Rooij, 2017.

glimpse of the kind of history folded into each still-life painting. In this light, salt becomes more than just an item displayed on a table. It becomes a gateway for a better understanding of the past. At the same time, it becomes apparent that these same questions i.e. where does my food come from, how is it produced, and what is the environmental, social, and economic impact of its production were as relevant four centuries ago as they are today.

Occupying two separate physical locations in Haarlem, the Frans Hals Museum and the De Hallen Haarlem, required conceptualizing an exhibition with two constituent parts, each of which could stand alone but also corresponded to the other one. Given the condition restrictions inherent in displaying seventeenth-century painting, all the historical works in the exhibition had to remain in the FHM. This portion of the exhibition developed as a three-dimensional essay while the portion in de Hallen ranged more broadly. Whereas the focus in the FHM was primarily Netherlandish history, works in de Hallen looked at various colonial legacies (British, Soviet, Spanish, etc.) and took up the problem of trade in the twentieth and twenty-first centuries.[12]

'A Global Table' at the FHM opened with a thesis statement, providing an historical grounding, contained in two comparative presentations. The first, a side-by-side comparison of two paintings, Florisz Gerritsz. van Schooten's *Still Life with Ham and Cheese* (1680–1691) and Pieter Gijsels' *Still Life by a Fountain* (1638–1640). A modest scene of domestic products, bread, cheese, butter, and meat, comprise the first. Gijsels', on the other hand, contains an exotic array of corn, tomatoes, and guinea pigs from the Americas, Turkish carpets, exotic flowers, gold from Africa, imported birds and animals. Together the paintings are visual evidence of the epic transformation the exhibition sought to explore.

The second comparison brought together historical and contemporary works taking advantage of the opportunity to initiate a critical dialogue about the consequences of colonial trade. Personifications of the city of Amsterdam are at the centre of Claes Jansz. Visscher's *View of Amsterdam* from 1611 and Gerard de Lairesse's *The Patroness of Amsterdam* from 1665–1685. In both works, allegorical figures representing regions and continents bestow gifts and merchandise (including but not limited to pearls, ivory, shells, tobacco, and spices) upon a regally dressed Amsterdam. Like the still lifes that surround them, these images contain a wealth of historical information.[13] They are documents not just of the realities of colonial trade but of the worldview, one of ownership, superiority, and entitlement, which grew up around them. Implicit in their unflattering characterizations of distant continents and peoples is the fact that seventeenthcentury trade involved redrawing the map of the world. Lairesse's and Visscher's works hang opposite Nelson Leirner's *Untitled* photograph from the series *Right You Are if You Think You Are* (2003). Like his historical counterparts, Leirner's work traffics in stereotypes—the countries of the global North are covered in images from popular culture such as Tweety Bird and Mickey Mouse, while monkeys and apes stand in for the countries of Latin America and Africa, a tragicomic commentary on the dehumanization of non-European populations by the European colonial enterprise. Leirner's series borrows its title from a play by Luigi Pirandello, the plot of which revolves around a cast of characters trying to determine the veracity of a story told by three separate individuals, each one insisting their version is the truth. Like Pirandello's play, Leirner's work is a reminder that maps, like those he embellishes, and maps at large, are not benign objects but rather

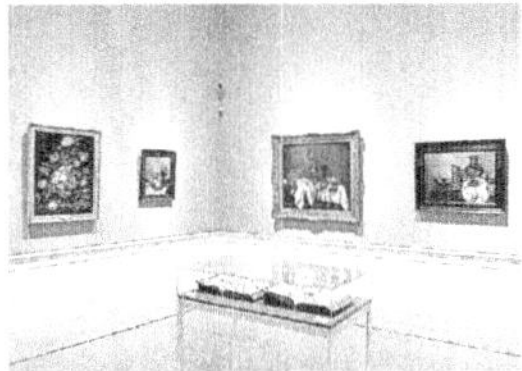

13 Abraham Mignon, *Flowers in a Metal Vase*, c. 1670, oil on canvas, 90 × 72.5 cm, Mauritshuis, The Hague; Willem Claesz. Heda, *Still Life with Silver Tazza*, 1631, oil on panel, 55 × 40 cm, Frans Hals Museum, Haarlem; Willem Claesz. Heda, *Still Life with Pie and Silver Ewer*, oil on canvas, 123 × 103 cm, Frans Hals Museum, Haarlem; Willem Claesz. Heda, *Still Life with Pasty*, 1633, oil on panel, 79 × 58.6 cm, Frans Hals Museum, Haarlem; Hendrik van Reede tot Drakenstein, Volume 7 and 9 of *Hortus Malabaricus*, 1678–1703, Library at the University of Leiden, installation view, 'A Global Table', Frans Hals Museum, Haarlem. Courtesy Frans Hals Museum | De Hallen. Photo: Gert Jan van Rooij, 2017.

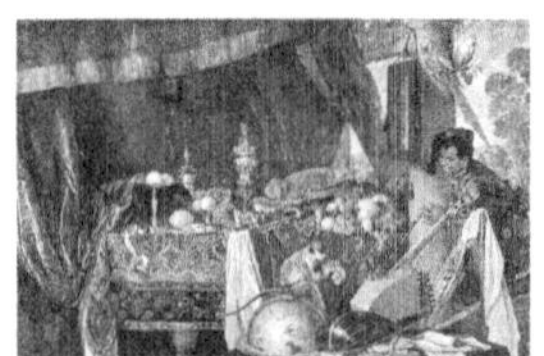

14 Jan Davidsz. de Heem, *Still Life with Moor and Parrot*, 1641, oil on canvas, 223 × 316 cm, Hotel de Ville (Maison du Roi), Brussels.

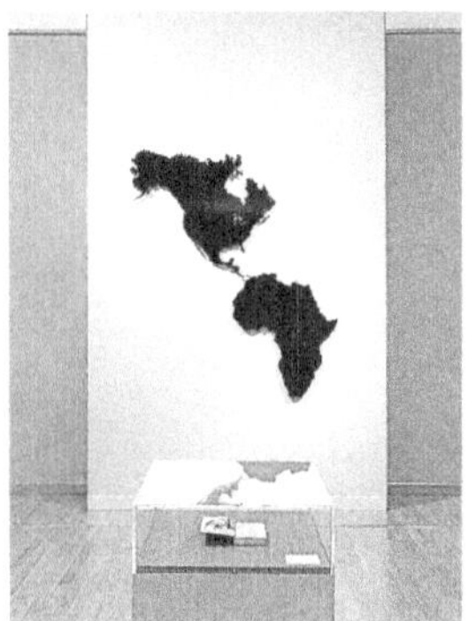

15 Hank Willis Thomas, *A Place to Call Home (Africa-America)*, 2009, polished aluminum with powdered coat, 203 × 167 cm; *Histoire Naturelle du Cacao et du Sucre*, 1720, book, Library at the University of Leiden, installation view, 'A Global Table', Frans Hals Museum, Haarlem. Courtesy Frans Hals Museum | De Hallen. Photo: Gert Jan van Rooij, 2017.

versions of the truth and, when placed in this context, a rebuttal to the worldview described above. Still-life painting in the seventeenth century reflected not just the fantastic accumulation of wealth but also the desire to embrace and collect the bounty of the globe, an acquisitiveness, Leirner reminds us, not viewed with such enthusiasm on the other sides of the ocean.

'A Global Table' endeavoured to unmask the benign domesticity of still life and to reveal the stark divide between 'reality' as it was perceived by the beneficiaries of and those devastated by colonial regimes. Achieving primacy in the global economy involved the brutal conquest of territory, the suppression of local populations, the use of slave labour, the import and export of African slaves, and the exploitation of natural resources. The transatlantic slave trade brought people from Africa to the Americas where they were forced to work in fields tending cash crops such as sugar (indigenous to South East Asia), cotton (native to India and Pakistan), and tobacco (a native American product that would transform the habits of the Old World). Their labour produced raw materials that were then transported to Europe where they were processed and shipped to Africa to be sold in the form of textiles, alcohol, etc. The brutal logic of the early modern economy transformed people into commodities. Eventually, individuals of African descent came to be displayed alongside the goods their bodies laboured to produce in paintings intended to display the abundance of the age. Two such paintings, one by Jurriaen van Streeck (*Still Life with Moor*, n.d.) and the other by Jan Davidsz. de Heem (*Still Life with Moor and Parrot*, 1641),[14] were presented alongside Hank Willis Thomas' *A Place to Call Home (Africa-America)*, 2009.[15] In the seventeenth-century paintings, we see the consequence

(African figures depicted as symbols of status) without any indication of the mechanism by which their likeness came to be synonymous with wealth. Thomas' work, a visual representation of his own hybrid identity (African and American) in the form of a redrawn map connecting North America to Africa, bridges the historical gap and refuses that ambiguity. Where did the two nameless figures come from? They were brought from Africa to the Americas. They were slaves, taken against their will. The consequence is encapsulated in *A Place to Call Home*.

Literature

Crosby, Alfred W. *The Columbian Exchange: Biological and Cultural Consequences of 1492*. Westport, 1972.
Mintz, Sidney. *Sweetness and Power: The Place of Sugar in Modern History*. New York, 1985.
Schama, Simon. *The Embarrassment of Riches: An Interpretation of Dutch Culture in the Golden Age*. New York, 1987.

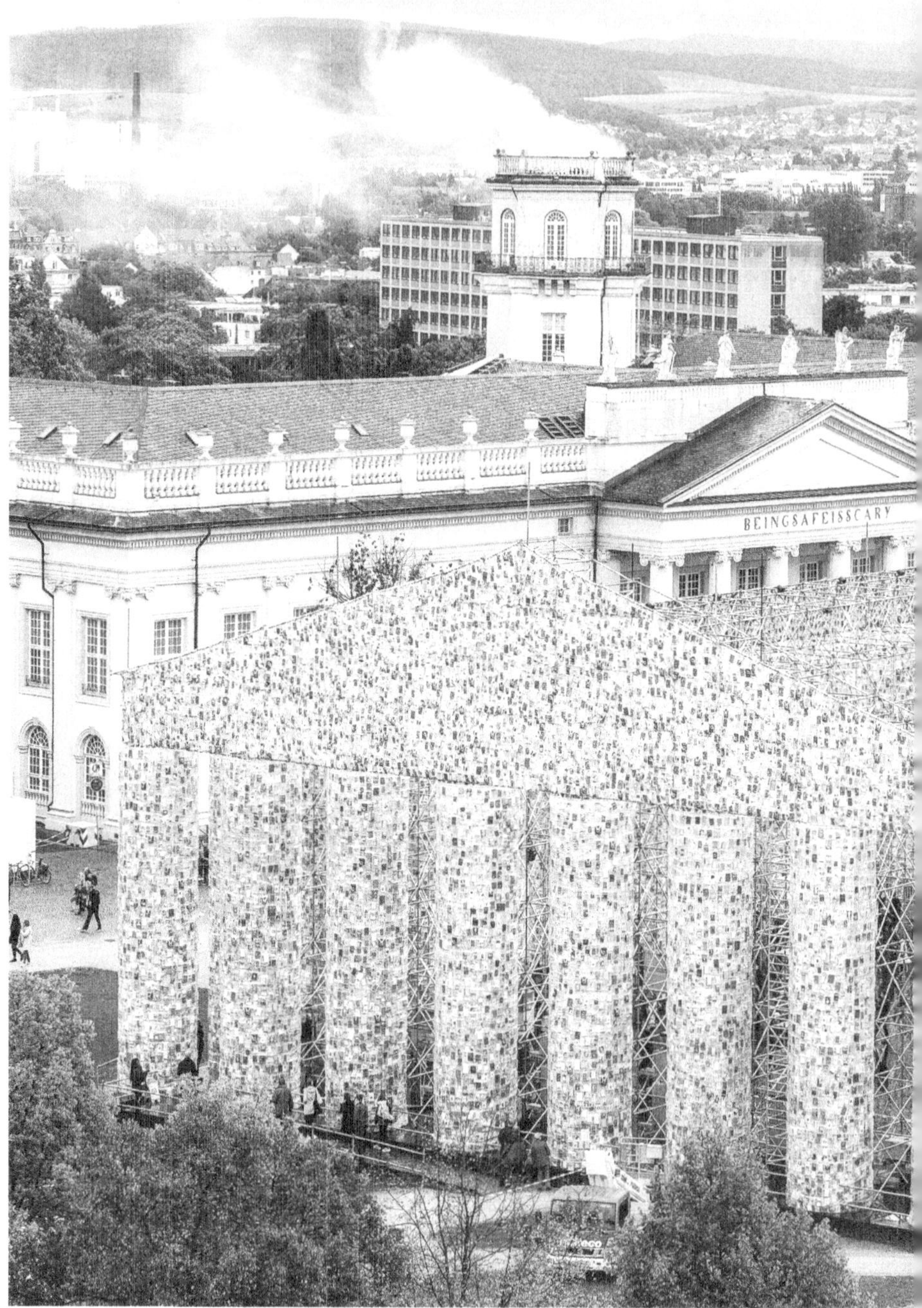
BEINGSAFEISSCARY

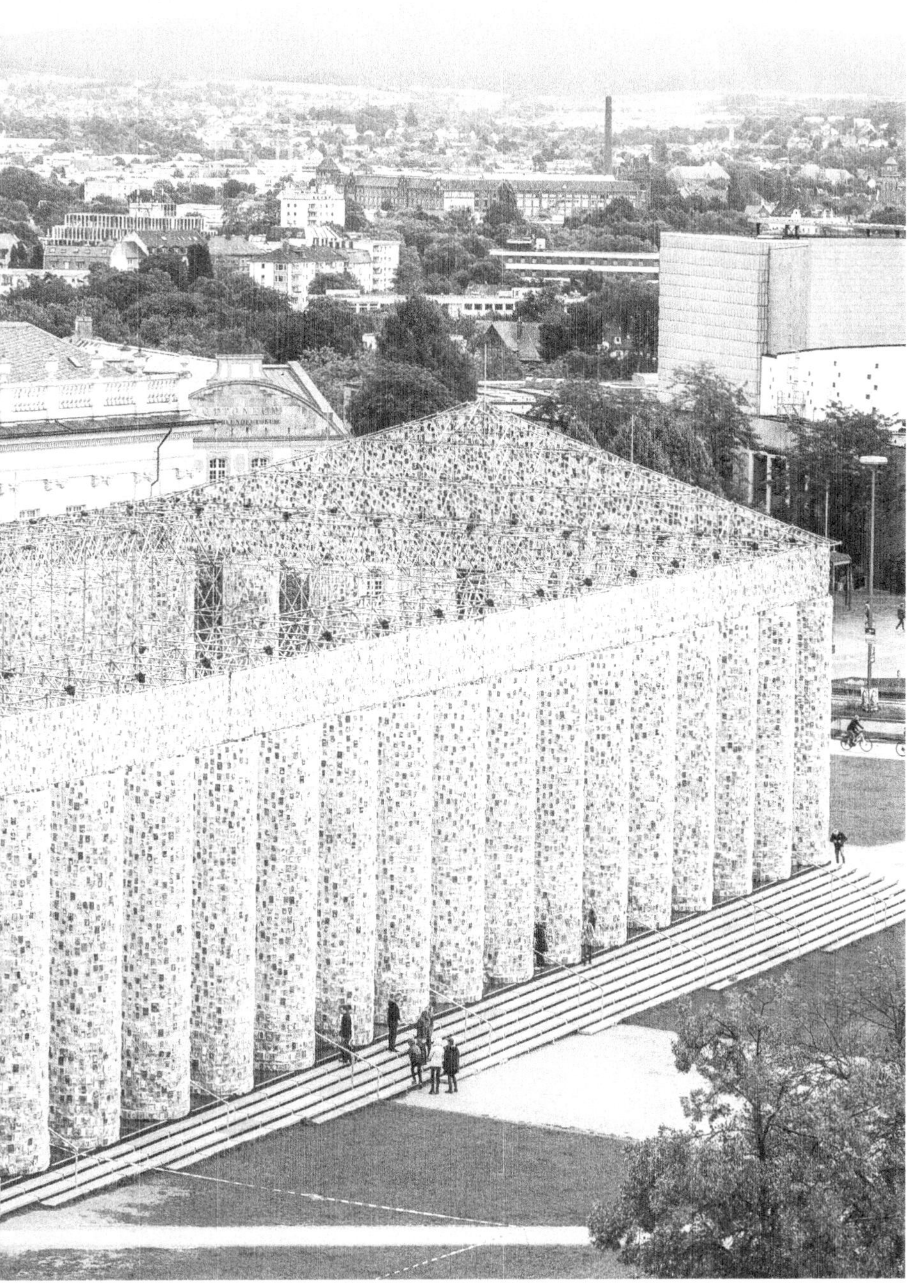

The Friedrichsplatz in Kassel during documenta 14 with Marta Minujín's *The Parthenon of Books*, 1983/2017; Banu Cennetoğlu, *BEINGSAFEIS-SCARY*, 2017, and Daniel Knorr, *Expiration Movement*, 2017. Photo: Mathias Völzke, 2017.

documenta 14

A Transhistorical Dérive

Hendrik Folkerts

Space is not a scientific object removed from ideology or politics. It has always been political and strategic. There is an ideology of space. Because space, which seems homogeneous, which appears as a whole in its objectivity, in its pure form, such as we determine it, is a social product.[1]

Nothing disappears completely. … In space, what came earlier continues to underpin what follows. … Pre-existing space underpins not only durable spatial arrangements, but also *representational spaces* and their attendant imagery and mythic narratives.[2]
—Henri Lefebvre

documenta 14 sees itself as a theater of actions—a performative, embodied experience available to all its participants. Moreover, while thinking about the seemingly immutable spectacular order, in which documenta 14 is perceived as an 'exhibition' conceived by its 'curators' for an 'audience', we believe it is possible to think beyond that narrow definition, toward other models and modes of production of meaning that would entail producing situations, not just artefacts to be looked at.[3]
—Quinn Latimer and Adam Szymczyk

At the heart of documenta 14, an exhibition that took place—in part, simultaneously—in Athens, Greece, and Kassel, Germany, was an acknowledgement that the space of an

1 Lefebvre, 'Reflections on the Politics of Space'.

2 Lefebvre, *The Production of Space*, pp. 229–230.

3 Latimer and Szymczyk. 'Editors' Letter'.

exhibition is always and fundamentally a political space. As the two passages from Henri Lefebvre's 'Reflections on the Politics of Space' (1976) and *The Production of Space* (1991) demonstrate, space, as a physical entity and metaphysical construct, is imbued with ideological purpose as well as historical significance that continues to produce meaning in the present. Lefebvre's text can easily be read alongside Anthony Bennett's seminal essay 'The Exhibitionary Complex' (1992), foundational for the analysis of exhibition history and curatorial practice. Bennett observes a shift in the nineteenth century from presenting art in the privacy of, for instance, a monarch's cabinet to art's public exposition in exhibitions and world fairs. He suggests that this 'exhibitionary complex' proposed knowledge and pedagogy as instruments to render visible to its constituents the state's cultural, architectural and industrial power and accomplishments, in order to infuse spectatorship with the awareness of power and consequently, exercise control through the populace's self-regulation.[4] As such, the space of the exhibition is not only a site of political significance, but also of power.

This essay aims to reflect on documenta 14 as an exhibition that operated through a transhistorical mechanism, within the political histories and contemporary realities it encapsulated. Any definition of the 'transhistorical' is necessarily unstable. In its most rudimentary form, as a juxtaposition of historical and contemporary objects or images, it invites us to consider the past through the present and vice versa. Its challenge to the temporal continuity of past, present, and future invokes Walter Benjamin's reading of Karl Marx's historical materialism. Benjamin saw history not as a stable continuum or linear progress, but rather as a reciprocal relationship between the 'now' as an ever-shifting perspective and the 'what-has-been'. The event or image in history is thus

4 Bennett, 'The Exhibitionary Complex'.

5 Benjamin, *The Arcades Project*, p. 462 N2a, 3.

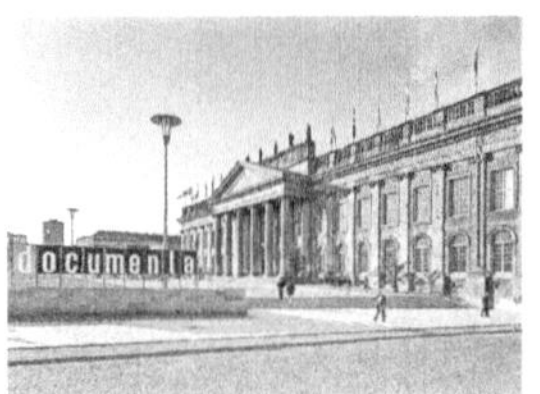

6 documenta 1, 1955. © documenta archiv/Günther Becker. Photo: Günther Becker, 1955.

no longer isolated in time, approached with our desire to see it for what it really was, but exists in a constellation with other temporalities:

> It is not that what is past casts its light on what is present, or what is present its light on what is past; rather, an image is that wherein what has been comes together in a flash with the now to form a constellation.[5]

Benjamin's complex theory of history allows us to consider the transhistorical as a methodology in exhibition-making and curating; a comprehensive approach to how history is entangled with our present experience of the world in which neither of these temporal coordinates are stable signifiers. These considerations on the materialities of history, alongside the spatial dimensions constituted by two geographical anchor points (Athens and Kassel), formed the artistic and political axes on which documenta 14 unfolded.

Our story begins, inevitably, in Kassel, at various intersections between 1945 and 2017. A city in ruins following the destruction of World War II, as it had been such an important military and strategic hub for the Nazi regime, Kassel became an icon of the reconstruction and cultural rematerialization of post-war Germany. Considering its geographic location at the border of the newly formed German Democratic Republic in the East and the Federal Republic of Germany in the West after 1949, it is important to consider Kassel's symbolic placement of a city in the West facing the East during the emergence of Cold War cultural politics. In this political imaginary, Kassel became the birthplace of documenta, organized by curator, designer, and educator Arnold Bode and a team of art historians in the reconstructed Fridericianum in 1955.[6] Coinciding with the German

National Garden Show—a major horticultural event instituted in 1951—documenta 1 had a guaranteed audience and, indeed, turned out to be a major success and continued as a not-for-profit institution after 1955.

The first iteration of documenta intended to build a bridge between the art of the historical avant-garde and the post-war moment, diametrically opposite to the 'Degenerate Art Exhibition' the Nazi's had mounted at Munich's Haus der Kunst in 1937. As such, in a carefully curated display and accompanied by lecture series on the history of the avant-garde, documenta 1 presented artworks from the late 1940s and early 1950s alongside works from the first half of the twentieth century, including not only European artists, but, significantly, a number of American artists, making it one of the first exhibitions on the continent to align European and American histories of the avant-garde. Although such an alignment emerges from the (forced) migration of many artists and intellectuals from Europe to the United States before and during World War II, I would argue that Bode's editions of documenta also need to be understood in the larger context of Transatlantic cultural politics, anchored in the Marshall plan to rebuild Europe and the covert American cultural programmes during the Cold War.[7]

While documenta 1 as well as Bode's subsequent documentas 2, 3 and 4 may have been the most political exhibitions in Europe of the twentieth century, the genesis history of this exhibition continues to linger in how documenta manifests today, as inextricably tied to German national identity—the furious responses to organize the exhibition elsewhere, such as Athens, are surely a testament to that. Over time, documenta changed. It became an increasingly global event, a recurring landmark of contemporary art and theory, the growing scale of which corresponds to its conscious or

7 See Mühlmann, *Der Kunstkrieg*; for a more general discussion on the relationship between the American Secret Service and the advocacy of abstract art as an American 'product', see Saunders, *Who Paid the Piper?*

unconscious relationships to the tourist industry, city branding mechanism, and the global art market.[8]

In many ways, documenta 14 began where documenta 1 ended, in the words of then chair of the organizing committee, Heinz Lemke: 'In our time, which again questions all human standards and intellectual paradigms, we must—continuously—try to determine our own position and location.'[9] To move documenta's geographic and ideological centre from its homestead in Germany and thereby define a future direction was fully materialized through Adam Szymczyk's proposal for documenta 14 in Athens and Kassel. The choice for Athens was motivated by myriad concerns and political stakes; I will focus on one singular thread.[10]

This particular story of Athens begins, tellingly, in Germany, when Johann Joachim Winckelmann published his *Reflections on the Painting and Sculpture of the Greeks* and the magnum opus *History of the Art of Antiquity*, in 1755 and 1764 respectively.[11] Considered landmarks in the study of the Greek Classical period as well as foundational texts for the academic disciplines of art history and Antiquity studies (in German, *Altertumswissenschaft*), these publications put Winckelmann at the heart of what classicist Katherine Harloe describes as an 'imagined community of classical scholarship' in eighteenth- and nineteenth-century Germany.[12] Celebrating Greek Classical sculpture and painting as the most ideal form of beauty, Winckelmann constructed a framework of historical interpretation infused with desire—a passionate longing for a time and a place connected to an art form that was long gone, infused with homoerotic desire.[13] His scholarly devotion was integral to constituting the art and architecture of Greek antiquity as the principal references for German art history (and well beyond); a vision of the

8 Andrew Weiner's analysis of documenta 14 offers valuable insights into these relationships through the question: is documenta too big to fail? See Weiner, 'The Art of the Possible'.

9 Lemke, 'Vorwort', translation by the author.

10 For a more elaborate exposé on why documenta 14 took place in Athens, in addition to its traditional Kassel venue, see: Szymczyk, '14: Iterability and Otherness'; and Latimer and Szymczyk, 'Editors' Letter'.

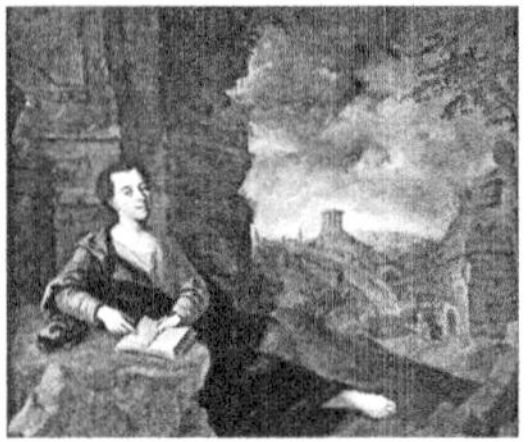

11 German School, *Johann Joachim Winckelmann Shown against an Italian Landscape*, early 19th century, oil on canvas, 71 × 85 cm, The Royal Castle, Warsaw. © Haupt & Binder.

12 Harloe, *Winckelmann & the Invention of Antiquity*, pp. 13–19.

13 See Potts, *Flesh and the Ideal*; and Davis, *Queer Beauty*, in particular pp. 23–49.

South of Europe and its past imbued with Northern projections.[14]

Winckelmann's work existed in a much broader context of European Neoclassicism that dominated intellectual and artistic production in the second half of the eighteenth century. It should also be noted that Greek Revival architecture and Neoclassical architecture in Europe were the preeminent forms in which power was expressed; the Greek temple as a blueprint for the architecture of the European nation states. Such archaeologists and architects as the Frenchman Julien David Le Roy and his bitter British rivals James Stuart and Nicholas Revett, travelled to Athens and other parts of Greece to survey the ruins of antiquity in meticulous architectural treatises. Stuart and Revett's *The Antiquities of Athens Measured and Delineated* (1762)[15] is richly illustrated with surgical renditions of Greek Classical architecture, which they regard as the most just and beautiful form, infusing their observations with sentimental affect for the ruins of Greece. One finds a remarkable dyssynchrony in some of these illustrations. In the background of the temples or in the dress of the people in the images, there are clear indices of the actual political geography of Greece at that time, as part of the Ottoman Empire. Here, the 'pure' vision of Athens as Northern and Western European heritage is complicated by the image of Greece as a transitional zone between the Middle East, the Balkan area, and Europe.

Transforming cultural desire into political reality, the year 1832 marks the next point on our journey: the second son of King Ludwig I of Bavaria became King Otto of Greece following Greece's independence from the Ottoman Empire. At the time, Athens was a relatively small and rural settlement around the Acropolis of little economic or political consequence, yet due to its major cultural relevance it was instated

14 For a more detailed analysis of how the mirage of Greek Classical antiquity captured the minds of German intelligentsia in the nineteenth century, see Roelstraete, 'A Mighty Forest'; and on the notion of philhellenism (the love for anything Greek in the nineteenth century) in the context of German nationalism and cosmopolitanism, see Most, 'Philhellenism, Cosmopolitanism, Nationalism'.

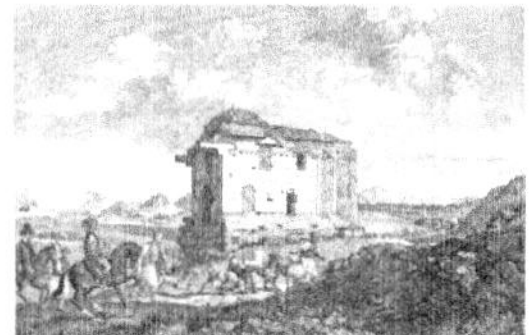

15 James Stuart and Nicholas Revett, *Ionic Temple on the Illissus*, in *The Antiquities of Athens Measured and Delineated*, 1762.

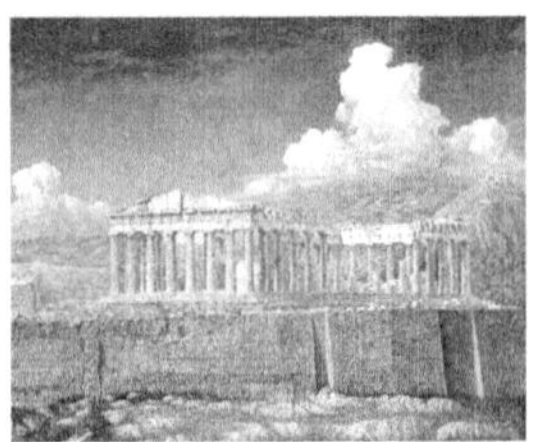

16 Alex Kalderach, *Der Parthenon*, 1939, oil on canvas, 100.5 × 124 cm, Belvedere, Vienna.

17 Szymcyzk, '14: Iterability and Otherness', pp. 25–26; Latimer and Szymczyk, 'Editors' Letter', p. 5.

as the capital of modern Greece. The celebrated Bavarian architect Leo von Klenze devised a massive new urban planning programme for Athens based on previous plans by Stamatios Kleanthis and Eduard Schaubert, which was implemented in the years following 1834. Athens as we know it today is a product of German intervention—in more ways than one, as argued in the previous paragraphs. Throughout the nineteenth century and well into the twentieth century, Athens continued to play a pivotal role in the German and European cultural imagination, from Romantic landscapes to the ominous renditions of the Parthenon in such Nazi paintings as Alexander Kalderach's *Der Parthenon* (1939).[16]

While maintaining the exhibition's function as 'mirror, witness and commentator', documenta 14 operated, per Antonin Artaud, as a 'theatre and its double', a *mise en scène* of two venues in two cities that radicalized the relationship between the exhibition as a representative sphere and life as the domain of direct action, toward the exhibition as a 'theatre of action'—across a historical spectrum and political reality that mutually affects both sites.[17] The historical constellation of Winckelmann, King Otto and Leo von Klenze in documenta 14 invokes an image of Europe's South through the eyes of the North, whereas Bode, documenta 1, and the exhibition's subsequent history illustrate how from the ashes of the German empire arose the Cold War separation between East and West, as well as how documenta has always (consciously or unconsciously) been the stage of political theatre. Blurring the lines between history as representation and the present as an opportunity for intervention, artists, exhibition curators, visitors, and spectators alike were addressed as active agents in considering numerous junctures from the point of view of 'what-has-been' alongside the perspective of the 'now': the economic violence inflicted by neoliberalism, the financial criminalization of the Southern European states by the European Union, the politics of debt and restitution, the histories of colonialism and techniques of neo-imperialism, displacement and dispossession, global diasporic networks, and so forth.

In concreto, consider the image printed with this essay. We see Marta Minujín's *The Parthenon of Books* for documenta 14, a 1:1 scale reproduction of the Parthenon in Athens, constructed with banned books donated by a predominantly German public to re-enact the initial *Parthenon of Books*, which Minujín mounted in her native Buenos Aires in 1983 against the censorship of the Argentinian military dictatorship (1976–1983). In 2017, the work was located on the Friedrichsplatz, a space in the city of Kassel that once connected the old medieval city with the Huguenot settlement in the late eighteenth century and was the site of military parades and massive book burnings by the Nazis, prior to being split up into two parts by a highway to accommodate the car-driven urban planning of post-World War II Kassel. A number of shops are clustered around the city square; small shops that designate a slowly disappearing local market place and corporate fashion and food chains that show the increasing presence of the global economy. Minujín's reproduction of the Parthenon faces its Neoclassical counterpart, the Fridericianum, the first public museum in continental Europe and then a library, reconstructed after World War II to become the birthplace of documenta in 1955. Across the Fridericianum, next to *The Parthenon of Books*, we see a large statue of Friedrich II, one of the most successful landgraves of Kassel in the eighteenth century, largely thanks to his economic programme that rented out soldiers to Britain to fight in the American Revolutionary War. His Friedrichsplatz and his

Fridericianum stand as testaments to the wealth he brought to the city, fuelled by a war machine that is still an important engine for the city's economy, with Rheinmetal and other companies producing tanks for global defensive and offensive missions. On the façade of the Fridericianum, artist Banu Cennetoğlu has replaced the letters that spell MUSEUM FRIDERICIANUM with *BEINGSAFEISSCARY*, a commentary on how our incessant desire to be safe is not only an illusion but in fact produces violence; and from the Fridericianum's tower white smoke signified the opening hours of the exhibition in Athens, a take on the *habemus papam* by artist Daniel Knorr. All of these images and elements are surrounded with visible and invisible public sculptures from documenta's past, from *The Strangers* (1992) by Thomas Schütte to Walter de Maria's *The Vertical Earth Kilometer* (1977).

This allegorical image summarily encapsulates some of the mechanisms of documenta 14 that question when and where this exhibition 'belongs' while also proposing it as a situation rather than a representational space. Perhaps most important for the context of this essay, this image, embedded in documenta 14 at large, demonstrates that history and the present are always and continuously in motion, changing with every shift in perspective.

Literature

Benjamin, Walter. *The Arcades Project*. Cambridge, 2002.

Bennett, Anthony. 'The Exhibitionary Complex.' *New Formations* no. 4 (Spring 1988), p. 76.

Davis, Whitney. *Queer Beauty: Sexuality and Aesthetics from Winckelmann to Freud and Beyond*. New York, 2010.

Harloe, Katherina. *Winckelmann & the Invention of Antiquity: History and Aesthetics in the Age of Altertumswissenschaft*. Oxford, 2013.

Latimer, Quinn, and Adam Szymczyk. 'Editors' Letter.' *South as a State of Mind* #6 [documenta 14 #1]. Kassel: documenta und Museum Fridericianum, 2016, p. 5.

Lefebvre, Henri. 'Reflections on the Politics of Space', *Antipode* 8, no. 2 (1976), p. 31.

———, *The Production of Space*. Oxford, 1991.

Lemke, Heinz. 'Vorwort.' In *documenta. kunst des XX. jahrhunderts*. Munich, 1955.

Most, Glenn W. 'Philhellenism, Cosmopolitanism, Nationalism.' In *Hellenisms: Culture, Identity and Ethnicity from Antiquity to Modernity*. Edited by Katerina Zacharia, pp. 151–167. London, 2008.

Mühlmann, Heiner. *Der Kunstkrieg: Das Haus der Deutschen Kunst, die Documenta und die CIA-MoMA-Connection*. Munich, 2014.

Potts, Alex. *Flesh and the Ideal: Winckelmann and the Origins of Art History*. New Haven, 2000.

Roelstraete, Dieter. 'A Mighty Forest.' *South as a State of Mind* #8 [documenta 14 #3]. Kassel: documenta und Museum Fridericianum, 2016, pp. 169–184.

Saunders, Frances Stonor. *Who Paid the Piper? The CIA and the Cultural Cold War*. London, 2000.

Stuart, James, and Nicholas Revett. *The Antiquities of Athens Measured and Delineated*. London, 1762.

Szymczyk, Adam. '14: Iterability and Otherness: Learning and Working from Athens.' In *The documenta 14 Reader*. Edited by Quinn Latimer and Adam Szymczyk, pp. 17–42. Munich, London and New York, 2017.

Weiner, Andrew. 'The Art of the Possible: With and Against Documenta 14.' biennialfoundation.com; ‹www.biennialfoundation.org/2017/08/art-possible-documenta-14/› (accessed on 3 February 2018).

Index

Contributors

Mieke Bal is a cultural theorist, critic, video artist and occasional curator. She works in cultural analysis, literature and art, focusing on gender, migratory culture, psychoanalysis, and the critique of capitalism. Her 38 books include a trilogy on political art. Her video projects, *Madame B*, with Michelle Williams Gamaker, is widely exhibited, in 2017 combined with paintings by Edvard Munch in the Munch Museum in Oslo. Her most recent film is *Reasonable Doubt*, on René Descartes and Queen Kristina (2016).

Melanie Bühler is the Curator Contemporary Art at the Frans Hals Museum in Haarlem, the Netherlands since 2017. Prior to this, she worked as an independent curator, her most recent project being 'Inflected Objects', an exhibition series at Future Gallery, Berlin (2016), De Hallen Haarlem (2016), Swiss Institute, Milan (2015). She founded Lunch Bytes (2011–2015)—a project on digital art and culture for which she collaborated with the Haus der Kulturen der Welt, Berlin; ICA, London; and Hirshhorn Museum and Sculpture Garden, Washington, D.C., and other institutions. She edited *No Internet, No Art. A Lunch Bytes Anthology* (2015) and her writings have appeared in exhibition catalogues and magazines.

Peter Carpreau is the Curator in charge of the Old Masters and collection department of M-Museum Leuven. At M, he was also responsible for the reinstallation of the collection presentation in 2017. Carpreau studied art history at the KULeuven and the Sorbonne, Paris IV. His research focuses on perception, visual literacy, and the value of art. Recent exhibitions include 'Crossing Borders: Medieval Sculpture from the Low Countries' (2017), 'Edgard Tytgat, Memory of a much-loved window' (2017) and 'Michiel Coxcie, The Flemish Rafael' (2013).

Bice Curiger is an art historian and curator. Since 2013, she is the Artistic Director of the Fondation Vincent van Gogh Arles. From 1993–2013 she worked as a curator at Kunsthaus Zürich, where she organized numerous monographic and essayistic exhibitions, such as 'Birth of the Cool' (1997), 'Hypermental' (2000), 'Georgia O'Keeffe' (2003), 'Sigmar Polke' (2005), 'The Expanded Eye' (2006), 'Peter Fischli/David Weiss' (2007), 'Katharina Fritsch' (2009), and 'Riotous Baroque' (2012/2013). In 2011 she served as the Director of the 53rd Venice Biennale. She has published numerous books and essays on contemporary art, such as *Meret Oppenheim* (MIT Press, 1989), and *Rebecca Warren*, (Fuel, 2012).

Penelope Curtis is the Director of the Calouste Gulbenkian Museum in Lisbon. She previously directed Tate Britain, London and the Henry Moore Institute, Leeds. In 2017 she published *Sculpture: Vertical, Horizontal, Closed, Open* with Yale University Press. Earlier monographs were published with Oxford University Press (1999) and Ridinghouse/Getty (2007/2008). She regularly writes on and for contemporary artists, including, most recently, Per Kirkeby, Aglaia Konrad, Thomas Schütte, and Heimo Zobernig.

Ann Demeester is the General Director of the Frans Hals Museum | De Hallen Haarlem, the Netherlands, since 2014. From 2006 until 2014 Demeester was director of De Appel arts centre Amsterdam. Together with Kestutis Kuizinas she was the curator of 'X Baltic Triennial of International Art', Vilnius, Lithuania, in 2009. From 2003–2006, she was the director of the contemporary art centre W139, Amsterdam. As the assistant curator of Jan Hoet in Ghent (Municipal Museum for Contemporary Art, SMAK) and his deputy director in the German Museum MARTa Herford, she realized solo exhibitions with artists such as Luc Tuymans, Raoul De Keyser, Royden Rabinowitch, Rob Birza, Joe Scanlan, and Bjarne Melgaard.

Olga Fernández López is a researcher and a curator. She works as an Associate Professor at the History and Theory of Art Department of Universidad Autónoma de Madrid where she lectures on contemporary art history and curatorial studies. Her research focuses on the specificities of the exhibition medium and its critical possibilities for curatorial practice. She has recently curated 'One thousand roaring beasts. Exhibitions devices for a critical modernity' at Centro Andaluz de Arte Contemporáneo, Sevilla (2017). Together with María Íñigo Clavo she was the co-founder of the independent research group 'Península. Colonial processes and artistic and curatorial practices' in collaboration with Museo Nacional Centro de Arte Reina Sofía.

Hendrik Folkerts is the Dittmer Curator of Modern and Contemporary Art at the Art Institute of Chicago and one of the curators of documenta 14 (2017). He studied art history at the University of Amsterdam, specializing in contemporary art and theory, feminist practices and performance. From 2010 until 2015 he was curator of Performance, Film & Discursive Programs at the Stedelijk Museum, Amsterdam. Prior to this, Folkerts was co-ordinator of the Curatorial Programme at De Appel arts centre, Amsterdam. He frequently publishes in journals and magazines, as well as monographs and exhibition catalogues. Folkerts is (co)editor of *Shadowfiles: Curatorial Education* (2013) (with Ann Demeester) and *Facing Forward: Art & Theory from a Future Perspective* (2015) (with Christoph Lindner and Margriet Schavemaker). He is one of the founding editors of *Stedelijk Studies*.

Hanneke Grootenboer is a Professor of the History of Art at the University of Oxford where she teaches early modern art and contemporary theory. She is the author of *The Rhetoric of Perspective* and *Treasuring the Gaze*, winner of the Kenshur book prize and recipient of various research fellowships from the Leverhulme Trust, Clark Art Institute and the NIAS. Currently she is completing *The Pensive Image*, in which she argues that painting is a form of thinking. Recent publications include 'The Self-Conscious Image: Painting and Hegel's Idea of Reflection', in *The Art of Hegel's Aesthetics* (2017) and 'Arresting What Would Otherwise Slip Away: The Waiting Images of Jacob Vrel' in *Time in the History of Art: Temporality, Chronology and Anachrony* (2018).

María Íñigo Clavo is a researcher and curator. She works as Associate Professor at Open University of Catalonia Department of Arts and Humanities. Her research focuses on power colonial relationships, museum and gallery studies, and art in Latin America. She has collaborated with a variety of publications, such as *e-flux*, *Stedelijk Studies* and *Afterall*. She has recently edited the magazine *Re-visiones*, which was launched in December 2017, on the topic: 'Is It Possible to Decolonize Western Methodologies? The South as Interlocution.' Together with Olga Fernández López she was the co-founder of the independent research group 'Península. Colonial processes and artistic and curatorial practices' in collaboration with Museo Nacional Centro de Arte Reina Sofía.

Xander Karskens is Artistic Director at Cobra Museum in Amstelveen (NL). He is an art historian with a focus on contemporary art, who has worked as curator of contemporary art at the Frans Hals Museum | De Hallen Haarlem from 2006-2016. Here, he was responsible for programmes and collections, and worked on exhibitions and publications with many artists, including Erik van Lieshout, Roger Hiorns, Nathaniel Mellors, Cécile B. Evans, Michel Auder, Charles Atlas, Guido van der Werve, Maaike Schoorel, and Andro Wekua. Among other international projects, Karskens curated the Finnish national pavilion at the 2017 Venice Biennale with Erkka Nissinen and Nathaniel Mellors.

Christa-Maria Lerm Hayes is Professor of Modern and Contemporary Art History, University of Amsterdam. Until 2003–2014 she worked at the University of Ulster, Belfast, leading a Research Graduate School there (2007–2011). Her books include: *Brian O'Doherty/Patrick Ireland: Word, Image and Institutional Critique* (2017), *Post-War Germany and 'Objective Chance': W.G. Sebald, Joseph Beuys and Tacita Dean* (2011), *Beuysian Legacies in Ireland and Beyond: Art, Culture and Politics* (ed. with Victoria Walters, 2011), *Joyce in Art* (2004), and *James Joyce als Inspirationsquelle für Joseph Beuys* (2001). She curated exhibitions at RHA Gallery, Dublin; Goethe Institut, Dublin; Tolstoy Estate, Russia; MoA, Seoul; GTG, Belfast; LCGA, Limerick; CCI, Paris; M HKA, Antwerp.

Jean-Hubert Martin has been director of several museums: the Kunsthalle Bern, Musée d'art moderne Centre Pompidou, Musée des arts d'Afrique et d'Océanie, Paris and Museum Kunstpalast, Düsseldorf. He has been in charge of the artistic programmes of Château d'Oiron and of PAC, Milan. His interest in non-Western cultures led him to conceive transcultural and transhistorical exhibitions confronting heterogeneous artworks in order to favour a new approach. He has been curator of numerous biennales and large exhibitions, including: 'Carambolages' (2016), 'Une image peut en cacher une autre' (2009), 'Partage d'exotismes' (2000), 'Magiciens de la terre' (1989), 'Paris–Moscou' (1979).

Alexander Nagel is Professor at the Institute of Fine Arts, NYU. His interest in the multiple temporalities of art led to the publication of *Anachronic Renaissance* (co-authored with Christopher Wood, 2010) and *Medieval Modern: Art out of Time* (2012). His current work addresses questions of orientation and configurations of place in Renaissance art and culture. In 2016, he received an NEH Fellowship for a collaborative project (with Elizabeth Horodowich, NMSU) entitled *Amerasia: A Renaissance Discovery.*

Ruth Noack, author, art critic, university lecturer and exhibition maker since the 1990s, trained as a visual artist and art historian. Noack was curator of documenta 12 (2007). Currently, she is developing *Ghosting the Nation*, for the Frans Hals Museum, Haarlem, the Netherlands, and creating a new institution *A Museum In A School* (to open in 2020). Since 2015, she has been teaching at the DAI/Arnhem. Head of the Curating Contemporary Art Program, RCA/London (2012-13), Noack acted as Research Leader for the EU-project *MeLa—European Museums in an age of migrations*. She was Šaloun professor at AVU/Prague (2013–2014) and lead the Gwangju Biennale International Curator Course (2014). Her publications include *Sanja Ivekovic: Triangle* (Afterall Books) and *Agency, Ambivalence, Analysis: Approaching the Museum with Migration in Mind* (both 2013).

Nicola Setari is a researcher, curator, and writer based in Brussels. He holds a PhD in the History of Architecture, Art Sciences and Restoration from Ca' Foscari and IUAV University, Venice. Since November 2016, he is the Head of Visual Arts and of the Research Unit Intermedia at LUCA School of Arts in Brussels. He was the curator of 'CONTOUR 7', the moving image biennale in Mechelen (2015) and was a member of the curatorial team of dOCUMENTA (13) in Kassel. With Hilde Van Gelder, he is the co-editor of the book *Allan Sekula: Mining Section (Bureau des mines): Collaborative notes* (2016).

Jasper Sharp is a British art historian, and the Adjunct Curator for Modern and Contemporary Art at the Kunsthistorisches Museum, Vienna. Recent exhibitions include surveys of Lucian Freud and Joseph Cornell, and projects with guest curators Ed Ruscha, Edmund de Waal and Wes Anderson. He worked at the Peggy Guggenheim Collection, Venice, from 1999–2005, was Commissioner of the Austrian Pavilion at the 55th Venice Biennale in 2013, and was nominated by *Apollo* magazine in 2014 as one of the ten most promising museum curators in Europe under the age of 40. He is also the founder and director of the philanthropic organization Phileas, based in Vienna.

Abigail Winograd is an independent curator and writer. Most recently, she was the Transhistorical Curatorial Fellow at the Frans Hals Museum | De Hallen Haarlem, the Netherlands, where she organized 'A Global Table' (2017). She was the Research Associate for 'Kerry James Marshall: Mastry' (2016) at the MCA Chicago where she also was the Marjorie Susman Curatorial Fellow. Winograd served as a graduate curatorial fellow at the

Hirshhorn Museum and Sculpture Garden in Washington, D.C. and the Blanton Museum of Art in Austin, TX. She earned a PhD in art history at the University of Texas at Austin and holds additional degrees from the University of Wisconsin, Madison, and Northwestern University.

Eva Wittocx is an art historian, curator, and writer based in Brussels. In 2009 she was appointed Senior Curator at M-Museum Leuven, where she developed the institution's contemporary art programme focusing on solo exhibitions by both emerging and established artists. She curated shows at M by Mika Rottenberg, Dirk Braeckman, Guy De Cointet, Sol LeWitt: Walldrawings (with Béatrice Gross), Markus Schinwald, Patrick Van Caeckenbergh, and many others. Together with artist Dirk Braeckman, she was nominated as the curator to represent Belgium at the 2017 Venice Biennale. Wittocx was curator at SMAK Municipal Museum for Contemporary Art in Ghent (1997–2006) and curator at the STUK arts centre Leuven (2006–2009).

Editors: Eva Wittocx, Ann Demeester, Peter Carpreau, Melanie Bühler, Xander Karskens

Contributors: Mieke Bal, Melanie Bühler, Peter Carpreau, Bice Curiger, Penelope Curtis, Ann Demeester, Olga Fernández López, Hendrik Folkerts, Hanneke Grootenboer, María Íñigo Clavo, Xander Karskens, Christa-Maria Lerm Hayes, Jean-Hubert Martin, Alexander Nagel, Ruth Noack, Nicola Setari, Jasper Sharp, Abigail Winograd, Eva Wittocx

Copy-editing: Leo Reijnen

Proofreading: Els Brinkman, Leo Reijnen

Index: Elke Stevens

Design: Sam de Groot

Typefaces: Eldorado (William Addison Dwiggins, 1953), Computer Modern (Donald Knuth, 1984), SKI DATA (Tariq Heijboer, 2014)

Lithography: Mariska Bijl, Wilco Art Books

Printing and binding POD edition: Scanlaser, 2023

Publishing partners: M-Museum Leuven, Leuven (BE), Frans Hals Museum, Haarlem (NL)

Publisher: Astrid Vorstermans, Valiz, Amsterdam, 2018/2023 ‹www.valiz.nl›

This publication has been generously supported by the Van Toorn Scholten Stichting.

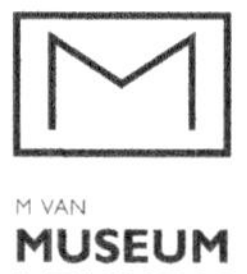

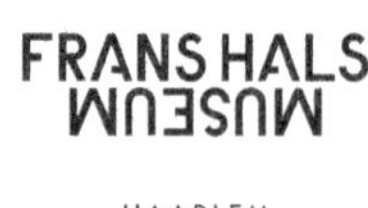

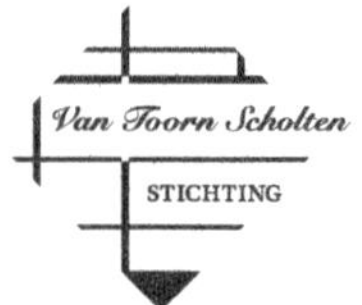

Distribution
USA: DAP, ‹www.artbook.com›
GB/IE: Anagram Books, ‹www.anagrambooks.com›
NL/BE/LU: Centraal Boekhuis, ‹www.cb.nl›
Europe/Asia: Idea Books, ‹www.ideabooks.nl›
Australia: Perimeter, ‹www.perimeterdistribution.com›
Individual orders: ‹www.valiz.nl›, ‹info@valiz.nl›

ISBN 978-94-92095-52-7
Printed and bound in the EU

Project 'The Transhistorical Museum: Objects, Narratives and Temporalities'

The publication is part of the long-term research project 'The Transhistorical Museum: Objects, Narratives and Temporalities', an initiative by the Frans Hals Museum, Haarlem and M-Museum Leuven on the subject of transhistoricity in museological and curatorial practices. Initiated in 2015, and made possible by the Van Toorn Scholten Stichting, the project has resulted in two conferences, held in November 2015 in Haarlem and in May 2016 in Leuven; a workshop, also held in Haarlem in 2016; and a keynote lecture by Jean-Hubert Martin at the Oude Kerk, Amsterdam in November 2016. Further part of the project is the Fellowship Transhistorical Curating at the Frans Hals Museum that invites emerging museum professionals to organize a transhistorical exhibition at the museum. The first exhibition as part of this program was 'A Global Table' (2017–2018), curated by Abigail Winograd, who held the fellowship in 2016/2017.

More information and resources on the topic can be found at ‹www.franshalsmuseum.nl/en/› and ‹www.mleuven.be›.

Thanks to Suzanne Sanders, who was responsible for the production of the conference and workshop 'The Transhistorical Museum' at the Frans Hals Museum | De Hallen Haarlem (2015–2016) and Lore van Hees, the producer from the side of M-Museum Leuven without whom this project could not have been realized.

vis-à-vis

The vis-à-vis series provides a platform to stimulating and relevant subjects in recent and emerging visual arts, architecture and design. The authors relate to history and art history, to other authors, to recent topics and to the reader. Most are academic researchers. What binds them is a visual way of thinking, an undaunted treatment of the subject matter and a skilful, creative style of writing.

Series design by Sam de Groot, ‹www.samdegroot.nl›.

2015

Sophie Berrebi, *The Shape of Evidence: Contemporary Art and the Document*, ISBN 978-90-78088-98-1

Janneke Wesseling, *De volmaakte beschouwer: De ervaring van het kunstwerk en receptie-esthetica*, ISBN 978-94-92095-09-1 (e-book)

2016

Janneke Wesseling, *Of Sponge, Stone and the Intertwinement with the Here and Now: A Methodology of Artistic Research*, ISBN 78-94-92095-21-3

2017

Janneke Wesseling, *The Perfect Spectator: The Experience of the Art Work and Reception Aesthetics*, ISBN 978-90-80818-50-7

Wouter Davidts, *Triple Bond: Essays on Art, Architecture, and Museums*, ISBN 978-90-78088-49-3

Sandra Kisters, *The Lure of the Biographical: On the (Self-)Representation of Artists*, ISBN 978-94-92095-25-1

Christa-Maria Lerm Hayes (ed.), *Brian O'Doherty/Patrick Ireland: Word, Image and Institutional Critique*, ISBN 978-94-92095-24-4

2018

John Macarthur, Susan Holden, Ashley Paine, Wouter Davidts, *Pavilion Propositions: Nine Points on an Architectural Phenomenon*, ISBN 978-94-92095-50-3

Jeroen Lutters, *The Trade of the Teacher: Visual Thinking with Mieke Bal*, ISBN 978-94-92095-56-5

Ernst van Alphen, *Failed Images: Photography and its Counter-Practices*, ISBN 978-94-92095-45-9

Paul Kempers, *'Het gaat om heel eenvoudige dingen': Jean Leering en de kunst*, ISBN 978-94-92095-07-7